Saints As They Really Are

MICHAEL PLEKON

# Saints As They Really Are

VOICES OF HOLINESS IN OUR TIME

University of Notre Dame Press

Notre Dame, Indiana

*Library of Congress Cataloging-in-Publication Data*

Plekon, Michael, 1948–
Saints as they really are : voices of holiness in our time / Michael Plekon.
    p.   cm.
Includes bibliographical references (p.      ) and index.
ISBN-13: 978-0-268-03838-0 (pbk. : alk. paper)
ISBN-10: 0-268-03838-4 (pbk. : alk. paper)
E-ISBN: 978-0-268-08982-5
1. Christian biography—United States.   I. Title.
BR1700.3.P585   2012
277.3'0820922—dc23

                                                      2012006670

CONTENTS

## ACKNOWLEDGEMENTS

—

First I want to thank Jeanne, my dear spouse of more than thirty years, for this book, not to mention everything else good in my life! Actually, strange as it may sound, I thank her herniated disc that erupted in terrible pain for her in the spring of 2009. Fortunately surgery and recuperation followed, but her being home where I acted as her caregiver sat me down to work on these chapters that follow. If holiness, as I have learned from Paul Evdokimov and so many others, is to be found in the ordinary, in the tasks and joys of everyday living, then there is no better place than our home and no other person to start with in expressing gratitude than the one, Jeanne, who has shared with me life, children, careers, and family dramas.

The list of others I have thanked earlier and must thank again: Barbara Hanrahan, former director of the University of Notre Dame Press, has believed not only in my writing but in that of a number of others whose work I have proposed as projects. She has made the UND Press truly and expansively catholic! I also owe a great deal to Matt Dowd, also of the press, who has collaborated in copyediting various manuscripts and served as my editor in this project. Many other staff members at UND Press have been supportive. I mention Rebecca DeBoer, Kathryn Pitts, and Emily McKnight, among others. Some of the writers I listen to here responded to inquiries—Andrew Krivak, Nora Gallagher, Barbara Brown Taylor, Sara Miles, Patricia Hampl, and Darcey Steinke. I am also grateful to friends who were willing to read, comment on, and criticize rough drafts—William Mills, Jerry Ryan, Rachelle Linner, Robert Thompson, Sarah Hinlicky Wilson, and John Bostwick, and then those who shared time and memories of Carmelite days—especially James Hess and Bob Linderman, as well as John Ramsay, James Miller, and Creig Doyle. As always, I thank my friends Alexis Vinogradov and Seraphim Sigrist for conversations that educate and change me.

I would also like to thank my own teacher, now emeritus university professor at Boston University, Peter L. Berger. His book *Questions of Faith* was very helpful here, and not just the questions either. Not only his books but sitting in his classroom as a student and years later around a seminar table were always feasts of listening and conversation. For the most part, courses with him dealt with classical and contemporary social theory, issues of modernization, and topics in the sociology of religion. He was willing to accept a dissertation from me on the Danish theologian, philosopher, and social critic Søren Kierkegaard, and there is a line running from that to my recent efforts to understand holiness in our time. Vielen Dank.

# Real Live Saints

Naturally speaking, people are filled with repulsion at the idea of holiness. . . . After the last war, everyone was talking about the lost generation. After this war [World War II] thank God, they are talking more about saints. . . . Archbishop Robichaud, in his book *Holiness for All,* emphasizes the fact that the choice is not between good and evil for Christians—that it is not in this way that one proves one's love . . . but between good and better. In other words, we must give up over and over again even the good things of this world, to choose God. . . . It is so tremendous an idea that it is hard for people to see its implications. . . . We have not begun to live as good Jews, let alone as good Christians. We do not tithe ourselves, there is no year of jubilee, we do not keep the Sabbath, we have lost the concept of hospitality. . . . We devour each other in love and in hate; we are cannibals. There are, of course, the lives of the saints, but they are too often written as though they were not in this world. We have seldom been given the saints as they really were, as they affected the lives of their times—unless it is in their own writings. But instead of that strong meat we are too generally given the pap of hagiography. Too little has been stressed the idea that all are called.[1]

The sometimes cantankerous, often discerning Dorothy Day wrote these lines in her column in *The Catholic Worker* in May 1948. A political radical, writer, the cofounder of the Catholic Worker movement and newspaper, and an activist for social justice all her life, she grounded all these commitments in a deep relationship with God and an energetic life of prayer. These words echo her notorious comment that many are fond of quoting: "Don't call me a saint; I don't want to be dismissed that easily." Given all the wildness of her youth and her radicalism, it remains astonishing that then Cardinal John O'Connor of New York officially submitted her case for the Roman Catholic process of canonization on February 7, 2000.[2]

Dorothy Day's "attitude" was not just her own irascible but compassionate personality once again showing. The problem is what we have done to saints—lifted them so high above us, made them so different from ourselves, so heroic and unusual that at best we can only admire them from afar. The universal call to holiness had been forgotten, as far as she saw it. But Dorothy knew better. Digging deeper into this is what I am about here. To do so, as will become clear, I want to extend the meaning of that line of hers about "saints as they really were." This book is about saints—few of them canonized, all of them our contemporaries, and we have to number ourselves among them—"saints as they really are."

This book proceeds from earlier ones as well as talks, articles, and works in translation, not to mention sermons, class presentations, and quite a few conversations. In *Living Icons,* I profiled a number of persons of faith from the twentieth century, looking for the distinctive features of their spirituality, their work for others.[3] These were for the most part from the Eastern Church in the twentieth century. In a sequel, *Hidden Holiness,* I moved on to identify a much more diverse twenty or so writers, activists, and artists who embodied holiness without the patterns of sainthood of the past.[4] Unlike the earlier book, these women and men were from various church traditions, and in a couple of cases not Christian either. But all were from the twentieth and the twenty-first centuries. Quite a few are still very much alive. What they spoke of and lived out was a holiness both everyday and diverse, less noticeable while nonetheless real and powerful.

## To Whom Shall We Listen? A Shift of Focus

In what follows I want to move on from my previous focus on holiness and persons of faith, looking at even more ordinary lives and experiences, and looking from some different perspectives. Saints have a great deal to tell us about the kind of persons of faith we ourselves are. By this I mean, of course, those few women and men elevated by the ecclesiastical process of canonization, after popular veneration, to official sainthood. These are the saints of our icons, frescoes, stained glass windows, and holy cards. But I certainly do not mean *just* these canonized saints. As Kenneth Woodward, James Martin, Elizabeth Johnson, Robert Ellsberg, and others have emphasized, the process of recognizing people as saints—the formal ecclesiastical process of canonization—over time restricted the kinds of women and men who could be so recognized.[5] The development of this process, both in the Eastern and Western churches, came to demand extraordinary things of saints, both heroic virtue and often unusual activities in their own lives and then miracles that could come under scrutiny and be verified and attributed to the intercession of the individual in process. Recently, for example, an unexpected and medically unexplainable healing is being used in the process for John Henry Cardinal Newman, and the remission of Parkinson's disease for a French nun in the process for Pope John Paul II.

But I shall not primarily be examining individuals who meet the standards for canonization, and I certainly will not focus on what happens to their reputations after their deaths. I am calling the book you are reading *Saints As They Really Are*. I want to see what holiness looks like in contemporary lives by listening to voices of those seeking to live such a life in our time. But rather than pursue themes and values in the abstract, I have chosen instead to go to individuals, to listen to writers and what they have said about their efforts to find God.

## Saints As They Really Are: Holiness in Our Culture and Society

I want to follow Dorothy Day's lead: "Communitarians, we will find Christ in our brothers and sisters." My focus will be on persons of faith shaped in and by our time, culture, and society. All have written about their experiences searching for God and trying to live the life of holiness. Yet not all would call themselves "writers" in any professional sense. I want to listen both to their accounts of what got them going in the search as well as what put them off, discouraged them from it. I want to hear what lifted them up on the journey, but I am also interested in what dragged them down, what they found poisonous and destructive while living in their communities of faith. Without necessarily being conscious of it, their lives reveal their effort to live the life of the Spirit.

This will be an ecumenical endeavor. It will also need to be selective, because some figures, important as they are, have been the subjects of a great deal of study, for example, Thomas Merton, Dorothy Day, Dr. Martin Luther King Jr., and Flannery O'Connor.[6] My plan, for the most part, is to listen to voices and track lives less often studied, and perhaps therefore less known.[7] I have some material of my own for you to listen to here, as well as my commentary on what these authors say. But my discussion of their experiences cannot be a substitute for actually reading their beautifully crafted writings— though I have tried to select passages that reveal the power of their words. I hope that the writings themselves will entice readers to go directly to the writers' essays and books; the endnotes to this volume will help you find them.

I want to track the life of holiness in the experience of those who have been able to express all the turns and twists of this journey with clarity and beauty. Each writer will offer us something different. My strategy is to generously cite these writers, thus allowing them to speak in their own voices and giving us all the chance to listen and take their experiences to heart. More often than not, we will also hear about the details of their lives, since spiritual autobiography and memoir writing converge in many of the individuals we will examine.

I always field test what I am reading and writing with my students at Baruch College of the City University of New York, where I have been teaching for more than thirty years. With more than a hundred languages represented among the more than seventeen thousand students and several hundred faculty members, it is an understatement to say it is a diverse community of learning. In any class I teach there will be at least a dozen ethnic groups represented and perhaps half a dozen or more different religious traditions. True, there are requirements for majors and minors, and optimal class times and days, but I find that every time I present women and men of our time talking about their search for God in the reading list, the texts are devoured, debated, and discussed with passion in class. So this book is aimed not only at those generally interested in spirituality but for use in courses that connect religion and literature, church and society, as well as the search for meaning in life in the twenty-first century.

Lastly, I found it made most sense to stay within the tradition I know best, Christianity, fully aware that there are many paths to God. As will be clear, however, I placed no boundaries and did not rule out questions of faith or doubt or points of view divergent from the tradition or the contemporary mainstream. It is an ecumenical collection of writers we will listen to—some from the Episcopal Church, others Catholic, Eastern Orthodox, Lutheran, and a few who do not have a particular tradition with which they exclusively identify. Boundaries or defining lines may be necessary for other reasons, but because we are thinking here about holiness in the lives of human beings, and since holiness is a gift of God, something of God's very self, well, then, there can be no boundaries except those that an individual raises for him- or herself. If a writer or a reader so chooses, so be it.

*Writers, Voices, Memories*

As will be apparent, I am not interested in simply summarizing and then criticizing the works of these writers. Rather, I want to invite readers to the conversation and reflection I have had with them myself. I want readers to be able to listen, to hear these voices in their own words—thus, the use of generous quotations from their writings, as well as the gallery of images, their faces. Mother Maria Skobtsova, herself a gifted poet and theologian, called the faithful, the people of God, "living icons."[8] She observed that in the Eastern Church liturgical services, after censing the icons of Christ and the Mother of God and major saints on the icon screen and the walls of the church building, the deacon or priest then bowed to and censed the men and women gathered there in prayer just as those in the heavenly kingdom, the saints recognized by the church, had just been reverenced. Those of us who gather to hear the scriptures and preaching, to sing hymns of praise and thanksgiving and to share the bread and cup—we are not canonized, that is, officially recognized saints. Yet we are indeed saints because God made us in God's own image and likeness, and in baptism came to dwell in us, and works in, with, and through our voices, eyes, hands, and ears. We are, at the very least, "saints in the making."

I am convinced that as living icons of God, we reflect God's presence in us in the unique quality of our features, as well as our experiences and actions. It is not so much that the writers I assemble here are models of holiness or even necessarily teachers of the holy life. Most of them are not trained theologians. Only a few are ordained to ministry in the church. Yet all of them chronicle their own failings and weaknesses. Each is the product of very particular experiences of family, marriage and friendship, of education, and, yes, of prayer and church life. Every one has a story to tell that is idiosyncratic and yet offers us new perspectives, different choices, deaths and resurrections. The motif of dying and rising, so central to the gospel, to the major sacraments of baptism and the Eucharist, to Christian life, I discovered was a theme common to all of these individuals. It was there in their writings, whether intended or not, and it needed little excavation, surely no imposition or interjection by me.

I am privileged to have met and corresponded with a few of the writers surveyed here. I have learned a great deal from what they have had to say about their searching for God and trying to live a holy life. Most of them are alive and working. Not one would fit the caricature of a saint that Dorothy Day attacked in frustration, in the passage quoted above. None speaks officially for his or her church. It is true that the writers have a lot to say about their own lives, the people close to them, about experiences of joy and sadness, of rage and rejoicing. Is it that we will hear too much about the writers and not enough about God? Not at all! How else does God communicate with us except through us—our words and actions, our feelings. I do not hold up these women and men as models of heroic virtue or extraordinary holiness. Yet I do think they are people looking for God and trying to live accordingly. Their attempts to write about their own experience are not to be taken as recipes. We shall soon see that most all of them would warn us not to follow them but whatever path we find before ourselves. Nevertheless, there is much we can learn from them. Struggling with discouragement and their own weakness, with both the support and sometimes the dysfunction and destructiveness of the church, these women and men have much to share with us. We will see ourselves in many of the situations and feelings they describe. We will also have sides of ourselves illumined, whether we like this or not.

*Kathleen Norris* is a poet, but also a student of monastic spirituality in particular and the spiritual geography of America more generally. Her latest book is an autobiographical contemplation of life as a writer, a spouse, now a widow and the adult caregiver to an ailing parent, and on the spiritual aridity and suffering that comes with aging, illness, and loss.[9]

Although I sampled their work briefly in an earlier publication, I would like to return to two powerful writers on belief and unbelief. *Sara Miles* has shared her own rich life and conversion and now her ongoing struggle with religion as she serves in a parish.[10] The daughter of a Lutheran pastor, *Darcey Steinke*'s childhood was saturated with church services and Christian texts and symbols. Yet she saw her parents' marriage dissolve and her father's faith seriously challenged, and her own passion for writing and music took her far from her roots. But her memoir chronicles a recovery of faith that is most relevant to the religious doubt, indifference, and fanaticism of our time. Sara Miles, on the other hand, grew up without religious formation of any kind, her parents wanting to undo the upbringing they were put through. Nevertheless, her own experience during a Eucharistic liturgy one Sunday morning became an encounter with Christ that reshaped her entire existence. A writer, she is also a deacon and the administrator of the food pantry at St. Gregory of Nyssa Episcopal Church in San Francisco. In these spiritual memoirs, both writers share the beauty of faith traditions and communities as well as their toxicity, and discuss religious loss, recovery, and conversion.

Close to these memoirs are those of *Barbara Brown Taylor* and *Nora Gallagher*. These writers chronicle their journeys toward and away from the ordained ministry, both, coincidentally, in the Episcopal Church. Barbara Brown Taylor has been an Episcopal priest for more than twenty years. But after a profound crisis, perhaps a "burnout" in parish ministry, she has been a professor of religious studies alongside her lecturing and writing. The story of her failure in ministry is a courageous revelation but, as we will discover, most constructive, healing for us all. Nora Gallagher began but did not complete the process toward ordination in the Episcopal Church, and as she said in correspondence, she "continues to live in the space(s) between ordained and non-ordained priesthood, experiencing the priesthood of all believers." Their stories confront us with what no one expects to find in the life of faith—not just what is wonderful but also what is destructive. Both, however, find their way through to a deeper, more discerning life in the Spirit.

*Diana Butler Bass* is by profession a church historian. She has produced a fascinating look at healthy, creative communities of faith. But she also crafted an account of how her own life and a failed marriage took her on a pilgrimage through the American religious landscape.

*Patricia Hampl* has written fiction but also specialized in the genre of memoir. While her memories of growing up Roman Catholic in the pre–Vatican II years are strong, equally powerful and beautiful are her accounts of "pilgrimage" in search of a faith lost, the revelation of idiosyncrasies of nuns and monks, and her discovery of silence and prayer.

The similarly memoir-like accounts of her youthful pilgrimage into Orthodox Judaism and out of it into mainstream Christianity have made *Lauren Winner* a voice not to be ignored. She also confronts traditional teaching with the tough attitude and experiences of a young adult. She is by profession a church historian and is a member of the Episcopal Church.

The spiritual autobiography of writer *Andrew Krivak* is likewise sensitive and articulate in examining what led him into the long formation process of the Jesuits and then out, into married life. Moved by so many of these honest accounts and nudged on by a couple colleagues, I will reflect on some of my own experiences in religious life.

Ninety-five years old when he died in 2011, Trappist monk *Matthew Kelty* took up over the years all kinds of issues of our time from war to sexual identity, social justice, and individual depression, not unlike his much better known comrade at Gethsemani monastery (and former novice master), the great writer Thomas Merton.

My own teacher is the well-known sociologist of religion and Lutheran lay theologian *Peter Berger*. He has spent almost a half century scrutinizing the American social and religious landscapes. In addition to questioning his own earlier conclusion about secularization in our time, he recently produced a most intriguing reflection on belief and doubt. His voice adds a distinctive perspective to those already mentioned. There are several others whose accounts will also appear, if briefly. The effect is a kind of chorus of voices, not blended in close harmony, but nevertheless singing the same song, albeit with parts that diverge as well as converge.

In the first chapter we will consider that we have become stuck on saints, but mostly the official ones—on walls and atop pedestals. But what would we find if we looked into the experiences of ordinary people instead? Official recognition of people as saints usually requires the demonstration of out-of-the-ordinary achievements both within their lives and after death. We will instead follow the road of experience, as suggested in Peter Berger's reflection, *Questions of Faith*. A basic pattern will emerge in his look at what we believe and what can be questioned in the faith. A leading writer in the genre of memoir, Patricia Hampl, will orient us toward hearing from others working in that genre, tracking back through their spiritual journeys.

From that we will move, in chapter 2, to what most of us are first aware of—that our lives are a mess, that we are very imperfect people, subject to innumerable weaknesses. We are often our own worst enemies. We will listen to Kathleen Norris's account of her own struggles with the aridity or spiritual emptiness known as *acedia*. But at the same time we will encounter other traumatic events in her life and see how she dealt with these. Then we will follow Barbara Brown Taylor's riveting but disturbing retelling of her own path both in parish ministry and beyond. And we will accompany Nora Gallagher through the liturgical year and beyond as she faces the death of her brother as well as a rediscovery of her own faith in Trinity Church, her home parish in Santa Barbara. Part of this will be her experience of internship as she discerns whether to continue as a candidate for ordination.

In chapter 3 we will confront the reality that religion, in many different ways, can be toxic, that the institutional church can work at cross purposes to its ideals, that people of faith can do great harm to others as well as to themselves. Once again we will hear Barbara Brown Taylor on losing one's calling and one's way, from Sara Miles and Darcey Steinke on other sides of parish life, and from Sergius Bulgakov and Alexander Schmemann on the perils of clericalism and power.

In chapter 4 we move to the other side of what is toxic and destructive—joy in the pursuit of holiness. In the search for God and the effort to lead a holy life there is happiness, peace, and fulfillment alongside struggle and loss. Here Andrew Krivak's memoir of his years in formation in the Jesuits will be a source, along with accounts from two pastors, Lillian Daniel and Martin Copenhaver. I entitled chapter 5 "You want to be *happy?*" This was the response from a wise and discerning priest to me when I was a very naive eighteen year old. Of course we all want to be happy, but this is just the start of the conversation. What follows is a remembering of my own time in the Carmelite Order as a high school and minor seminary student, then a novice and student friar. I want to remember Fathers Vincent McDonald and Albert Daly, among others, and many of the good things I learned and received in pursuing the Carmelite life of prayer and work. It is also necessary to remember some of the painful, not-so-positive aspects as well.

Another experience is that of searching for communion with God and with others. This we will examine in chapter 6. But sometimes it is searching in all the wrong places and being found by or finding God nonetheless. Patricia Hampl's account of several attempts at pilgrimage, at finding the contemplative life and a life of the Spirit, is a very rich source to explore. Likewise, Lauren Winner's account of her conversion experience, told with ample dollops of both Orthodox Judaism and Christianity, makes for the most unusual and extreme spiritual memoir we will encounter here, yet a very moving one.

A discovery in the path of searching for God is that God "is everywhere, filling all things," as the Eastern Church prayer invoking the Holy Spirit puts it. This we will pursue in chapter 7. Darcey

Steinke absorbed this sensitivity to God's omnipresence from her experience as a pastor's kid, and it radiates not only in her own memoir but in her fiction too. Barbara Brown Taylor presents a number of practices in the spiritual life, ways of experiencing the presence and action of God in the everyday world around us. Listening to her again is in itself a fascinating counterpoint to her prior account of the toxic possibilities of the church and religion.

In chapter 8 I want to bring together the many threads of experience at which we have looked. Diana Butler Bass will be an important source, first taking us on her own personal spiritual journey, then taking us through the experiences and practice of some living communities, local churches, and parishes that have intentionally tried to grow, reaching out for God and for the neighbor. We will also listen to Matthew Kelty, a Trappist monk with the gift for bringing together liturgy and life, faith and work, the church and the world in his preaching.

These two voices and other conversations return us, in the final chapter, to where Dorothy Day's comment launched us. No one finds God by him- or herself. *Solus christianus, nulla christianus,* in Tertullian's words: "You can't be a Christian alone." What is happening to communities of faith in the twenty-first century? A great deal has already changed, even more is changing around us, yet with a few exceptions, most in institutional church positions either cannot see or do not wish to see these changes.

## So What?

Peter Berger used to routinely throw this fairly ultimate question out at us in class as we wound our way through Marx or Weber, George Herbert Mead, Durkheim, Simmel, Freud, Arnold Gehlen, or Alfred Schutz—great classical and contemporary social thinkers. But in addition to this "canon" he would also swirl in whatever other authors he was reading, whether novelists or poets, theologians or political scientists. For me, at least, this was proof positive that to educate oneself, it was necessary to forget about disciplinary boundaries or labels, much less a particular "school" or approach such as "structural functionalism" or "symbolic interactionism." Like the very best writers, Berger was constantly reading, listening to new, different voices.

I think the "so what" was, at least in my memory, a way of bringing both research findings and theory back to everyday life. It was a question of what meaning or significance could this idea or connection have for not just the way I look at the world but for decisions made, actions taken corporately. I am convinced that it was a consulting of experience as well. Since this is not the first time I have pursued either holy people themselves or mere mortals thinking in their writing about the search for meaning, for God, I myself have thought many times in the writing of this volume, "So what?" While memoirs like those of writers such as Joan Didion, Mary Karr, and Elizabeth Gilbert sell and are read, [11] and while there has been a small renaissance of interest in saints, is there really need for yet another book along those lines, like this one? I decided that there was, as the response to the "So what?" question pulled me personally in. In trying to remember and then record memories of the years I spent in formation in the Carmelite Order, I had the welcome admonishing of my daughter Hannah to dig deeper and not just describe events but to offer up what I felt and thought, what I still delighted in, and what I still was disgusted by. In so doing and reconnecting through Facebook with some comrades of those Carmelite days, I realized that I was not just proceeding as a teacher and scholar for over thirty-five years. I was coming to terms, even if in a small way, with my past and my present and not in the usual location for so many of us—a therapist's office. I was coming to terms with pastoral ministry many years after ordination—asking why we continue to operate with models of parish life that are more than five hundred years old in a context that is no longer rooted in the agrarian economy, small town society, and homogenous ethnic communities in which those models were rooted. In all honesty, several years of grappling with the scandal of financial mismanagement and abuse of authority in my own church body also was pressing on me.

What is more, because the parish in which I serve always has seminarian interns, I realized I was helping to prepare young people for a very uncertain future in the church. When asked what I relied on, what encouraged, sustained, and, yes, also comforted me, I kept going back to those whom I had read, studied, and written about: Sergius Bulgakov, Alexander Schmemann, Paul Evdokimov, Mother Maria Skobtsova, Nicholas Afanasiev, and beyond them those I actually had met and knew—all almost five feet of Elisabeth Behr-Sigel, Darcey Steinke, Vincent McDonald, Albert Daly, Matthew Kelty, and Patrick Hart, at eighty-eight, a senior monk at Gethsemani monastery, where he was once Thomas Merton's secretary.

Thus in what follows, some of the ideas and lives that spoke to my "So what?" question I share with you—beautiful experiences of looking for and finding joy in the liturgy, the scriptures, in community and friendship within the church. But I had to include the pathological, destructive, and lethal realities too. And as those who know the ancient ways of studying the sacred texts, it was both necessary and good to end up not with answers or recipes but with numerous questions. To be disappointed and then be reminded of the likes of Mother Maria Skobtsova and her sufferings and courage, to be challenged about what the point of the all-too-human church is—and then to read the hundreds of entries of Alexander Schmemann's journal, be slapped in the face, as it were, by Darcey Steinke's strength despite what she experienced . . . So what? So there is a point to keep on reading, listening, talking, and living after God.

# CHAPTER ONE

# Bringing Saints down from the Walls and Pedestals

*Dorothy's Lament*

It was Dorothy Day who lamented that we seldom know holy women and men in their authentic humanity, in the actual context of their lives as women and men, but rather according to their miracles, the extraordinary feats they performed, or their "heroic virtue." The passage quoted at the start of the introduction is but one instance of her point of view. In her recently published diaries as well as in her columns in *The Catholic Worker* paper, there are many similar passages recognizing the universal call to holiness and the need to see the human sides of holy people.[1] Robert Ellsberg has also edited her letters and the same holds true for them.[2]

Dorothy was on to something. It came out of her faith, out of her daily praying the liturgy of the hours and participation in the Eucharist, not to mention her reading, which was prodigious! Official recognition of people as saints often requires the demonstration of out-of-the-ordinary achievements, both during their lives and after death, upon their invocation by the faithful. Miracles during the saints' lives abound in their "official" biographies—walking on water, bilocation, floating in the air, astounding healings of the sick, existing sometimes on nothing but holy communion.

Dorothy Day, of course, knew better. Her reading told her that great saints suffered doubt, depression, and all kinds of eccentricities. They could be nasty, impatient, forgetful, and clueless when it came to the people around them. Saints could be arrogant in self-confidence and learning or illiterate and out of touch with their worlds. They could also be quite normal, ordinary, and flawed. She saw this in great figures from the past such as Augustine and Francis of Assisi but also in a modern saint like Thérèse of Lisieux. Dorothy knew the singularity of sanctity in her brilliant but eccentric collaborator Peter Maurin. She also recognized the spirit of holiness in nonbelievers from her past.[3] Even when she tangled and strongly disagreed she saw the flame of the Spirit in her co-workers and correspondents.[4]

Dorothy's own life was a weave of contradictions and affirmations. She never let go of the radical vision of social justice that was ignited in her youth as a political journalist. She criticized the indifference, the political conservatism and clericalism of her Catholic Church. Having had an abortion, several affairs, and a child who she raised by herself as a single parent, she found the sexual openness and rebelliousness of the young people who flocked to the Catholic Worker houses in the 1960s and 70s repulsive. She seemed at times to cling to her faith and devotional practices almost irrationally.

And yet as one hears her taped interviews and reads her columns, diaries, and letters, there were still other sides to this fascinating, amazing woman. Her diaries confirm what is also there in several filmed interviews—a rich, deep, sometimes contradictory personality. The closer one gets to Dorothy the better one comes to know a generous soul, a stunningly passionate woman emerging. What is telling is that many conservative Catholics find her objectionable, think her official cause for canonization misguided and inappropriate.[5] But it is precisely the clash of characteristics, the flash of radicalism and traditional piety that reveals Day's singular character. Her complex personality and rich life, focused however on love for God and for the neighbor, make her very much a saint for our times. The same I think is true of a number of others, including Thomas Merton. In Merton's case, twenty-five years after his death in 1968, when his literary estate opened his unpublished writings for study and publication, an intricate, surely not typical image of Merton emerged. Audiotapes of his classes at Gethsemani monastery reveal a profound grasp of the sources of not just monastic life but the wider Christian tradition—the scriptures, the entwining of prayer and contemplation with life, the crucial connections between the church and the world. And mixed in to all these were his own volatile emotions, his clashes with his abbot, James Fox, even his falling in love with a student nurse who cared for him in the Louisville hospital—the joy and the pain and the resolution of this relationship, and Merton's commitment to his monastic vocation. When the full sweep of Thomas Merton's humanity was revealed in his journals and letters, some who formerly regarded him as a spiritual master were scandalized that he was a human being, with great gifts but also inadequacies, weaknesses, difficulties. Recently Mark Shaw has tried to upend Merton's figure precisely by appeal to these aspects of his humanity.[6]

Years ago something similar occurred when it became clear that there were different versions of the diaries and letters of Thérèse of Lisieux, the censored version and the unexpurgated, the latter of which revealed, again, the humanity of their author. Almost a decade ago the publication in English translation of selections from the journal kept by Alexander Schmemann, the Orthodox priest and theologian, in the last ten years of his life offered a fascinating portrait of this gifted man. But this has more recently been countered by the release, both in the original Russian language and in French translation, of a more complete version of the journal.[7] Not surprisingly, there are sides of Schmemann here not previously known: a harsh critic of many things in the church, society, politics, and literature; a person with a great deal of self-awareness, self-criticism, strong positions, and equally strong changes of heart. In sum, the picture will be disturbing to those who preferred the essentially positive, even heroic profile hitherto provided. Yet, the more complex, even problematic individual who put down so many reactions and insights is far more fascinating. Moreover, he is, once more, an example of how our personalities and experiences are essential in our life with God.

*Saints in Our Own Image?*

One could multiply examples here. Well-known priest, sociologist, and writer Andrew Greeley's multivolume memoirs are enormous, often self-serving and self-obsessed. Yet they are rich in evoking the Catholic Church in American society in the post–World War II years, all through Greeley's view. Also well known for his courageous civil rights and social justice advocacy, Episcopal bishop Paul Moore's memoir is striking. After his death it was countered by the far more provocative memoir of his oldest daughter, a revelation of Moore as even more complex and burdened than his own account. I add to this the biography of his colleague and social activist pastor William Sloane Coffin—a portrait of a very complicated and not always likeable or compassionate man.[8] Add to these some of the other writers we will sample or briefly mention: bestselling memoirs by retired Archbishop Rembert Weakland, theologians Stanley Hauerwas and Eugene H. Peterson, and writers like Mary Karr, Elizabeth Gilbert and Anne Lamott.[9] There is a lot of glitter and adventure, but considerable mess in their lives, as in our own. Recently the release of Mother Teresa's letters, containing a great deal of her own spiritual agony and doubt, depression, and aridity were a shock to many.[10] How could this heroic little woman, whose life was an icon of caring for the outcast, the sick, the dying also suffer real doubt in God's plan, and experience God's absence more than God's presence?

The reactions of well-meaning, even faithful people to apparent imperfections, difficulties, fears, and doubts in individuals such as Mother Teresa, Dorothy Day, Thomas Merton, and others, tells a great deal about what we carry around as definitions of holiness. In both Dorothy Day and Thomas Merton's journals and letters there are numerous instances of anger at injustice and political policy choices in the Cold War era, but also admissions of personal weakness and impatience, in short, fallible humanity. Yet for all of these and for others, Christ remained at the center. Prayer was the air they breathed, the Eucharist their sustenance, the scriptures their language. For all their blots and blemishes, they were with the grace of God striving to live holy lives.

None of these—not to mention others on the margins or outside the church such as philosopher Simone Weil and writer Etty Hillesum, or those very much within it: Dietrich Bonhoeffer, Alexander Men, Brother Roger Schutz—correspond to ancient classes or categories of holy people. Bonhoeffer, and with him Martin Luther King Jr., Men, and Skobtsova, died for their positions and work. Yet some would say they were not really martyrs because they did not die specifically for the faith. Weil and Hillesum never were baptized. Roger Schutz spent his life nurturing the ecumenical monastic community and center of Taizé. And after all the decades he devoted to ecumenical prayer and conversation, the churches remain divided, some would say less inclined to further ecumenical work than they were a half century ago. Alexander Men had and still has many enemies in his Russian Orthodox Church, those who reject his work to reconnect society and the church. Holy people are not always successful, popular, or recognized. Desert hermit and mystic Charles de Foucauld had no followers at his death, only after which did the little brothers and sisters come into being. Yet today their numbers are few, and one of the brothers asked in an open letter whether the vision of Brother Charles was lost or never comprehended—to live the hidden life of Jesus in his family and home at Nazareth.

Look at other traditional categories and much the same holds true. The calendars of most churches are full of martyrs in the first place, the highest regarded form of witness in the earliest days, but even then not the only one. There have always been teachers and theologians, as well as other confessors of the faith. Particularly in the Catholic and Orthodox calendars monastic women and men abound. But who are the teachers we look up to today? Many would point to John Paul II. Those more academically experienced might name Karl Rahner, Sergius Bulgakov, Paul Tillich, John Courtney Murray, or Teilhard de Chardin, to name just a few. There has been a rediscovery of Reinhold Niebuhr, perhaps the leading American theologian of the last half of the twentieth century. Though he was a Baptist pastor and prolific writer, most would recognize Martin Luther King Jr. for his civil rights work and great preaching. As difficult as his writings are, I myself revere the witness and vision of Edward Schillebeeckx, the controversial Dominican theologian recently deceased.[11]

Every name that could be mentioned here will have critics. Each of those named above I have heard dismissed, both in calm objectivity or with considerable emotional force. Nowadays there are not as many monastics to recall. But if Merton, de Foucauld, or Maria Skobtsova are named, likewise, every one will be rejected for one or another personal attribute or the lack thereof. It is also important to note how very few husbands and wives, mothers and fathers, scientists, lawyers, physicians, business people, or political leaders are to be found in church lists. Perhaps only in the provocative frescoes of "dancing saints" at St. Gregory of Nyssa Episcopal Church in San Franciso will one find Ghandi, Malcolm X, Eleanor Roosevelt, Ella Fitzgerald, and Thurgood Marshall among theologians, martyrs, and monastics.[12]

### The Communion of Saints—A Failed Symbol or a Symbol Renewed?

Elizabeth Johnson has been one of the most discerning students of the rise and fall and rise again of saints and their recognition as well as their veneration. She has looked both back to the historical development of the canonization process as well as forward to a renewed understanding of the communion of saints. Johnson does not hold back on what went wrong over time regarding the clear distortion of the vision of holiness in those officially selected in overwhelming numbers to be called saints.

> Public recognition of worthiness, including a place in the calendar of saints, was now to be granted from a single authoritative source, thus shifting what had been an acclamation close to the spiritual life of the people to an increasingly bureaucratized process. . . . Since the right to name the community's exemplars reinforces the authority of the one who canonizes, this was one more element in the centralization of power in the hands of the papacy. . . . Inevitably the process became political.[13]

Those with more funding and influence were able to push their candidates more effectively, this being the case with religious orders as well as individual bishops and interested wealthy sponsors. Though a centralized and ordered process controlled the naming of truly inappropriate people for reasons other than their sanctity, the process also began to distort the understanding of what a holy person's life, personality, and ideas were, or ought to be. Obedience and loyalty to the hierarchy, extraordinary fasting and prayer, extreme sacrifice, even physical and emotional suffering became synonymous with holiness, while creativity, critical thinking, and ordinary vocations of marriage and parenthood disappeared for all practical purposes from the lists of saints. While the record-breaking numbers of individuals beatified and canonized by Pope John Paul II gave the nod to more lay people, even married couples, looking at his more than one thousand additions it is still clear that founders and members of religious communities and the clergy, along with martyrs, dominate.

> While canonization developed in response to historical forces, its exercise at this point in time also has a negative impact on popular and theological awareness of the communion of saints. Saints have become an ever more elite group, proclaimed for their heroic virtue and their power to produce spectacular miracles. The unfortunate result has been that meaning of the term "saint" itself has shrunk in Christian usage to refer mostly to those who have been named as a result of this official juridical scrutiny. Not only does this overshadow the theological meaning of the term "saints," which embraces all persons of love and truth, but existentially the official ideal of perfection rewarded by this process becomes rarified to the point where people reject their own identity as holy and blessed: "I'm no saint." . . . Product of a clericalized culture, both the roster of canonized saints and the liturgical calendar of saints drawn from it reflect a worldview that is overwhelmingly favorable toward men who are priests or bishops and toward persons of aristocratic and upper-class origins. These "canons" are likewise biased against the full and legitimate use of sexuality by both women and men.[14]

Johnson cites several studies which verify these claims. From the tenth to the nineteenth centuries 87 percent of Roman Catholic canonizations were of males. In the twentieth century it fell slightly to 75 percent male. From the tenth to the nineteenth centuries, 82 percent of canonized saints were clergy; in the twentieth century this falling to 79 percent.

> Glaringly missing from the canonized lists are married people honored for the goodness and exemplarity of their lives precisely as actively

married. The official ideal of holiness thus marginalizes lives in which sexual activity in integrated rather than excluded, sending a message that most people live in a less-than-holy way. . . . It is obvious from this roster that the history of women's holiness is given extremely short shrift. . . . Another flag raised is by the fact that saints must pass muster before a narrow definition of doctrinal orthodoxy, thereby largely excluding pioneering thinkers, intellectuals, artists or anyone with a critical or challenging spirit.[15]

Add to this that the process must be instigated by the hierarchy, is expensive, slow, requires scrutiny of everything a person ever wrote or said publicly, everything they were witnessed to have done—it is no wonder that the official saints do not reflect the diversity of the whole people of God. It is no wonder either, that for so many today, such saints have become at best irrelevant and at worst problematic and alienating.

While Elizabeth Johnson and the authors cited above focus upon the canonization history and process in the Roman Catholic Church, there is little essential difference from that in the Eastern Churches with one exception: it is still possible, in principle, for a truly "local church," say a diocese, to canonize one of its own, the recognition then spreading gradually to the rest of that national church as well as others. A number of contemporary figures in the Eastern Orthodox Church have been canonized locally. Raphael Hawaweeny was the Lebanese bishop of Brooklyn, New York, and was canonized by two American Orthodox church bodies, one the direct successor of his own church. Nikolai Velimirovich was a Serbian bishop who spent a number of years in America. He was canonized by his home diocese of Zicha in Serbia. Poet, social activist, and nun Mother Maria Skobtsova and her companions in Paris were made saints by their own western European archdiocese headquartered in Paris. The cases of Olga Michael Arsumqaq, a Yup'ik priest's wife and healer, and widower Metropolitan Bishop Leonty Turkevich are still pending in the Orthodox Church in America. Both were extraordinary—in their very ordinary lives.[16]

So, we could speak of a "crisis" of sanctity, not of the reality of lived holiness by any means, but of the church recognition of sainthood—who makes the cut, who does not, and why. Related to this, as Elizabeth Johnson and other students of holiness observe, is the effect of official models on ordinary believers—how meaningful or irrelevant the saints are to them, to the extent that the very identity as "saint" would be seen as something distant, strange, unattainable.

There have been efforts to reform, that is, to change how saints are venerated and for what purposes, as well as the ways in which we recognize them, not just formally and ecclesiastically, but locally, informally and privately.[17] Linked to this is a trend in the liturgical calendars of such as the World Council of Churches, the Episcopal Church in the USA, the Evangelical Lutheran Church in America, and the monasteries of Bose in northern Italy and New Skete in Cambridge, New York, namely, the deliberate addition of saints of other church bodies to their calendars.[18] Likewise, Elizabeth Johnson discusses at length and provides many examples of ever expansive lists of holy women and men commemorated by gatherings and conferences, mostly informal. Dorothy Day may have been officially entered into the process toward canonization despite some opposition by family members and some co-workers. Yet if Thomas Merton's name was excluded from a Catholic catechism, the likelihood of Dorothy Day's canonization, at least in the near future, would not appear to be great. Nevertheless, one can find icons of her in several venues, a custom that is of ancient precedent in the church, where persons of faith and holiness were locally venerated long before official recognition.[19]

I agree wholeheartedly with Johnson that the symbol of the communion of saints is again alive and well, full of meaning and strength. As contemporary martyrs are named and invoked, the diversity and the expansiveness of their holiness are attested.[20] Figures in the ancient church are being remembered too—women leaders of congregations such as Phoebe and Lydia, married couples such as Prisca and Acquila, Junia and Andronicus. They join ranks with our contemporary teachers.[21] Having looked at the lives and listened to the voices of a number of holy people both well known and obscure, I have come to the conclusion that the real issues and thus the work belong to us. Those of us who want to hold onto conventional examples of holiness are finding this preference rebounding into our faces. A kind of dissonance then dominates. We lash out at a secular or worse an immoral culture around us, but when we look to the saints we find ourselves escaping our own worlds. We come to see the saints as unlike ourselves, their heroics unattainable. Thus holiness becomes out of reach.

The path toward saints who are accessible, who are identifiable as our brothers and sisters, who are really human, goes in several directions. As I have done before, and as quite a few others too—James Martin, Robert Ellsberg, George Fedotov—it is very useful to go back and retell the stories of the saints' lives.[22] And if, as these writers and others like Elizabeth Johnson suggest, the range of holy people is broadened, expanded to include those beyond our own communities and those outside the traditional categories already mentioned, there is much to be learned. Looking in unexpected places and for the less well known brings us to an Olga Michael, Joanna Reitlinger, or Paul Anderson, and perhaps here to some others.[23] This is not to reject the saints recognized and glorified in the past. Local as Peter and Paul maybe have been to Jerusalem and Rome, they are apostles to all. Likewise other locals have become universal—Monica and Augustine, Benedict and Scholastica, Francis and Clare of Assisi, John of the Cross and Teresa of Avila, Thomas Aquinas, Julian of Norwich and Hildegard of Bingen, Seraphim of Sarov and the "good pope" John XXIII.

### Saints in the Making?

However, telling the stories of those who have already passed into the heavenly kingdom should not cut us off from all the saints still living. St. Paul addresses the members of the communities he founded as "the holy ones" or "saints" (*oi agioi*). Here we have the fundamental and important reality, recognized in apostolic times but forgotten later on. Sanctity is not just heroics. As Paul Evdokimov wrote, paraphrasing Berdyaev, I think, the opposite of evil is not virtue but goodness, Godliness, holiness. Holiness is a gift, and it is given to every child of God. The often criticized Matthew Fox was right to emphasize "original blessing" rather than original sin.[24] The Eastern Church has been better in sensing this than the West.

We will always lift up extraordinary, exemplary people in our traditions. At the same time we must recognize that there are innumerable others, a huge cloud of witnesses, whose efforts to search for God and live out the gospel will never be widely known. But there remains a third category—saints in the making. I want to focus upon these in this book. Here, all the voices we will listen to are of people still very much alive and engaged in the struggle of the life of holiness. They are still on the way, searching for God. Rather than retelling the stories of their lives, we rather will listen to their first-person accounts. We will try to learn from their experiences and their recounting of them.

There is a considerable literature of this kind. I earlier mentioned the memoirs by Mary Karr and Elizabeth Gilbert. But there are so many other fine writers along these lines. Among Karen Armstrong's formidable publications is a powerful personal recollection.[25] Theologian Roberta Bondi produced her account.[26] Tony Hendra's memoir was a bestseller, though later his daughter's claims about his abuse of her did it damage.[27] Throughout his later life the acclaimed spiritual writer and priest Henri Nouwen chronicled his spiritual journey.[28] Thomas Merton's autobiography, though strongly qualified and contextualized by the author himself in his journals in his later years, remains a modern classic of the genre, and remains in print sixty years after publication.[29]

The writers I have chosen to listen to are diverse, intriguing, and in ways disturbing, too. One converted from Orthodox Judaism to Christianity, confounding family and friends. Several others went public with real and painful failures in their lives, personal and professional. Still others chose to write about their parents, warts and all, and their childhood with them. We do live in a time where it is not self-revelation or confession that are controversial, rather more crucial are issues of accuracy and authenticity in telling one's story.

I selected the writers because they speak powerfully, in very different ways, of their experience in living out their faith. Some tell more details of their lives than others. Some make more connections among their discoveries, joys, and disappointments, assess them more carefully. And others surely tie their experiences to larger issues or problems more explicitly. But I think all of them have much to share about the search for God and the effort to live in light of that search, lives of holiness.

## Questions of Faith

Peter Berger has had a great deal to say in the past several decades about religious institutions and belief in what he has characterized as a secularizing modern world. More recently, though, he has qualified this characterization, and he is in the good company of Charles Taylor, Philip Jenkins, and José Casanova, among others, who recognize that the diagnosis of progressive and, for the churches, destructive secularization was not accurate.[30]

Berger has something more to say. While always acknowledging his Lutheran roots, he has over the years also claimed freedom in theological perspective, aligning himself neither wholly with liberal nor conservative poles.[31] But over a decade ago he began to examine the possibilities of faith in a supposed time of unbelief.[32] And at the same time he, along with others, started questioning the dogmatic status supposing secularization to be an unstoppable, inevitable process in our time.[33]

In *Questions of Faith*, Berger employs the Apostles' Creed as the framework for a probing examination of what is not believable or, at the very least, is open to serious debate and criticism in the Christian tradition. Berger had already engaged in this insider's confrontation with Christian faith, the scriptures, the sacraments, the church, and ethics for quite awhile beforehand. However in asking quite a few provocative questions about the claims of the Christian tradition, he does something he had only tentatively attempted earlier. Anyone involved in the administration of a church body today, in coverage of American religious news, or in ecumenical activities will surely find much to affirm in his thoughtful questioning about the claims churches make over against the testimony of the scriptures and the historical record. For example, he contrasts the radical challenge of the reformers in his own Lutheran tradition—Luther and Melanchthon—with the later institutionalization of the movement and the development of various Lutheran orthodoxies. He also sees through the often made claims that the Eastern Orthodox churches have never been reformed and have never needed any reformation. Berger is fair, though. No denomination is immune to his discerning reflection, whether the massive Roman Catholic Church or dynamic Pentecostal congregations. It is worth noting that, at the Boston University Institute for Religion and World Affairs he had directed until recently, research on Pentecostals in South America has gone on alongside examination of religious fundamentalism and the possibility for a more moderate path.[34]

Berger has always posed questions for religious institutions and their members. Over the past four decades he has left a remarkable trail of books on religion in modern society and life. Early critical studies brought both sociological and theological challenges to the comfortable situation of American churches at the end of the 1950s.[35] Later, he would add a major statement about the place and role of religion in society alongside an equally major vision of the constructed nature of social institutions.[36] Berger continued to focus on the rediscovery of the sacred in supposedly secular society. He persisted in scrutinizing possibilities of religious affirmation even if not completely orthodox. After reflection on the ways in which modernity changed consciousness with a number of other religious thinkers, he and Richard John Neuhaus drafted a kind of manifesto, an affirmation over against both conservative and liberal factions.[37] The difficulty as well as the complexity of faith in a secular, pluralist, credulous, and incredulous culture was also a focus.[38] In addition to pushing the hard questions that many churches and Christian believers cannot bring themselves to raise or even to face, Berger also makes a strong profession of his own Christian commitment. He never characterized himself as outside the Christian tradition. A questioner of parts of it, a skeptic about some of its claims and efforts to legitimize them, he nevertheless, like Kierkegaard, offered a critique from within. He is as much a critic of denominationalism as he is a longtime observer of the behavior of religious groups in a kind of market economy of diverse beliefs and rituals.

## The Experience of Faith

Why have I drawn Peter Berger into our reflections here? Precisely because he has always brought together faith and reflection, the content of religious tradition with human experience. He is hardly original in this, for a train of thinkers throughout the centuries have realized that it is not just that Christ the risen lives, but that he lives, is to be found in, with, and through our experience, our thinking and feeling, what we have seen and done in our lives. Berger once thought that a Lutheran variation on the interpretation of Christ's presence in the Eucharistic bread and wine might illustrate what he meant. Over against the approach of "transubstantiation" that sees the bread and wine transformed completely, turned into the body and blood of Christ, "consubstantiation"—in fact a much more ancient perspective one finds as early as the apostolic teachers—sees the body and blood of the Lord in, with, and under the physical substance of bread and wine. I turn to Peter Berger then, to start us off on the road of experience in the search for God and the living of the holy life.

Christianity, as the very texts of the New Testament amply attest, is *not* just a set of truth claims to be assented to intellectually. It is first and foremost a community that is gathered not only by the word of God but also by worship. Alexander Schmemann insisted that the ancient formula *lex orandi, lex credendi* meant that liturgy was the "primary theology." And distancing himself from exclusive, sectarian versions, Berger's experience says that Christianity must be cosmic.

> If Christianity is true, then the universe is in the final analysis a vast liturgy in praise of its creator. It was created for this purpose and it is this purpose. This liturgy includes all human beings who have been brought to this understanding and (in the "inclusivist'" version of religious pluralism) it also includes those who praise God under strange names. The cosmic liturgy includes the living and the dead, and it includes angels and all beings in this or any other world. If Christianity is true, then the one who affirms this truth must necessarily join the community of praise. This community must have embodiments in the world of human beings—that is, there must be places where people gather to worship, by whatever means available. In other words, the cosmic community of praise must necessarily have empirical manifestations.[39]

The empirical community, with its preaching and services and other institutional components cannot help but be deficient. Yet though inadequate and finite, it is nevertheless a bearer of the infinite (*Finitum capax infiniti*). As Berger puts it, the bread may be stale, the wine sour, and yet, "in, with, and under" them and all the other elements of ecclesial existence, Christ is present.[40] This is so, despite such diversity of language, ritual, so many theological debates, and other human inadequacies.

Now while Berger's focus admittedly was on the question of the church as an empirical, very human, and imperfect dwelling for the Spirit, he points us to the two dimensions we will be looking into in what follows here. The first is that of our surroundings: our *culture, society, and time period*. Yet it is not only these immediate, contemporaneous settings but also the historical tradition that went before. Here in particular is *the church*—the community of faith, worship, and fellowship, the "local church" of the parish or congregation to which I belong, with all its attractive and not so pleasant aspects. But here also is the church long before my lifetime, the one I have read about and studied. And while I might believe there is but one church of Christ, in reality there are many churches. Some still divided by doctrine, decision, and practice, others "in communion" technically, but operating like the many retail chains, fast food franchises, or convenience stores and gas stations. This dimension is that of the formally organized religious institution, but also that of a theological tradition—Catholic, Orthodox, Lutheran, Reformed, Evangelical, and so on. (Not to mention all the communities, traditions and institutions beyond the Christian ones!)

Communities of faith can be life giving, but as we know and will hear, they can be toxic, destructive. Just as much as supporting or inspiring a pilgrimage of faithful living, they can poison our hunger for God, discourage our desire to serve God and the neighbor, even disorient our vision of human relationships. One of the pitfalls we will examine is mistaking the institution—the church and its structures, especially its customs and rules—for the "way," the life of the gospel itself. Religious leaders can demand more of us than God, equate growth in membership and giving with authentic discipleship. As the scandals of abuse by clergy—sexual and financial, among others revealed in recent years—make clear, those set apart by ordination or religious vows are not immune to greed and cruelty. Several of the writers whose voices we will hear will have stories ranging from the horrible to the humorous about the failings of people of the church, both leaders and rank and file members.

Also implied in Berger's words above is that the boundaries or limits of the church have been drawn too tightly, too exclusively. Nowhere could this be more the case than with holiness. St. Gregory of Nyssa Episcopal Church is but one example of sinning in the opposite, inclusive direction in its generous choices of holy women and men for the frescoes of the "dancing saints" in its sanctuary. Of course the entire Christian tradition is represented: East and West, Protestant and Catholic, martyrs and teachers, scientists and artists, social activists and ordinary people are there. There are holy folk from the ancient, medieval, Renaissance, Enlightenment, and modern periods. But this sacred procession crosses over boundaries to encompass the Old Covenant and Islam, even Hinduism, Buddhism, and humanism as well.

Holiness on first view we take for granted as originating within our tradition and history, even if we expand this to include all of Christianity. But if holiness is indeed of God, a gift from God, its giving must be universal, according to the overflowing love and the wisdom of God! So to set out to look at holy people and their experience will of necessity be provocative. It will shock and sadden us as we see what is done "in the name of God," even what we sometimes do to ourselves because of distorted understandings of the meaning and rules of our tradition.

The second dimension that we will track in further detail is that of *experience*—the personal encounters and confrontations, the doubts and confidence, the joys and fears by which individuals travel the paths of holiness. We will listen not only to Berger, but to many others already mentioned who are not, like him, professional and academic students of the sacred. Their accounts are their own, of course, subject to all the conditions of memory, later interpretation of earlier incidents, changes in viewpoint, the emotional weight of things said and done to them. But those sampled here I think pass the test of authenticity and discernment. Whether Barbara Brown Taylor's account of her failed ministry, Darcey Steinke's memoir of growing up as a "PK" ("pastor's kid"), Andrew Krivak's account of his formative years in the Jesuits, or Nora Gallagher's chronicling of her return to church in troubled times—to mention a few—my wager is that there is much to learn from these spiritual journeys of experience.

*Experience and Connections*

There are many competing images of the modern (some would say, postmodern) world in which we live in America. The late Richard John Neuhaus did not hesitate, in his posthumously published book, to call it "Babylon."[41] Radical conservative that he was, Neuhaus long argued that the prevailing culture was not just secular but militantly so, and that quite a few Christian thinkers as well as communities had sold out to the permissive, skeptical worldviews of the American left. (He was scarcely as critical of the right as he was of his former liberal culture.) But I would side with Berger in seeing not a secular waste-land in America but if anything a veritable marketplace of religious communities, rituals, and traditions, and a wildly diverse one at that.

It is not a recent phenomenon that preachers and politicians see the Antichrist lurking behind an American president, or creeping and godless socialism embedded in domestic policies for extension of health insurance, reform of the public schools, and stimulation of the recession-damaged economy by public work projects. The New Deal of FDR was similarly attacked, and most overviews of American religious history reveal ongoing fear of alien ethnic groups and their faiths, of free thinking and atheistic threats to the "city on a hill," the great spiritual experiment of America. Gary Wills' *Head and Heart: American Christianities* is one such study, but in it he forces us to see the diversity of belief and unbelief that characterized the very beginnings of the American project, Thomas Jefferson, Thomas Paine, and Benjamin Franklin but three notable examples of skepticism toward organized religion and traditional faith.

One could become convinced that Americans were either inherently, irrevocably godless or God-obsessed. The realities are of course far more complicated.[42] Houses of worship until the very end of the eighteenth century were for the most part cheaply built and poorly attended. Despite the mythology of a "Christian nation," the conflict among Christians in the colonies, and not just between Protestants and Catholics but among the descendants of the Reformation, was intense. From the outset, it is important to acknowledge that in America there has been a climate for belief and active religious life, as well as the other realities of religious diversity and conflict, and last but not least, skepticism and unbelief.

Although many challenges are raised in Berger's *Questions of Faith,* it is significantly subtitled "A Skeptical Affirmation of Christianity."[43] As problematic as traditional doctrine and dogma may be, the content of their claims for Berger is not as crucial as the personal connection with them. Having worked through Rudolf Bultmann's challenge to New Testament Christianity and church formulations thereafter, Berger writes:

> But there is also something very right about Bultmann's project: Faith cannot be based on any historical construction. My faith in Christ can only be based on the recognition of "Christ for me." . . . I do indeed encounter this Christ in the kerygma, but this encounter will only be meaningful to me if I can find the *nexus* between it and my own experience of reality.[44]

A bit further on, he makes it clear that it is not a one-sided subjectivity that is at issue, not only his own perception but what is experienced. And this is what is experienced:

> *An affirmation of faith in Jesus Christ hinges on the Resurrection as an event, not in human existence or consciousness, but in the reality of the cosmos.* Put differently: *Not Good Friday but Easter morning is pivotal for Christian faith . . . Only through the Resurrection is Jesus perceivable as the Christ—that is, as cosmic redeemer, and as victor over all the evils and sufferings of this world.*[45]

The nexus or connection has to do with the *kenosis*—God's self-emptying, self-giving in the suffering and death of Jesus and his glorification. For Berger, this action, which we also know as the "paschal mystery," bridges between ourselves and God, enables us to put the riddle of human suffering and death together with a supposedly merciful, loving creator.

The dramatic tension and link between Good Friday and Easter, between kenosis and cosmic victory . . . bring us back to the . . . tension between the benevolence and the omnipotence of God. Kenosis is the utmost stretch of the benevolence, the Resurrection the utmost expression of the omnipotence. I have suggested that the agonizing problem of theodicy can only be addressed ("solved" would be an inappropriate word to use here) if God is perceived as suffering within creation; if that suffering is understood, however falteringly, as necessary for the redemption of flawed creation; and if God is also perceived as the one who, at the end of time, will be judge and ruler of all.[46]

Berger does a theology not from above nor just from below, but one that is truly incarnational. It honors both the integrity of the human subject who is not asked in the Bible to simply believe but who, rather, is always encountered by God, given the experience that then is to be grasped, made part of one's own being because it is cosmic, real in itself.

In Christ's suffering and death on the cross, the extreme point of God's humiliation (*kenosis*), God both shares all the pain of creation and inaugurates its repair. And Christ will return as victor and restore the creation to the glory for which God intended it.[47]

## Patterns and Paths

It is all too easy to reduce sanctity to heroic virtue, to extraordinary actions on the part of unusual people, to fulfilling agreed-upon requirements. Saints are therefore the highly accomplished witnesses, servants, renewers, teachers, and so on. As I suggested in my previous book, we then nurture a "cult of celebrity," the spiritual equivalent of television shows such as *The Insider* or *Entertainment Tonight*. We can get as obsessed with saints as we do with actors and athletes, investors and politicians, both the admirable and the nasty.

But holiness is first and foremost a characteristic of God and a gift of God to those made in God's image and likeness. Is not the path of holiness, then, both one of personal experience and God's action? Women and men connect with God as they perceive his reality both around them and within them. In the Christian vision, God's very becoming one with creation, a sharer in time and space, presumes the goodness of creation. Hence Irenaeus of Lyons' dictum: "The glory of God is the human person fully alive." Note it does not say heroically virtuous, magnificently accomplished.

The plan of God may have begun with the birth of the Virgin Mary, the archangel Gabriel's announcement to her that she would bear the son of God, and the birth itself, but it did not stop there. Rather it went on to the other events remembered in the Eucharistic prayer: "the cross, the tomb, the resurrection on the third day, the ascension into heaven, the sitting at the right hand and the second glorious coming" (Liturgy of St. John Chrysostom).

Berger rightly insists that *kenosis,* the self-emptying suffering of God and victory of resurrection, is the center of faith. In the first half of the twentieth century, the Russian Orthodox priest and theologian Sergius Bulgakov also put *kenosis* at the heart of all Christian doctrine, at the heart of God's plan of salvation, and thus at the core of the church's tradition and Christian life. His students and friends, such as Mother Maria Skobtsova and Paul Evdokimov, likewise affirmed the self-giving of God as the pattern for Christian service and forgiveness, both in their writings and in their own lives of service to the poor and marginal. And if this is so, it must also be the principal pattern for holiness.

### *"You're history!" Patricia Hampl and Memoirs*

"You're not writing another memoir, I hope," a celebrated novelist friend whose work I treasure said one day, as if he'd given me long enough to get over my bad habit. "When are you going to get to the real books?" Meaning the novels.[48]

This was quite a shot to receive from a colleague with more name recognition as a writer than yourself. But it is only one of the succulent lines in Patricia Hampl's essays about the genre of which she is a leading practitioner here in America today—the memoir. Here several memoirs are written with gorgeous attention to detail, with emotional finesses, and with a tough, clear honesty even when the moment or relationship she describes is troubled, painful, crushed with sadness.

Usually when we hear "You're history," it is a put-down, a dismissal as too much in or of the past, too old, too dated, useless. In her essays about the ins and outs of writing memoirs Hampl stresses that memoirs are not indulgent nostalgia about the past, nor are they an idolatry of days gone by and the people in them. If anything, the blend of remembering, fact checking, and creativity — the use of imagination in reconstructing one's childhood bedroom or piano lessons, one's parents and other relatives' personalities and ways — enables us to know ourselves through our past.

We store in memory only images of value. The value may be lost over the passage of time . . . but that's the implacable judgment of feeling. This, we say somewhere within us, is something I'm hanging on to. And of course, we cleave to things because they possess heavy negative charges. Pain has strong arms. . . . True memoir is written, like all literature, in an attempt to find not only a self but a world. The self-absorption that seems to be the impetus and embarrassment of autobiography turns into (or perhaps always was) a hunger for the world. Actually it begins as a hunger for *a* world, one gone or lost, effaced by time or a more sudden brutality. But in the act of remembering, the personal environment expands, resonates beyond itself, beyond its "subject," into the endless and tragic recollection that is history. We look at old family photographs in which we stand next to black, boxy Fords, and are wearing period costumes, and we do not gaze fascinated because there we are young again, or there we are standing, as we never will again in life, next to our mother. We stare and drift because there we are historical. It is the dress, the black car that dazzle us now and draw us beyond our mother's bright arms which once caught us. We reach into the attractive impersonality of something more significant than ourselves. We write memoir, in other words. We accept the humble position of writing a version, the consolation prize for our acknowledgement we cannot win "the whole truth and nothing but." I suppose I write memoir because of the radiance of the past — it draws me back and back to it. Not that the past is beautiful. In our communal memoir, in history, the darkness we sense is not only the dark of forgetfulness. The darkness is history's tunnel of horrors with its *tableaux vivants* of devastation. . . . But still, the past is radiant. It sheds the light of lived life. One who writes memoir wishes to step into that light, not to see one's own face — that is not possible—but to feel the length of shadow cast by the light. No one owns the past, though typically the first act of new political regimes, whether of the left or of the right, is an attempt to rewrite history, to grab the past and make it over so the end comes out right. . . . No one owns the past, but it is a grave error (another age would have said a grave sin) not to inhabit memory. Sometimes I think it is all we really have. But that may be melodrama, the bad habit of the memoirist, coming out. At any rate, memory possesses authority for the fearful self in a world where it is necessary to claim authority in order to Question Authority.[49]

Spoken like the true baby boomer she is, the sixties child who had a war-protesting boyfriend much to her parents' disapproval. (There was lots of disapproval in the sixties—of saying you would no longer be going to church on Sunday, that you would not be attending a Catholic college, that you really wanted to be a writer—where is there a job for a writer?) Patricia chronicles her Greyhound pilgrimage to visit her boyfriend in prison, but also sketches what is for me one of the most memorable days in her twenties—the day she went to get her first prescription of birth control pills and then devours, in a Minneapolis deli, a Reuben sandwich "that could feed two," as well as a serious slice of five-layer chocolate cake while reading Walt Whitman in the time of the Vietnam War. It was for her, amid all the generational and value conflicts of the late sixties, part of a desire for purity, for a "*Mayflower* moment," in which the original innocence and goodness of America could be grasped again amid all the conflict—in that time not unlike today—over the war, over establishment priorities, racism, the plight of the poor, between those of the parental generation and their way of life.

Antiwar, a feminist, an agnostic, dedicated to the vocation of writing, thus does she head out in life, as several short memoir essays and her larger ones—*A Romantic Education* and *Virgin Time* (to which we will listen later)—chronicle. No wonder, as a fellow child of the sixties, I am pulled toward her memoir writing and her ideas, both about remembering the past, accepting that one is identified with and by it, but then sorting out the meaning of all that turbulence and idealism of the sixties for not only me but for others today. Yet beyond the biographical bonds I might feel, Hampl is a muse for the very reason that she provided for writing memoir. Whether in my own life, in my family, my church and its tradition of faith, my parish, the school where I have taught for more than thirty years—in all these I find what made me what I am. I trace in those experiences, as Berger says, where God is at work, who God is, what is the point of searching for and trying to make sense of God and of the life of holiness that leads to him.

> There may be no more pressing intellectual need in our culture than for people to become sophisticated about the function of memory. The political implications of the loss of memory are obvious. The authority of memory is a personal confirmation of selfhood, and therefore the first step toward ethical development. To write one's own life is to live it twice, and the second living is both spiritual and historical, for a memoir reaches deep within the personality as it seeks its narrative form and it also grasps the life-of-the-times as no political analysis can. Our most ancient metaphor says life is a journey. Memoir is travel writing, then, notes taken along the way, telling how things looked and what thoughts occurred. Show *and* tell. But I cannot think of the memoirist as tourist. The memoir is no guide book. This traveler lives the journey idiosyncratically, taking on mountains, enduring deserts, marveling at the lush green places. Moving through it all faithfully, not so much as a survivor with a harrowing tale to tell as that older sort of traveler, the pilgrim, seeking, wondering.[50]

Hampl's most recent memoir, *The Florist's Daughter,* is beyond summary. She begins and ends in the hospital where her elderly mother is dying and then dies. From this recent location, off flies the memoir to the city of St. Paul in which her Irish American mother and her Czech American father married in August 1940 in the cathedral very close to where Patricia Hampl lives today. In between is a whole lifetime with these now deceased parents, a great deal of their personalities, their attitudes toward work, marriage, the children they raised, the church, life in America in the second half of the twentieth century.

St. Paul is neither New York nor Los Angeles, neither Paris nor Moscow. Growing up in a middle-class home there, going to a Catholic convent school, then the big, bad University of Minnesota, and still living there over a half century later, Hampl holds out the puzzle—maybe better the contradiction—that so ordinary a place and people could yield so rich a story.

> These apparently ordinary people in our ordinary town, living faultlessly ordinary lives, and believing themselves to be ordinary, why do I persist in thinking—knowing—they weren't ordinary at all? What's back there? Back there, I say, as if the past were a location, geographic rather than temporal, lost in the recesses of old St. Paul. And how did it become "old St. Paul," the way I habitually think of it now, as if in my lifetime the provincial Midwestern capital had lifted off the planet and become a figment of history, and from there ceased to exist except as an invention of memory. And all the more potent for that, the way our lives become imaginary when we try most strenuously to make sense of them. It was a world, old St. Paul. And now it's gone. But I still live in it. Nostalgia, someone will say. A sneer accompanies the word, meaning that to be fascinated by what is gone and lost is to be easily seduced by sentiment. A shameful undertaking. But nostalgia shares the shame of the other good sins, the way lust is shameful or drink or gluttony or sloth. It doesn't belong to the desiccated sins of the soul—pride, envy. To the sweet sins of the body, add nostalgia. The sin of memory.
>
> Nostalgia is really a kind of loyalty—also a sin when misapplied, as it so often is. But it's the engine, not the enemy, of history. It feeds on detail, the protein of accuracy. Or maybe nostalgia is a form of longing. It aches for history. In its cloudy wistfulness, nostalgia fuels the spark of significance. My place. My people.[51]

Patricia Hampl's memoirs and discerning thinking about memoirs make her my muse here. For a great deal of the material to which I will have us listen are voices remembering swaths, pieces, whole segments of their lives in search of God and trying to live a life of holiness. As Hampl notes of her place and her people, their supposedly ordinary status obscures extraordinary qualities of their personality. Read *The Florist's Daughter* and you will not forget "Leo the Lion," her Dad and "Mother." Stan Hampl's steady, understated figure asserts itself nonetheless whether in the floral shop or the greenhouses or at home. The restless, ambitious, surging personality of Mary Marum Hampl, her ever-present cigarette and ever-running commentary on everyone around her—no wonder Patricia had to excavate them from their youth, their dreams and sense of duty, their towering presence in her life. Of course, she found from whence a great deal of her own indomitable character, wonder, and feistiness came—if not just from that couple, then in sheer resistance to and affection for them.

I am powerfully drawn to Patricia Hampl's remembering—to her youthful rejection of her Catholic upbringing and her complicated rediscovery of the contemplative life, of the psalms and the liturgy, of the scriptures and the holy women and men who form a long procession from the first days of Christianity down to the present. Hampl's writing about Francis, as we shall see, as well as her essays about Edith Stein, now canonized a saint, and Augustine, not to mention her own spiritual director Sister Madonna, have the aroma not just of honesty but more, the sniff of real comprehension. This writer is so good at crawling back into "old St. Paul" and the lives of Stan and Mary and the rest of the relatives that, whatever she has to say about a Francis or a Clare or for that matter the friars and sisters she encounters at Assisi and the Redwoods monastery—well, I really want to listen. We will join Hampl's pilgrimages later.

∞ Every one of us has a story, many stories actually, to tell. In our time so many theologians have not only stressed that experience is for us modern people the highway to God. They proceeded on this path themselves. And we will as well, following the paths of some articulate writers who chose to explore the paths and past that brought them away from and back to God. But it is neither just the origins nor the destinations, the end points that are important. The journey in experience is everything.

# CHAPTER TWO

# Messy Lives, Imperfect People

Among authors who write about their religious lives, few could be said to have an easy go of it in those lives. Whether Kathleen Norris or Barbara Brown Taylor, Darcey Steinke or Sara Miles, Patricia Hampl or Nora Gallagher, their memoirs are sometimes hilarious, always poignant but often painful. In many cases, there is a great deal of suffering and not all of it of the authors' own making. Starting with what is messy, imperfect, wrong, even tragic and destructive might not seem the best beginning in trying to follow holy lives. Yet Elizabeth Gilbert's *Eat, Pray, Love*, for example, takes off from her traumatic divorce, the end of a post-divorce relationship, and severe depression. There is a movement from darkness to light, sickness to healing, death to life in the lives of those seeking God, becoming holy. The movement is not once-and-for-all, certainly not just progressive or linear, as if religion were the Bayer aspirin Dietrich Bonhoeffer once noted many modern Christians wanted it to be. The journey is everything because in the traveling, in the experience, we do not just arrive at the heavenly city, do not simply become the new person in God. Rather the traveling is the process of being born and dying many times, growing and regressing. It takes most of us many years to intuit that there is a pattern of rising and falling, dying and rising, as St. Paul describes what being baptized into Christ will mean.

### *Kathleen Norris:* Acedia *and Her Life*

Kathleen Norris has been for some decades now an unusually lyrical voice about the spiritual life and the monastic way but also the small-town simple existence she and her husband chose in Lemmon, South Dakota. She chronicled some of this return to simplicity in *Dakota: A Spiritual Geography*. Her encounter with Benedictines, first in South Dakota then at St. John's Abbey in Collegeville, Minnesota, where she spent some time in residence, resulted in an exquisite collection of essays, *The Cloister Walk*. These were reflective essays on time spent in monastic communities, on monastics themselves, and on the tools of the spiritual trade such as *lectio divina* and the regular praying of the psalter. I would say that Kathleen Norris is second only to Thomas Merton as an interpreter and point of entry for many to the monastic tradition and its charisms, or gifts, for the spiritual life of prayer, study, and work in community.

To these publications she added a remarkable primer on the spiritual life, *Amazing Grace: A Vocabulary of Faith*. This dictionary enabled her to share the rich heritage not only of monastic spirituality but also of the wider Christian tradition. It is rare that a respected writer is able to do this, and moreover in a sustained way. She delivered the Madeleva lectures, which were published as *The Quotidian Mysteries,* contemplations of the spirituality of everyday life. Her contribution to a Trinity (Church) Institute conference on Benedictine spirituality in 2003 was entitled "Holy Realism"—meditations, again, on ordinary holiness. She also has published several volumes of poems as well as a memoir of her earlier life as a student and writer, *The Virgin of Bennington*. The memoir genre continues in her most recent book, *Acedia and Me: A Marriage, Monks, and a Writer's Life*.

In many ways this must have been a very difficult book to write. It is also painful to read. Norris takes us on a demanding yet revelatory exploration of the condition known in ascetic experience as *acedia*. This term is notoriously difficult to translate into English or, more broadly, into twenty-first-century terms. It may include what we understand as clinical depression, but it is both less than this and yet much more than spiritual aridity, indifference, inertia, lack of energy, or desire. Norris wraps an historical, theological, as well as psychological analysis around, first, a memoir of her existence as a writer and then a series of traumatic turns in her own life. These centered on David Joseph Dwyer, her husband and a writer also, and his struggle with profound depression, drinking, and a cluster of medical conditions including cancer, over the course of their married life. These illnesses contributed to his rapid decline over the last ten years of his life. He died at the age of fifty-seven in 2003.

In addition to the end of their life together, Norris being alone and choosing to be the caregiver for her aging mother would have seemed to set the stage for her descent into what most would describe as depression but which she presents as *acedia*. She returns to her childhood, adolescence, and student years to track the pattern of being a loner, moody, but observes that such tendencies work well for a writer. But the description of her *acedia* is meant to communicate the pain.

> One of the first symptoms of both acedia and depression is the inability to address the body's basic, daily needs. It is also a refusal of repetition. Showering, shampooing, brushing the teeth, taking a multivitamin, going for a daily walk, as unremarkable as they seem, are acts of self-respect. They enhance ability to take pleasure in oneself, and in the world. But the notion of pleasure is alien to acedia, and one becomes weary thinking about doing anything at all. It is too much to ask, one decides, sinking back on the sofa. This indolence exacts a high price.[1]

Whether one sees *acedia* as a form of depression, with spiritual roots and manifestations, or sees it a simply one of the many forms depression takes, it is a brutal experience. But as Norris forages through the ascetical literature, it is not rare. Rather, many monastic authors see it as virtually an occupational hazard of their monastic way of life. Beyond that, others see it as part of the journey in search of God, the pilgrimage of holiness. The effects of *acedia* seem severely debilitating and destructive, so much so that Norris connects the condition with suicide, referencing Sylvia Plath's *The Bell Jar*. What is most valuable from her lengthy examination of *acedia* and her autobiographical narrative, however, is that one can turn from it and, with God's help, be healed.

Norris's suffering with *acedia,* as it turns out from her account, is neither the result of the very difficult aspects of her marriage and profession as a writer nor due to the sad turns in her husband's health in the last decade of his life. *Acedia* was present independent of these factors and both before and through them. But running through a grim narrative, laced with citations from desert mothers and fathers, quotes from theologians and psychologists, there still is a will to live, to fight, to be healed.

> If only I could free myself from . . . acedia! Often I can. But if I become too weary, I care for so little that it becomes hard to care even whether I live or die. I need to learn to see again, and to reclaim my life through ordinary acts: washing my hair, as well as the dishes in the sink, and walking out of doors and enjoying the breeze on my neck. I may attempt to regain my ability to concentrate by taking on a good book of poetry. And I will certainly answer that ringing phone. . . . When I stop running from my life, I can return to living it, willing to be present again, in the present moment. But this means embracing those routine and repetitive activities that I scorn.[2]

Interspersed with detours exploring the many writers who have tried to define *acedia* and respond to it, Norris very courageously and honestly narrates the last years of the life she shared with her husband. There were many joys in their life together in her grandmother's house in a small South Dakota town. Kathleen discovered Benedictine monasticism after returning to her Presbyterian church and eventually became a Benedictine lay associate, or oblate. She has kept this relationship to monastic life now for over twenty years.

Norris describes the crisis brought on by David's disappearance from home, which was accompanied by a suicide note. He was located, and psychiatric hospitalization and treatment followed. She then chronicles his continuing decline, the effort to fully live their last years together, and finally his death. Her pages on the shock of losing a spouse and redefinition as a widow are gripping.

In the wake of David's death and in the context of beginning to care for both her challenged sister and elderly mother, Norris brings all the pain of living with loss and *acedia* into connection with the search for God and life in God—connections always present in her research findings on *acedia*. Commenting on Psalm 90 she says:

"Our span is seventy years or eighty for those who are strong. And most of these are emptiness and pain. They pass quickly and we are gone." Savoring this stark truth in a holy book, I am better able to confront my acedia, and ask myself why I am so willing to waste time, as if it were not a gift, mindlessly consuming and discarding my precious mortal life. . . . I may feel lost and weary, but these words provide hope. If the life of faith, like depression, is a cycle of exile and return, I am a prodigal become pilgrim, if only I can come to my senses and remember to come home. The Christian spiritual tradition employs several biblical metaphors for acedia: the Israelites' wandering through the desert and despairing of God's continued guidance; the disciples' falling asleep in the garden of Gethsemane, their abandoning Jesus on the night before his death. Each of these stories holds meaning for me, but another has become more significant, that of the childless woman, seemingly barren, whose unexpected motherhood becomes an essential part of salvation's story. It is as a childless widow that I embrace these women of Scripture—Sarah, Hannah, Leah; Elizabeth, the mother of John the Baptist; and Mary, the mother of Jesus—with their apparent dead ends and their harsh circumstances. We encounter each woman at a time when she is certain that she is incapable of being a mother. Yet each becomes a bearer of the promise, carrying within herself the mystery of transformation as Thomas Merton described it: "Prayer and love are learned in the hour when prayer has become impossible and your heart has turned to stone."[3]

Kathleen Norris's very personal story bears the marks of the pattern Peter Berger identified at the heart of Christian faith: the *kenosis* of suffering and the ultimate triumph of resurrection—Christ's as well as our own. Norris is not a Benedictine of the eleventh century though, but a Bennington graduate, a writer acclaimed by reviewers and readers, represented by a major publicity firm, a familiar face in religious publications and institutions. She is very much a woman of the twenty-first century, surely no paragon of perfection or heroic virtue, as her forthright tales of her own life and experiences indicate, both in *The Virgin of Bennington* and *Acedia and Me*. I suspect if we were to ask her, she would say she suffered a great deal but learned, with God's help, to struggle with the *acedia* that drained her of pleasure and life. I think she would also say that being a writer, always observing, thinking about how to describe and express a feeling, place, or person also helped greatly. I somehow sense she is a fighter and recognize it in her solidarity with the childless women of the Bible. (Dorothy Day expressed just such a connection.) Listen to her continue from the last citation about the movement toward healing and life.

> A way where there is no way; this is what God, and only God, can provide. This is salvation, which in Hebrew means to widen or make sufficient. As we move from death to life, we experience grace, a force as real as gravity, and we are reminded of its presence in the changing of the seasons, and in the dying of seeds from which new life emerges, so that even our deserts may bloom. It permeates the very language we use, and we are fortunate indeed that our words are far wiser than we are. Any poet knows that they can speak with new meaning, even years after we have written them, and tell us what we most need to know. Poetry might not seem like much in an unjust and violent world, in which acedia tempts us to give up the fight for something better. But poetry — psalms and hymns — can offer a remedy for the human tendency to take refuge in indifference.[4]

The movement in the journey of holiness is from death to life. This is not just at the end of one's life. As so many holy women and men remind us, this is the movement all through our lives.

*Barbara Brown Taylor:* Leaving Church

Another unembarrassed narrator of her own difficulties and failures is Barbara Brown Taylor. One of the best-known preachers in America, usually in the top ten list, she is a priest in the Episcopal Church and now professor of religion at Piedmont College in Georgia, as well as an adjunct professor at Columbia Theological Seminary. The author of over a dozen books, she has been granted numerous awards and honorary doctorates, and is a much sought after lecturer and preacher.

Brown Taylor is also a former parish pastor. By her own admission, and in great, haunting, painful detail in her "memoir of faith," she failed in the parish of her dreams. She knew this had happened when she described what daily life had become for her. But before this, she shared the path that led her first into ordained ministry and then into Grace-Calvary Church in Clarkesville, Georgia. Her account, not unlike that of Nora Gallagher, gives real insight into what the experience of discerning a vocation to ordained service entails, just as in Darcey Steinke's and Patricia Hampl's memoirs one can also follow the calling to be a writer. (Barbara has much of this too since she became in time a writer and lecturer.)

Even once the direction of the call has been detected, the factors that lead one to ordination are not always evident. There may have been interest in theology or in church history. Very often the liturgical services are quite important to the one discerning a vocation to ordained ministry. For some, the principal attraction might be pastoral work. One reads, asks questions of those already serving in the priesthood, and eventually makes the desire known to the local pastor and other church authorities. Then there is a fairly complex path to pursue and complete. Often before embarking on applying to theological education or seminary, there is a process of postulancy or asking to be considered as a candidate for ordination. We follow Barbara through this, in flashbacks. Nora Gallagher went through this too. It entails meeting with a committee from the diocese and a spiritual director, a priest. During a time called "discernment," while not yet a seminarian and surely not ordained, a postulant shadows a pastor, dipping a foot, as it were, into the kinds of activities that will be part of a vocation to ordained ministry. These can include attending parish council meetings, going along on visits to shut-ins and hospitalized people, participating in services as a reader, teaching religious education classes, all the while checking in regularly with one's director and future sponsor. If all goes well, there follow several years' worth of academic and further practical preparation. Theological study includes not only biblical, church historical, liturgical, and preaching training but intensive pastoral formation too.

Barbara zoomed right into Yale Divinity School straight out of undergraduate work at Emory, much to the surprise of her family and friends. But as she remembers growing up, there was some pull toward "The Presence," as she puts it, in a field of prairie grass behind her home, looking up at the sky while lying buried in the growth or looking up at stars and planets in the night sky, close by her father. Raised without church membership or attendance, it is only in college that she discovers actual religious belonging and in seminary the liturgy, the church year, and sacraments at Episcopal Christ Church in New Haven. It was the first of many fallings in love, which took her through the rest of the formation period, to ordination as deacon and priest and work as an assistant at an urban Atlanta parish and at last to the little clapboard small town parish of Grace-Calvary in Clarkesville.

Once there, the dynamo personality simply took off. Barbara and her husband, Ed, found a beautiful piece of rural property, built their own house, tended gardens, and kept horses. Her energy and dedication were greeted with reciprocal affection, and within a few years the small parish had so grown in size that a mission offshoot was planted. She describes lovingly, colorfully, vividly exactly what draws people to ordained ministry—the tapestry of Sunday liturgies, the smell of the home-baked communion bread and wine poured out, the howling of infants waiting to be baptized, the sicknesses that are healed and those that terminate in the new life of the heavenly kingdom.

> In years to come, when people would ask me what I missed about parish ministry, baptisms and funerals would be high on the list—that and the children who hung on my legs after the service was over, clinging to my knees when I shook their parents' hands at the door. Because they were not old enough to serve on committees or wrangle over the order of worship, the children often had a better grasp of what church was all about than the rest of us did. When one four-year-old rode by the church with his mother and her out-of-town friend, he interrupted them by tapping on the window. "That," he announced to the friend, "is where God gives us the bread." Because he was right about that, the congregation grew. God gave us the bread and we gave it to one another. Then we carried it into the community, dishing up soup at the soup-kitchen, handing out food at the food pantry, setting the table for mothers and their children at the women's shelter.[5]

She became known as a preacher and much loved as a pastor. And the small nave filled, and they went from three to four services, and her old back troubles returned.

> I was not doing so well on the inside either. In spite of my best intentions, I had dug myself into the same hole that I had left All Saints' to escape. My tiredness was so deep that it had seeped into my bones. I was out more nights than I was home. No matter how many new day planners I bought, none of them told me when I had done enough. If I spent enough time at the nursing home then I neglected to return telephone calls, and if I put enough thought into the vestry meeting then I was less likely to catch mistakes in the Sunday bulletin. . . . The demands of parish ministry routinely cut me off from the resources that enabled me to do parish ministry. I knew where God's fire was burning, but I could not get to it. I knew how to pray, how to bank the coals and call the Spirit, but by the time I got home each night it was all I could do to pay the bills and go to bed. I pecked God on the cheek the same way I did Ed, drying up inside for want of making love.[6]

When I first read this passage I had a very strong emotional and physical reaction. I myself have been ordained for thirty years, with some equally vivid memories of parish work and with several clergy colleagues having had vocational crises and personal breakdowns. One of them had sent me Barbara's book, recommended in a treatment center he had attended and from which he had received much healing. It was little consolation to keep reading Barbara's narration—about the need to add more space, raise money to do this, add staff, and then came the resentment: "We are not going into debt to build you a preaching emporium."

> Like most clergy, I know how to read the signs of depression, too many hours in bed, too little affect, too little hope that the deepening darkness will lift. . . . Behind my luminous images of Sunday mornings I saw the committee meetings, the numbing routines, and the chronically difficult people who took up such a large part of my time. Behind my heroic image of myself I saw my tiresome perfectionism, my resentment of those who did not try as hard as I did, and my huge appetite for approval.

I saw the forgiving faces of my family, left behind every holiday for the past fifteen years, while I went to conduct services for other people and their families. Above all, I saw that my desire to draw as near to God as I could had backfired on me somehow. Drawn to care for hurt things, I had ended up with compassion fatigue. Drawn to a life of servanthood, I had ended up as a service provider. Drawn to marry the Divine Presence, I had ended up estranged.[7]

I cannot do justice to the detail and honesty of her narrative here, I can only recommend it be read itself. Not having asked her, I can only imagine how much time, prayer, conversation, pondering, counseling in the years after this experience it must have taken Barbara Brown Taylor to be able to put it down in words, entrust it to all who would read her book. To be sure, she notes the less than supportive response of one clergy colleague. She also observes that her own difficulties personally as a pastor came exactly as a whole slew of "culture wars" and theological conflicts began to filter down even to the parish from the national church and societal levels—questions about the service of gay people in the ministry, the blessing or marriage of same-sex couples, abortion, and the question of whether the world around was a hell-hole of evil or God's good creation. Barbara did not blame her demise in parish ministry on the problems of the Episcopal Church or the administration in Washington or on anything around her.

Having tried as hard as I knew how to seek and serve Christ in all persons, I knew for sure that I could not do it. I was not even sure that I wanted to do it anymore, and I felt increasingly deceitful saying that I would. Feeding people was no longer feeding me.[8]

But out of this descent into doubt, depression, discouragement there came a rising, a new outlook, and a new life for her. Once again we find the pattern Peter Berger pointed to at the heart of it all—death and resurrection. Out of the loss, Barbara was to find a new calling, to continue writing and also to teach religious studies at the undergraduate level—the offer came close to her leaving the parish. And having announced her stepping down, she began the grieving as

well as the process of discovering so many things her pastoral preoccupations had obscured. We will draw on some of the fruits of that
discovery—of the need for rest, for a real Sabbath experience, of the
sacred character of ordinary everyday routines, of the presence of
God everywhere—later.

Her realization was not just of her own obsession with serving
and a need for approval. While we will look at it in another chapter
also, her recognition of the toxic possibilities of religion was also crucial for her.

> While I knew plenty of clergy willing to complain about high expecta-
> tions and long hours, few of us spoke openly about the toxic effects of
> being identified as the holiest person in a congregation. . . . Those of us
> who believed our own press developed larger-than-life swaggers and
> embarrassing patterns of speech, while those who did not suffered
> lower-back pain and frequent bouts of sleeplessness. Either way, we
> were deformed. . . . By fleeing the church to seek refuge in the world, I
> had reversed the usual paradigm, and I had to learn my way around the
> new one. For half my life, the axis of my world had run through the
> altar of a church. I spent most of my time in church, with church people,
> engaging in the work of the church. My view of reality grew from that
> center. I looked at life through the windows of the church, using the
> language I had learned there not only to describe what I saw but also to
> make sense of it. My context was so tightly focused that even my junk
> mail was Christian.[9]

The title of Brown Taylor's memoir is *Leaving Church*. She did leave
the parish but not the ordained ministry and surely not the church
or the Christian faith. In time she became reacquainted with ordinary
life and the presence of God in it without ecclesiastical labels. One
could write "January" and not "Epiphany time," granting autonomy
both to the world as well as to church, to life and to faith. It was much
like leaving the security of a backyard for the adventures of the rest of
the neighborhood, even the wild terrors of the nearby woods. After
having pounded doctrine into church-school kids, one could step
back and realize there were other interesting and beautiful things in
existence, more life than church life. And it was, all of it, very good.

Sunday morning was the Lord's day and good for the soul, whether or not one was in church all morning (which is why clergy need to spend some Sundays out of any church or service).

You could say that Barbara went through a most necessary process of "de-churching." Suffused with her sense of pastoral ministry and identity, she came to see that she had distorted the relationships between church and world, between liturgy and life, between the clerical collar and vestments she wore and her identity. The fruit of her process of healing and revisioning is the beautiful book about finding God everywhere—*An Altar in the World*— that we will consider. Teaching world religions as well as her own Christian tradition restored to her the sweep of spiritual experience in history, the women and men of faith from her own heritage as well as others.

Musing on the students struggling to stay awake in an 8:00 am class at her college, she sees that without the cross, candles, altar, and communion vessels, her hour and fifteen minutes with them had indeed been a liturgy.

> When I dismissed them at 9:15, I registered all that I had lost: my congregational base, my liturgical language, my exquisite vestments, my clerical distinction. . . . I saw that my humanity was all I had left to work with. I saw in fact that it was all I ever had to work with, though it had never seemed enough. There was no mastering divinity. My vocation was to love God and my neighbor, and that was something I could do anywhere, with anyone, with or without a [clerical] collar. My priesthood was not what I did but who I was. In this new light, nothing was wasted. All that had gone before was blessing, and all yet to come was more.[10]

*Nora Gallagher:* Things Seen and Unseen *and* Practicing Resurrection

Nora Gallagher and Barbara Brown Taylor have a number of things in common. Both are Episcopalians, both writers. Both have published widely but have chosen to expose their own troubles and joys in spiritual memoirs, and these have been well received. While Barbara pursued ordination to the priesthood and served two parishes before resigning from active ministry to write, teach, and lecture, Nora considered this path and went through the discernment stage, then withdrawing. Both weave together in their writing the pressures of marriage and career, of being in the church as well as in the larger world. Both attest to the seductive beauty of Christian faith and worship, the power of the community of faith to give individuals a sense of belonging and meaning. They catalog numerous examples of the diversity of religious belief and the respect in the Anglican tradition for this diversity, as well as for disagreement and doubt.

Both writers are courageous in revealing their own personal weaknesses and mistakes, the sorrows as well as the joys of their pursuing the life of holiness in contemporary America. And as the title of her second memoir, *Practicing Resurrection,* indicates, Gallagher, like Brown Taylor, has experienced not only the death of one close to her, her brother, but also the death of some religious ideals and consolations, only to experience resurrection from such depths.

If you tackle Nora's memoirs as well as look at some of her other writing and interviews, you surely come away with a sense of a strong, intelligent, and sensitive professional. I say this even though there is a great deal of inner doubt and personal unhappiness admitted, and on top of that, the tensions of integrating herself into a changing parish, the struggle of marriage, and the long, protracted sickness and death of not only her brother but a friend and co-worker.

Nora came to Trinity Episcopal Church in Santa Barbara as a visitor, but she was also looking for something.

I came to this church five years ago as a tourist and ended up a pilgrim. What I wanted at the time I walked in the door for the late morning Mass was peace, I told myself. I believe I understood peace at the time as comfort. What I got was "The peace of God that passes all understanding," as the Prayer Book says, or, as an old Irish hymn goes, "The peace of God—it is no peace." It was the late summer; I was greeted at the door by an African-American man with a sweet, vague smile and handed a bulletin by a thin woman with a sharp unhappy face. Inside, it was dark and cool; the altar stood beneath a stained glass window facing east, as is the custom in many churches. Men and women sat in lonely isolation in the mostly empty pews; the priest at the time, a dark-haired middle-aged man who looked depressed, preached a sermon about codependence. For the next few months, I dropped in on Trinity a few Sundays a month. I kept wondering why I was there but couldn't leave. The priest continued to seem depressed; the congregation dwindled: in a church that held four hundred, eighty to one hundred and twenty-five attended Mass on Sunday, five or six during the week. Very few people spoke to me at the coffee hour. Then, in the midst of this unhappy place, funny things began to happen. A couple of us started a soup kitchen in the parish hall. When the Jesuit priests and their housekeepers were killed in El Salvador in the spring of 1990, we held a candlelight vigil for them. We expected a hundred people; four hundred fifty—many from the community at large—showed up. A member of the parish wrote a letter to the Bishop of the Diocese of Los Angeles complaining about the priest and, after a long process, he eventually resigned. People were waking from a long sleep. During that time, I was often frustrated, disconcerted, even disoriented, but I was also waking to myself.[11]

Things got a lot better at Trinity and for Nora. A new priest came, Mark Asman, still the rector there. Eventually Nora becomes part of an intensely active community at Trinity, along with outreach organizer Ann Jaqua, associate priest Anne Howard, and retired but always radical Bishops Corrigan and Barrett, who constantly challenge the parish, both the clergy and laity. As the year progresses—and Nora titles the chapters of *Things Seen and Unseen* with the seasons of the liturgical year, from Advent to ordinary time—she is, one could say, baptized again, actually over and over with the many sides of life in a Christian community.

At Trinity, I learned how to speak to a crowd, how to write prayers, how to make soup for two hundred out of discarded vegetables. I cleaned up my act, stopped rebelling against everything in front of me (and/or leaving or hiding), and claimed my piece of the pie. I helped my friend Ben Nistal-Moret die—his was the first dead body I had ever seen—and I ran up against my own nature everywhere I went. "For now we see through a glass, darkly," said St. Paul, "but then face to face."

In the midst of it, I learned something about faith, its mucky nature, how it lies down in the mud with the pigs and the rabble. When Ben realized he was dying, he asked me to be his "alternate health care agent." As I signed that section of his Living Will, I imagined standing in the hallway of a hospital with perhaps a few doctors in white coats making compassionate and elegant decisions, gracefully. I did not imagine what came to pass. Instead of that antiseptic corridor, I sat in Ben's living room, jet-lagged, shoveling Chinese take-out food into my mouth, my own house strewn with dirty laundry and used cat litter boxes. I was deciding whether or not to ask a doctor to get a new drug that would help end Ben's life. I did not imagine being so tired I wanted Ben to hurry up and die. In short, I had imagined being a better version of myself. Instead I was the same old fucked-up woman.

In that time, I learned that everything is God's: my fucked-up self, my dirty laundry, my harrowing inability to be perfect for Ben. Everything is God's: shame, suicide, assisted death, AIDS. Because God is inside everything, findable in everything, because—I became convinced—I would not have made it through Ben's death without God. God is not too good to hang out with jet-lagged women with cat litter boxes in their dining rooms or men dying of AIDS or, for that matter, someone nailed in humiliation to a cross. God is not too good for anything.

I learned about community: that being faithful to God means being faithful to others, in sickness and in health, for better for worse. In my journal in July of 1990, I copied down a quote from the Czech president, Václav Havel: "By perceiving ourselves as part of the river," wrote Havel, "we take responsibility for the river as a whole."

I began to understand that the Holy Spirit (who is clearly a scatter-brained woman at a very large computer in Heaven) may or may not give a damn about results, but cares about the human process of getting there. Each time we met at Trinity to plan a worship service, to balance the budget, to decide how to decorate for Easter, we ran up against envy, pride and sloth. And we felt grace, learned compassion—for ourselves and for others—and sometimes, even sensed rebirth. "Be like the fox," writes Wendell Berry, "who makes more tracks than necessary, some in the wrong direction. Practice resurrection."[12]

In many ways these lines sum up much of what Nora chronicled in the first of her memoirs. She encountered street people previously rejected by the church, gay couples who at her parish at least felt welcome as part of the community of faith. The new rector felt compelled to tell the parish that he was gay, a process of inner reflection, debate, and prayer, some vestry members supportive, some not. When this tumultuous announcement was made and the community's acceptance and love for its pastor affirmed, did things quiet down and return to normalcy? There is no such thing in a real community of faith. The revival of the parish community was joined by the need to stabilize the church building's structure given the earthquake realities of southern California. Another controversial issue emerged, that of whether the parish would approve of the blessing of same-sex unions—marriage not then, in the '90s, the legal question it is now.

Nora also starts to observe the priests carefully, the beginning of her own movement toward preparing for ordination. She becomes a licensed chalice-bearer or lay communion assistant. Her actual distribution of the sacrament, along with her membership in a base community started at Trinity, and participation in weekday eucharists make her reflect incessantly on the connection between liturgy and life. Like Barbara Brown Taylor and Sara Miles, Nora is around the parish and the clergy enough to begin to see past the formal front. She follows the evolution of Mark Asman into a real shepherd for the community at Trinity, learning his own pilgrimage, as well as those of other priests, such as Anne Howard and Martha Siegel, and the retired bishops. Bishop Barrett was one of the ordainers of the first women priests in the Episcopal Church, and during the year Nora takes us through, he becomes involved in the ecclesiastical trial of Bishop Walter Righter, brought up on charges for the ordination of a noncelibate gay man. The nearby and now fire-destroyed Mount Calvary monastery of the Episcopal Holy Cross order is also a constant in Nora's account and the life of the people of her parish. The monastery is a frequent location for retreats and the brothers cherished counselors.

Nora creates in both memoirs beautiful quilts of her activities, the daily scripture readings, retreats, encounters with those who are fed, memories of her own growing up, the turbulence of her marriage, her ups and downs and now a rediscovery of community, faith, and work in the parish. The bad news of a diagnosis of terminal cancer for her brother, Kit, closes the first memoir and becomes the thread she continues into the second one. Stitched into this "memoir of work, doubt, discernment, and moments of grace," as in the first, are snatches of sermons and conversations, bits of authors' texts she is reading, and as the other thread pulling it all together, the rhythm of the church year and its feasts and fasts. Her brother's death opens the second memoir and the experience of his passing is a major theme—death but also resurrection, new life. The other principal adventure we follow is Nora's formal period of discernment or postulancy as a prospective candidate for ordination. It is a complex of silence sessions with her discernment group, various screenings and exams, her seeking one of the Holy Cross monks formally as her spiritual director, and then assignment as an intern to another parish, St. Columba's. Again I cannot and will not try to do justice to the beautiful pastiche of readings, conversations, observations, and sometimes tearful, at other times hilarious, events. Toward the end of the period covered in this second volume, she sums up.

> When I thought back on the last three years, it was as if I had crossed a series of invisible thresholds, passed through a series of new doors. When I visited the Bosque del Apache [where her brother had lived] after Kit's death, I thought, He is alive. Now I think, So am I. This, as it turns out, is my resurrection story. When I think about the resurrection now, I don't only think about what happened to Jesus. I think about what happened to his disciples. Something happened to them too. They went into hiding after the crucifixion but after the resurrection appearances, they walked back into the world. They became braver and stronger; they visited strangers, and healed the sick. . . . it was not only what they saw when they saw Jesus, or how they saw it, but what was set free in them. If there is some kind of life after death, what if it's not exclusively for the dead? What if it's a life available to us all . . . something the living can participate in too? . . . We spend so much time in the church "believing" in the resurrection or "not-believing" . . . that we may lose the point. What if the resurrection is not about the appearances of Jesus alone but also about what those appearances pointed to, what they asked? And it is finally what we do with them that matters—make them into superstitions or use them as stepping stones to new life. We have to practice resurrection. All the work of discernment led me to this place. I

had thought I was discerning a vocation to the priesthood, but in fact I had been discerning my relation to my brother's death, to my husband, to the world I live in, and finally, to myself. I had found the sacred again, but in different places. . . . I was not sure what I would do, finally. I was free to study for the priesthood. I had another book to write. Then it came to me, as I was writing these things down . . . that I was meant to remain in the middle for a while, between clergy and laity, a hybrid, a crossbreed, not the one and not the other. An inhabitant of the border-lands, in order to inform not only myself but the church, too. I needed to live the "priesthood of the laity" to find out how far it could be taken inside the church, and what it might mean outside her walls.[13]

Nora Gallagher responded to my inquiry about where she was and what she had done in the seven years since she wrote that. Her response:

You can say: Nora Gallagher continues to live in the space(s) between ordained and not ordained priesthood, experiencing the priesthood of all believers. She published a novel, *Changing Light,* about a physicist who leaves his work on the Manhattan Project, in 2006. Her book on taking communion as a practice, entitled *The Sacred Meal,* came out in the fall of 2009. She is at work on a third memoir.[14]

Once more, it is striking how the motif of death and resurrection emerges from the dense texture of a writer's effort to capture so much that she has experienced in a few years, from her return to Christian life and prayer, to the protracted sickness of her brother and his death, and the equally protracted exploration of a vocation to ministry. Beyond the central death and rising image, there are several others that seem to appear in most all the writers whose voices I have tried to listen to in this book as well as in the previous ones.

On returning to or rediscovering the life of faith, there is exhilaration but also, in time, the realization of the all-too-human aspects of church life. Members of Nora's Trinity parish can and do grow, venture beyond their vision of order and tradition in Christian life to accept a gay man as their pastor, along with others as members of their community. They learn to honor the chronically addicted and destitute as Christ himself, feeding them, occasionally having to control their behavior while hearing political talk-show hosts condemn the "coddling" of the poor. Next we will dwell on how religion can be at odds with its sources, toxic, destructive, inhuman, all in the name of God and his law. As Barbara Brown Taylor and Nora Gallagher, immersed as they have been in parish life, attest, very often people who have distanced themselves from church participation have themselves experienced the very negative side.

Yet even amid the mess of one's own personality, relationships, and fears, not to mention those of the community of faith, something is salvageable. Nora expresses a bit of disgust at the end of her first memoir; it is almost an exact echo of Sara Miles's frustration with the obstinacy of fellow parishioners to setting up the food pantry in her San Francisco parish.

On Nicholas Ferrar's feast day [a seventeenth-century deacon and founder of a lay community in the Church of England] I meet Ann Jaqua for lunch outside Brigitte's Café, two blocks down the street from Trinity. We refer to it as "our club." We're planning a project with two artists who've just joined Trinity and it's meeting with resistance from the liturgy committee. I order Brigitte's special, a half-sandwich and a salad, but they bring me a whole sandwich. "Sometimes I just can't stand church life," I say to Ann, biting into the sandwich half. "You have two options," she replies. "Live with it or start a new one." While we're talking, a crazy man with dreadlocks and a bare chest saunters by. He used to come to the Kitchen when it was housed at Trinity. When we are finished, I stand up, the half-sandwich still on my plate. "I don't know what to do with this," I say to Ann. "I'm going to see my therapist and she doesn't have a refrigerator." The crazy man walks back down the street. He stops near the table, looks at me. "You gonna eat that?" "No," I say, and hand it to him. It's a smooth motion without effort or hesitation. Ann grins. She says, "Nothing is lost."[15]

## "Nothing is lost," but There Are Losses

In the grander, eternal sweep of things, surely nothing is lost, ever. God is greater than our hearts, knows what we need before we ask. Love covers a multitude of sins the way a gracious person breezes over embarrassment or awkwardness to make one feel at home. I read once that a person truly in touch with his or her life, really comfortable in one's own skin, was able, most of the time, to do the same for you—make you feel like you'd known them for ages, that you were welcome, at home.

This is how it is supposed to be with God and in the family of God, the church. But the point Brown Taylor and Gallagher make we will hear made again in distinctive ways by others. It is surely not God, not the gospel, not prayer, not the Eucharist that are toxic, that drive people from religion, that destroy their souls. People do such damage, and I am not thinking only of clergy who abuse, sexually or otherwise, those in their care. Such abuse is the pinnacle of toxicity to be sure, and in recent church scandals as well as the normal operation of ecclesiastical institutions, there has also been the abuse of terror—threatening those who raise questions or protest with suspension, loss of their livelihood. Bishops, chancellors, even lower clergy have engaged in this to protect themselves and their friends. Others have so behaved to attempt to halt investigation and reform.

We have seen high-ranking church officials characterize the sexual abuse debacle as an unusual aberration in North American cultural contexts already sullied by permissiveness and promiscuity. Now the uncovering of abuse has moved across the Atlantic. The Irish hierarchy systematically refused to admit that clergy were guilty, criminally, of abuse, and used deception and legal maneuvers to avoid prosecution and legal penalties. All of this and the retention and moving around of abusive clergy were revealed in a massive report in the spring of 2010. In early 2011 the Irish Catholic church is described as in near collapse. No sooner was the Irish situation made public than cases of clergy abuse that went unattended surfaced across western Europe—in Austria, the Netherlands, and Belgium, as well as in Germany, and under the present pope's tenure as archbishop of Munich. Hot lines continued to receive allegations and reports for months afterwards. In October 2011 Bishop Robert Finn of Kansas City, Missouri, was the first American Catholic bishop to be indicted for alleged failure to report child abuse by a priest of his diocese to authorities. Vatican officials have made unprecedented defenses of the pope, at the same time attacking the media that investigated and reported the stories as anti-Catholic and biased and inappropriately singling out the pope. No longer was abuse merely a "North American" or "Anglo-Saxon" problem. Theologians and church leaders for the most part scrambled to urge laity not to abandon the troubled church, although a few admitted that the counterattack was part of the larger problem. Those who claimed absolute authority in the Catholic Church—the bishops—had failed in their handling of abusive priests and even more so in the treatment of the victims. Add to this numerous scandals of financial abuse—fraud, embezzling, mismanagement—and the charge of religion's toxicity is hardly exaggerated.

Sometimes the damage done in the name of the church, obedience, or the rules of a religious community was perpetrated with seemingly the best of intentions. The treatment novice and student sisters received in Karen Armstrong's memoir of her time in religious life comes to mind.[16] Superiors and other leaders were in their own minds striving to be faithful, to follow all the rules themselves as well as make sure you and I follow them just as carefully. Novices and perhaps the laity were simply assumed to be weak, compromised, incapable of acting with discernment on their own. Looking back, it is striking how the name of God or Christ never was mentioned in ecclesiastical enforcement, just "the rule" or the will of the superior or the need to be obedient.

Let's not kid ourselves. Anyone who has spent time in the church and even more so in ordained ministry knows that the definition of the church as sinners seeking forgiveness, the sick in need of a healer, are very neutral descriptions indeed. There are sadists as well as masochists there. There are power mongers and control freaks, those who get their kicks from the fear and even misery of others. Should anyone be scandalized or shocked by this? Then just page around in either the Hebrew Bible or the New Testament. Paul even names the perpetrators in local churches—the ones who sow division, who tyrannize the rest of the community. The historical books contain a sorry parade of failed monarchs and false prophets. It is not a question of which religious movement or wing you belong to for Jesus. He praises the good will and actions of those outside the house of Israel and celebrates their kindness and boldness. The Samaritan woman, known in the Eastern Church as Photini, the one who brings light, I imagine to have been quite an eyeful, given her string of spouses and lovers. Yet Jesus not only asks her for a drink, but his encounter with her is one of the longest in the entirety of the Gospels.

He invites himself to dinner at the house of a seemingly corrupt tax collector, allows women of questionable virtue to wash his feet, tells followers to feed themselves, and heals despite the Sabbath bans. And when the first-century equivalent of canon lawyers and chancery officials challenge him on all this deviant behavior he throws the scriptures back at them. With the exception of one Sabbath service at home in Nazareth, nothing else in the Gospels takes places inside a house of worship and that which does—teaching in the Temple precincts—could not be more provocative. To defy the ecclesiastical establishment was as threatening as opposing the state, perhaps more so. Over the centuries no matter what part of Christianity they come from, East or West, Reformation, Catholic, or Orthodox, scholars and preachers cannot help but see that most of Jesus's public ministry takes place far from the religious establishment, actually in consistent opposition to it, and in the company of both religious and social misfits and marginals. Jesus is almost never in church, yet most of us cannot get ourselves out of the building! Likewise, so many of the parables invert the usual religious and social perspectives—lepers and corrupt officials, prostitutes and heretics force their way into the kingdom. There is no respect for the powerful and the pious.

Later on Francis of Assisi strips off and tosses his clothes back at his wealthy father and the local church leaders. Sergius of Radonezh continued to use wooden liturgical vessels, threadbare vestments, and a monastic habit fit for a beggar. He likewise refused demands that he assume the leadership of the church. Mother Teresa—it is captured on tape—forced workmen to remove carpets and soft chairs destined for a house of her sisters of charity, loudly berating them for trying to pamper them. Dorothy Day calmly refused tax-exempt status and elegantly stepped up into police wagons both in Union Square and in the California growing fields in which she was arrested for nonviolent protest.

For all the destructive activity done in the name of religion by people of some religious standing, I want to say that there is also an equally long procession of women and men who spoke and stood against what was wrong, and they continue to do so fearlessly, boldly. No consideration of holiness or the search for God can really proceed without confronting this side of religion. It has many different faces and appears in diverse situations. The very writers whose voices we listen to are themselves witnesses to religion's damaging potential while at the same time showing us that such destructive activity can be opposed and overcome. There is only light and truth in God. Yet the fundamental expression or "Word" makes clear that both darkness and lies remain around us.

# CHAPTER THREE

# Dangerous Faith

*Religion as Toxic, Destructive, Pathological*

*Losing One's Calling and One's Way: Barbara Brown Taylor*

As one of four priests in a big downtown parish, I was engaged in work so meaningful that there was no place to stop. Even on a slow day, I left church close to dark. Sixty-hour weeks were normal, hovering closer to eighty during the holidays. Since my job involved visiting parishioners in hospitals and nursing homes on top of a heavy administrative load, the to-do list was never done. More often, I simply abandoned it when I felt my mind beginning to coast like a car out of gas. Walking outside of whatever building I had been in, I was often surprised by how warm the night was, or how cold. I was so immersed in indoor human dramas that I regularly lost track of the season. . . . What month is this? What year, for that matter? Most days I could name the president of the United States, but my daily contact with creation had shrunk to the distance between my front door and the driveway. The rest of my life took place inside: inside the car, inside the church, inside my own head. On the nights when Ed and I walked, I sometimes talked with my eyes fixed on the moving pavement for more than a mile before an owl's cry or a chorus of cicadas brought me, literally, to my senses. . . . On what grounds did I fast from the daily bread of birdsong and starlight? The obvious answer was that I was a priest, with more crucial things to do than go for a walk around the park. I had been blessed with work so purposeful that taking time off from it felt like a betrayal of divine trust. . . . Maybe I had read *The Diary of a Country Priest* too often, or maybe I was too much of a romantic, but I thought God would keep depositing funds in my account whenever my balance got low. I thought that all I had to do was give myself fully to the work, and God would keep me in business.[1]

If you thought that you'd heard all the bad news about the situation of clergy in the church from Barbara Brown Taylor's falling apart in her Clarkesville, Georgia, Grace-Calvary parish, the lines above are not about that. Rather they form an account of what her existence had been like at St. Luke's in Atlanta, before she and her husband headed for a simpler, slower life in the hills, in a more rural area. I omitted several passages of this extended description, a chilling one to any believer, ordained or lay, in which insomnia started to play games with her perception, making her think she'd seen a run-over dog's body before her vehicle when it was just a crumpled cardboard box. Or her admission that after hearing story after story of pain and suffering, it became difficult to imagine any good stories, so much is church a place for the broken and their healing.

Some might be tempted to interpret Barbara's torment as of her own making, a personal, idiosyncratic tendency to self-victimization, obsession with obligations, a control freak consuming herself in doing good for others. But the context and its legitimation are essential to the mix. I am thinking here about the ways in which suffering is too often viewed as good within Christian communities. I also have in mind the self-deprecating, self-loathing, perhaps passive-aggressive outlook of many clergy who rage at their abuse at the hands of their people but also glorify and valorize their abuse, a kind of sacred professional masochism. I heard a high-ranking church leader once at a national assembly describe the life of the priest in wretched terms: underpaid, endless criticism and blame for everything that went wrong in the parish, incessant calls for consultation, the expectation of 24/7 availability, the presumption that the pastor has no feelings, no boundaries, no life or family or friends or free time. Reciting this horrible litany of what people do to priests and what priests allow to be done to them, he smiled when he said in summation that all of us priests were like doormats for people to wipe their feet on, that we neglected our spouses and marriages, our children and families, our friends and own interests, even our health—and yet we somehow boasted and glorified, like St. Paul, in our afflictions.

It was a most embarrassing moment because of what all this said about the speaker, ordained for over thirty years, with a great deal of parish experience, and now a church executive. His presentation was good spirited but, without his realizing, it was a devastating indictment of what so many clergy allow to happen to them. It was also an incictment of the many laity, themselves active parishioners, and the bishops listening to this address at a major gathering. Bishops by inaction or disregard allow priests to burn themselves out or be terrorized by their parishioners. And parishioners themselves both unknowingly and deliberately take out frustrations on their pastors. The phenomenon of so-called "barracudas," also termed "clergy-killers," pathologically destructive individuals, who stalk, terrorize, and even smear the reputation of clergy when they relocate is all too real.[2] I know all too well a case in which after driving a pastor from a parish, several members called the search committee and parish council that were considering him in another state, attempting to destroy his reputation and chances to find another pastoral assignment.

The situation of the clergy in contemporary parishes and other levels of the church is complex and problematic. Brown Taylor's narrative provides concrete examples. She describes recruitment and training. We see in her breakdown how many clergy fail to maintain their physical, emotional, intellectual and spiritual health. We can see how entangled and volatile relationships among clergy, their parishioners, and the high level superiors such as bishops can be—all in Brown Taylor's story. As parishes shrink because of mobility of jobs and population, the seminarians graduating and being ordained, in many church bodies, are now finding there are few if any parishes to which they can be assigned. Neither their seminary faculty nor their bishops are able or willing to address the changes occurring in church life in the first decade of the twenty-first century. New clergy may very likely have to return to the most ancient models of being "worker priests," and this may be the most appropriate model of ministry, for many reasons, not just theological or financial, in the years to come. Our focus here however is not the clergy as such, but rather the life of holiness, of searching for God that is shared by all. Given their responsibility for both leading and teaching though, the clergy not only contribute greatly to the difficulties but serve as a distinctive and helpful gauge of the broader climate, spiritual health, or pathology of the community of faith.

Yet not all those who have found the negative side are ordained people. Darcey Steinke had little choice in being born as the child of a Lutheran pastor. Her account while searing and honest is also full of love, a compassionate portrayal of her father's inability to be attentive to both his congregation and his family, of her mother's being exhausted and worn down by the poverty and insecurity of parish life, and of Pastor Steinke then trying to earn a living in other ways.

*Taking the Bread, Giving the Bread: Sara Miles*

I included Sara Miles in an earlier book I completed on holiness hidden because it is ordinary. However, Sara is anything but ordinary. In her memoir, she recounts a colorful life, one very much of our time. Sara had been a cook and a freelance journalist, and was raised by parents who very deliberately exposed their children to nothing of institutional church life or belief. Their own parents, former missionaries, had done them in with way too much religion, a mistake they thought they would spare their own children from. Commitments to political and humanitarian action were Sara's religion, along with an interest in trying to communicate these as a writer. But the morning she drifted into St. Gregory of Nyssa Episcopal Church in San Francisco, she wasn't planning on an epiphany and conversion experience.

> One early, cloudy morning when I was forty-six, I walked into a church, ate a piece of bread, took a sip of wine. A routine Sunday activity for tens of millions of Americans—except that up until that moment I'd led a thoroughly secular life, at best indifferent to religion, more often appalled by its fundamentalist crusades. This was my first communion. It changed everything.

Eating Jesus, as I did that day to my great astonishment, led me against all my expectations to a faith I'd scorned and work I'd never imagined. The mysterious sacrament turned out to be not a symbolic wafer at all, but actual food—indeed, the bread of life. In that shocking moment of communion, filled with a deep desire to reach for and become part of a body, I realized what I'd been doing with my life all along was what I was meant to do: feed people.

And so I did. I took communion, I passed the bread to others, and then I kept going, compelled to find new ways to share what I'd experienced. I started a food pantry and gave away literally tons of fruit and vegetables and cereal around the same altar where I'd first received the body of Christ. I organized new pantries all over my city to provide hundreds and hundreds of hungry families with free groceries each week. Without committees or meetings or even an official telephone number, I recruited scores of volunteers and raised hundreds of thousands of dollars.

My new vocation didn't turn out to be as simple as going to church on Sundays, folding my hands in the pews and declaring myself "saved." Nor did my volunteer church work mean talking kindly to poor folks and handing them the occasional sandwich from a sanctified distance. I had to trudge in the rain through housing projects, sit on the curb wiping the runny nose of a psychotic man, stick a battered woman's .357 Magnum in a cookie tin in the trunk of my car. I had to struggle with my atheist family, my doubting friends, and the prejudices and traditions of my new-found church. I learned about the great American scandal of the politics of food, the economy of hunger, and the rules of money. I met thieves, child abusers, millionaires, day laborers, politicians, schizophrenics, gangsters, and bishops, all blown into my life through the restless power of a call to feed people, widening what I thought of as my "community" in ways that were exhilarating, confusing, often scary.[3]

At first Sara saw a community that was open, diverse, welcoming. It did not divide or judge people based on their income or gender, age or politics, sexual identity, and certainly not on their theology or church background. When it still requires letters of transfer in the same denomination to move from one parish to another, a program of catechizing if one had not been from that church body, perhaps even some rite of reception that rejects an earlier membership and tradition for commitment to a new one, St. Gregory's parish excluded no one from the Eucharistic table, on which were Jesus' words about coming for sinners.

Since Christianity presumes a community, church by definition involves other believers. Whether from the scriptures, the liturgy, or the teaching of its tradition, the church is at root a community of trust and sharing. However there is plenty of responsibility to go around for what is wrong, deceitful, toxic, and destructive in the words and actions of the members of the church, both the ordained and the lay.

Because the church is both divine and human, it has a dimension that is fallible, capable of weakness. Some would prefer to maintain that, as the pure Bride of the Lamb, the image of the church in the Book of Revelation, there can be no error or wrongdoing possible by the church.

Concretely, Sara discovered before long the St. Gregory culture of "process," in which any action or change required a great deal of discussion and debate. Even in a community that embraced diversity and change, actual changes and people who were "different" were still problematic. She also found that the food pantry feeding people on more than a weekday, on Sunday, really pushed the comfort zone of many. A visit with parish staff to the Episcopal conference center in North Carolina for a national meeting also confronted her with organizational formalities and a more traditional liturgical style than she had been used to. The church, not only the national denomination, but even her own community, turned out to be cantankerous, aggravating, and even mean.

"Sunday is too much!" an older woman nearly shouted at me, taking me completely by surprise. "I've been coming here for more than fifteen years, and Sunday is my day of rest." Carol was passionate. "Sundays are for church, art, and beautiful music. Everybody's afraid to say it, but we don't want our Sundays invaded!" Others were equally vehement. Most of them made a point of praising the food pantry, but their message was clear: Feeding the hungry belonged in its place, and "real church" belonged on Sundays. I was dumbfounded. I believed the food pantry represented the best of St. Gregory's practices and values: its openness, its inclusion, its beauty, and its invitation to participate in creating something together. I'd grown to know the church's members over years of Lents and Easters, funerals and weddings, sicknesses, stumbling, song. I'd listened to them tell dirty jokes and awkward truths, seen them suffer through the deaths of parents and children, cooked and eaten with them. Everything that had inspired me about this community had wound up expressed in the food pantry, and I'd wanted to return the favor, to give a gift back to the church. I felt as if I'd thought long and hard about a beloved friend, looking for the perfect present that would reflect her values and enrich her life—and then she'd spurned my offer. Angry notes began to circulate on an e-mail list of members, pitting those who enjoyed St. Gregory's long-standing Sunday-afternoon classical music concerts and painting classes against those who wanted to use that time for a pantry.[4]

Some of what is experienced in Christianity, in the community of faith, is not in itself malevolent. It can be loyalty to a certain way of doing things, comfort in particular arrangements, and fear of change. Inevitably, communities can become trapped in their own experience and point of view. No harm to anyone else is intended, no abuse takes place—of course this is not always the case, as recent church and clergy revelations of abusive behavior show. Just as with Barbara Brown Taylor, who admits part of her failure was her own doing, perhaps we could say the same for the others. She, along with Sara Miles, Nora Gallagher, and others like them venturing into the midst of church work, was bound to confront both the unintentional irritations and obstacles of community. One might suppose that it is through an asceticism of belonging to the church or a necessary process of growth in the Christian life that one learns to deal with the diversity and imperfection of the church, something present within the New Testament church communities themselves.

If I'd understood once that I couldn't be a Christian by myself, I was having my nose rubbed in that idea over and over again: My heart was breaking. I tried to talk to Donald Schell [one of the pastors] though, by now, I was suspicious of anyone in authority in the church. I sent him a nasty note when he said that maybe we should wait for a year or so, then try the proposal again. "I wouldn't be so disappointed if I didn't believe you see what's going on here," I wrote accusingly. "You created St. Gregory's with a risky vision of open communion and welcome. You fought with the established hierarchy; made a big beautiful room, put a Table in the middle of it; and opened the door to everyone. Years and years later I walked in; you put your hands on me and baptized me and asked me to accept a commission we share: to continue in the breaking of bread. Did you mean that? What the hell did you *think* was going to happen?"[5]

A fellow member explained to Sara that she was hardly the first person to become excited about Jesus and then be disappointed, discouraged in his church. "Get over yourself," he suggested. "Welcome to Christianity, this is just the beginning."

It was, in fact, the beginning of another story for me. Echoing everything that was wrong with churches and church politics, repeating in microcosm the ugliness of Christianity through the ages, I started to fight fiercely with the people I was supposed to be in communion with, struggled to institutionalize my own dogma and generally hounded people in the name of the Lord. I felt righteous when I listened to members plead for space for art or music or their own peaceful services. Hadn't St. Gregory's proclaimed God's Table was open to everyone? Hadn't we announced that welcoming strangers was at the heart of our mission? How could people cling to their comforting, cozy services, rejecting change and newness? Maybe, I told the pantry backers, I should just start a Sunday pantry at another church—peel off, split, find a more open-minded group. The seductive pull of the schismatic impulse grew stronger.[6]

Later, interrupted at the morning prayer service by a frequent and emotionally disturbed client of the pantry, Sara has what can rightfully be called a second epiphany and conversion.

You can't be a Christian by yourself. You can't be more special or holy. I was going to be changed, too, and lose my private church for a new one I couldn't control. I was going to have to work with people I liked at St. Gregory's, and the ones who irritated the hell out of me, and Veronica, and a bunch of strangers I hadn't even met yet. "In plain words," as the archbishop [of Canterbury, Rowan Williams] said, "unity is a gospel imperative to just the extent that we find it hard."[7]

We will rejoin Sara a little later, to hear how the life of being fed and feeding in Christ has gone for her.

*Clerics on Clericalism and Other Ecclesial Pathologies: Bulgakov and Schmemann*

Undoubtedly, examples of this passing through the toxic, troublesome sides of a community of faith could be multiplied. Nora Gallagher surely met enough of them. Much like Barbara Brown Taylor, while the vocation and life of ordained ministry seemed attractive from afar, the closer she got to it, the more she tried it on for size, the more her reservations grew. Remaining, as she said, in the "spaces" between the ordained and lay states, she did not have the more than two decades of experience that Barbara did. Nevertheless, she encountered not only the intolerance but also the sheer weight of process in the church—innumerable committees, meetings, reports, the results of which were often disregarded, the connection of which to actual situations was often tenuous. Like Sara, Nora experienced the distrust of parishioners with the poor, hungry, homeless folk coming to eat at their food pantry in Santa Barbara. She also heard the opposition of members to changes in parish practice, but she also saw the vision and openness of older members of Trinity Church, including the two retired bishops, Corrigan and Barrett, notorious as activists in their day in the civil rights, antiwar, and women's ordination movements.

　　While clergy are responsible for much that is toxic and destructive in religion, the ordained cannot be held to account for it all. In the accounts of the mostly lay writers we have listened to, surely this sad side of church life has plenty enough for all the people of God to share. However, some of the most trenchant descriptions of the dysfunctional and destructive aspects of church life are to be found in the writings of people who were themselves ordained, treasured the ministry, and themselves suffered greatly.

Many years ago the great theologian—some call him the greatest of the twentieth century—Father Sergius Bulgakov found himself facing as an adult the all-too-human misery of the church he fled in his youth. Russian bishops far distant from Paris, where he was teaching and writing, without even reading his demanding theological texts nevertheless passed judgment, condemning him as a heretic. Two young theologians, later to be acclaimed as major voices of the Eastern Church, turned on him. Georges Florovsky, invited to teach at St. Sergius Institute by Bulgakov, came to have no use for his colleague and dean's work, though his intellectual disagreement did not become personal. The other, Vladimir Lossky, wrote a pamphlet condemning Bulgakov's effort to express the relationship of God and creation through the figure of the Divine Wisdom, Sophia. Lossky's pamphlet served as accusation for Bulgakov's condemnation by the Moscow patriarchate. Later, towards the end of his life, Lossky is said to have regretted this action.

In his journals Bulgakov reflected on some of the aspects of church life that most pained him. Like Darcey Steinke, he grew up in a priest's family and in considerable poverty, his father not having a parish appointment but the administration of a cemetery chapel.

> Orthodoxy is grounded in *sobornost,* the communality of the body of the Church, and not in episcopacy, the bishop or bishops alone. . . . Nevertheless there is a peculiar kind of exaggeration prevalent in the Russian and other Slavic churches with regard to the episcopacy. . . . This slavishness is to be found first of all in the attitude of the bishops to secular power, in Caesaro-papism—the "union of the church with the state," in substituting the kingdom of this world for the kingdom of God. . . . While thus submitting to Caesar outside the Church, the bishops have demanded the same submission to themselves within the Church—not of course from the laity, who have remained free and in a sense exercise power over the bishops, but from the clergy bound by canonical obedience.[8]

Bulgakov goes on to note that the "despotic autocracy" and abuse of pastoral power by the bishops is further complicated by their status as pseudo-monks. They become monks, are tonsured only in order to be consecrated bishops. It is the rare case that a bishop was once a person with an authentic vocation to monastic life.

Bulgakov has in mind the latter decades of the nineteenth century, particularly in Russia, in which candidates deemed suitable for the episcopate were groomed and segregated, given the best education and training as if they were professional diplomats in the making. In fact they were religious civil servants in the making in the Russian context. The absence of real spiritual calling to be pastors of pastors and of many churches led to decadence and to numerous calls for reform in the Russian Church, culminating in the Moscow council of 1917–18. Bulgakov was an important reformer while yet a layman in this council, only being ordained later in 1918 after its final sessions due to the revolution.

The further account criticizes "episcopolatry" or the "bishop-worship" encouraged by the rubrics of the pontifical liturgy, for the false and empty impression it gives that the bishop is a person of great sanctity simply by virtue of his consecration and status.

> Enthusiasm for this pageantry is most frequently encountered among the less spiritual members of the episcopate, who assume the role of living icons. But, alas, the temptation is real for all, and the most difficult aspect of the matter is that all of this tragic glorification of the episcopate is based not upon recognized dogma but upon ecclesiastical psychology and is a matter of feeling. . . . In any case I must confess that for all my affection and respect for the bishops with whom I personally had contact, this ecclesiastical despotism was the heaviest cross I had to bear as a priest, and I feel guilty of passivity, of connivance.[9]

This is especially shocking given that Bulgakov was Patriarch St. Tikhon's righthand advisor at the Moscow council and that he was called to Paris and made dean of St. Sergius by one of the most enlightened and generous bishops of the modern era in any of the Orthodox churches, Metropolitan Evlogy Georgievsky. Bulgakov was, like Alexander Schmemann in his journal, anything but bishop-obsessed. Like his student, Bulgakov would also confide to his journals his reactions—angry, painful but also poignant—to the clericalism, the lack of education and even disdain for it in favor of a cultic performance of Christianity. Around him he found ritualist preoccupation, superstition, and formalism—all of which lacked the central element of the faith: love of God and of the neighbor. It is no surprise that another student and spiritual daughter of his, Mother Maria Skobtsova, would likewise point out the worship of form, rules, and clerical status among the Eastern Church clergy and laity, accompanied by disdain for the ordinary people, especially the poor and homeless.

Yet, for all the narrowness, all the accommodation to the state and culture, all the ritualism and clericalism Bulgakov saw suffocating his own Russian Orthodox Church and people, he was sustained by a far more amazing vision of God at work in the world, of God's unfathomable goodness and love, of all this contained in the Eucharistic bread and cup shared every liturgy, and even in the so cluttered, decadent, institutional church apparatus. Beneath, behind, and within it all was the eschatological reality of the faith and church—that the kingdom of God was present in it all.

> Tradition has ceased to be living and has become the depository of the faith, to be preserved but not developed creatively. Yet Orthodoxy demands not the mere possession of the inherited wealth of faith and life, but prophecy and apocalypse—a call and a promise. In this sense apocalypse implies a concern for the history of the present and the future as well as that of the past. The Church has no continuing city on earth, but seeks one to come. . . . It is not cowardly fear of life and flight from it, but the overcoming of all givenness, the longing for a new heaven and a new earth, for a new meeting and life with Christ. All this in ineffable and sounds like music in the soul; it is like a symphony of colors, like art and poetry. It is eager expectation of the promise. "Amen, come Lord Jesus."
>
> Much as I am "rooted" in the Church and at one with everything in it, in this feeling for her life I have remained solitary and alien to historical Orthodoxy, which has not satisfied me. Or rather, I feel that to accept this limited sense of Orthodoxy is to betray it and to lose something vital and precious. . . . I may refer to this experience as a Sophianic feeling for life which allows us to recognize the divine ground of the world under the crust of matter. I cannot say that I have been alone in this recognition—kindred spirits joined me and were near me—but so

far as the institutional Church is concerned, I am lonely and cold in it. And yet so firm is my hope, so apocalyptic my attitude towards life, that I am supreme and joyous in my expectation.[10]

There are others who, as he did, saw the mountain though they realized they would never get to it—Father Alexander Men, in Bulgakov's own Russian Orthodox milieu, assassinated for all his writing and teaching about the joy of Christianity in life, or our own Martin Luther King Jr.

Alexander Schmemann's journals are a poignant and provocative source on the toxicity of clericalism and other destructive aspects of ecclesiastical life.[11] He ranted against what he called "the whole vaudeville of *klobuks,* [monastic cowls] stylization"[12] and "the religious madness" he saw emerging around him, obsessed with details of dress and fasting rules and liturgical rubrics and clerical power, but uninterested in Christ or the actual human being there in front of oneself. Here is a passage from the journals and then another from unpublished lecture notes, used by William Mills in a paper.[13] Schmemann targets the same educational and career-preparation process for creating a clerical caste and identity that distorts Christian faith.

The tragedy of theological education lies in the fact that young people who seek priesthood are—consciously or unconsciously—seeking this separation, power, this rising above the laity. Their thirst is strengthened and generated by the whole system of theological education, of clericalism. How can they be made to understand, not only with their minds, but their whole being, that one must run away from power, any power, that it is always a temptation, always from the devil? Christ freed us from that power—"All authority in heaven and on earth has been given to me" (Matthew 28:18)—by revealing the Light of power as the power of love, of sacrificial self-offering. Christ gave the Church not "power," but the Holy Spirit: "receive the Holy Spirit." In Christ, power returned to God, and man was cured from ruling and commanding. In the sixty-first year of my life, I suddenly ask myself: How has it all become so perverted? And I become afraid![14]

A first-year seminarian has already a tendency to think that he is to learn to acquire something "specifically priestly," a way to walk and to speak, a way to behave that will make him "soon like a priest," and this feeling of belonging to a different and superior "caste" may obscure in him the very simple idea that to be a priest one must first of all be a Christian—in the full meaning of this word. And to be a Christian, means, above everything else, to take seriously, directly and literally the commandments of Christ and to live by them.[15]

I think that the best or, some would say, the most devastating indictments of ecclesiastical toxicity come from members of the clerical caste themselves. This is why Bulgakov and Schmemann—priests, theologians, seminary deans, and advisors of bishops—have been cited here. Schmemann's harshest comments about bishops, abuses of clerical power, and the sickness and pathology of church life have as of yet been kept from English language translation of his journals, though much, if not all, of his ruthless honesty in those entries have now appeared in Russian and French editions of the journals. Many more could be cited. Retired archbishop Rembert Weakland's memoirs are a witness to his own failings but also to the treachery against one labeled an outcaste in the church. Donald Cozzens, a high ranking monsignor and former seminary dean, has likewise pried open the clerical origins of the abuse scandals in the Roman Catholic Church in the US.[16] The otherwise careful scholar, mentor of Schmemann and colleague of Bulgakov, Nicholas Afanasiev wondered about the tinkling bells on the bishops's vestments, the special rugs cast wherever they stood in church, and the often-repeated chants of "Many years, O Master!" (*Eis polla eti Despota!*). All these standard elements of a hierarchical liturgy still today, he said, are the last vestiges, sounds, and sights of the long extinct Byzantine imperial court—from which the hierarchical *sakkos* vestment and miter, the garb of Imperial senators, and much else of the pomp derived. What are these trappings saying? Do they point, as liturgical imagery is supposed to do, to God at all?

Unlike the perspective of critics such as Richard Dawkins, Christopher Hitchens, and similar writers, it is not so much the content of Christianity—God, Christ, the scriptures, or the very existence of the church—that is on target as toxic here, by me at least. Rather I would say it is the inevitably fallible institutional apparatus and the human factor—the people within it—who abuse the teachings and structure.

The recent John Patrick Shanley play-become-film, *Doubt,* captures the toxicity, not so much in the figure of Father Flynn but in the rage of Sister Aloysius, the parochial school principal, who has without any proof accused and convicted the priest of an inappropriate relationship with a twelve-year-old boy. Perhaps because of a long, trusting relationship with one of the nuns who taught him as well as the experience of clergy abuse in his family, Shanley's writing makes the vicious wildness of a religious believable, even if it does not fully present the horrific accounts of the behavior of abusive priests all over the country in various dioceses as well as the refusal of superiors to remove them, sometimes villainizing the victims and their families.

The negative possibilities of clergy and laity in the institutional church run the gamut from sheer prejudice and timidity to ignorance and all kinds of obsessions. But they can include the kind of fixations on work, perfectionism, the neglect of boundaries and limits, the distortion say, of what it means to be a pastor of a community, or a priest, nun, monk—these can be profoundly pathological and damaging. There is no theologizing around them, no spiritualizing them away. Not only can these tendencies destroy faith and trust in religious leaders, they can deeply distort or destroy lives.

I doubt that there are many who have been in the ordained ministry or in religious life who have escaped contact with this toxicity. In what I see, all told, as a lengthy but not terribly exciting or eventful life in the church, I have surely encountered a religious superior far more toxic and vicious than Shanley's Sister Aloysius, a man who was an alcoholic, most likely schizophrenic, yet left in charge of a house of studies for years, tormenting the seminarians there. Later on after ordination, I saw bishops paralyzed by fear, unable to maintain order or say what they thought because of criticism. I know clergy colleagues whose physical and emotional health, as well as that of their families, were damaged by parishioners intent on destroying them. I suppose it is not even unusual to have confronted truly emotionally ill parishioners, unaware that their rage or their preoccupations, their attempts to manipulate me or others stemmed from their sickness. And in the name of fidelity to church teaching and rules, I have seen a cleric threatened with deposition or defrocking for a decision of pastoral discernment unless he begged forgiveness, acknowledging more than anything else disobedience to the bishop.

The destructive possibilities and actual toxic behavior of religious people, however, do not exhaust this book or its inquiry. For, as many of the writers we are sampling show, even the experience of such negativity is not an inevitable end to one's belief or spiritual life. In fact, the lives of many holy women and men are riddled with such toxic experiences of the church and religious leaders. Think of Dorothy Day and the chancery and officials of the archdiocese of New York. Consider Thomas Merton and his abbot general, Gabriel Sortais, and others who feared his concerns for social justice and church reform. Fear but also rejection of his point of view led to Merton being censored and banned by Abbot Gabriel from writing on war, peace, and nuclear weapons. Fortunately Merton did not stop thinking about such matters and found what he believed to be an honest loophole in the sanctions. He continued to write letters on these Cold War issues and then did not publish them in a press or publisher but informally. Mimeographed copies circulated among friends and correspondents of his.

Theologians of the stature of John Courtney Murray, Teilhard de Chardin, and Yves Congar were also silenced and sanctioned. All of them were later exonerated and their writings were part of the renaissance of religious thought that occurred after World War II, especially after Vatican II. Despite being ostracized, these and many other controversial theologians continued to shape debates, even when such debates were not supposed to be taking place. The bishops told Alexander Schmemann they no longer needed his counsel. Sergius Bulgakov to this day is accused of heresy by many who have never completed one of his books. Mother Maria Skobtsova, canonized by her church, was scorned by some of her comtemporaries in Paris and still is dismissed by traditionalists as being neither a real nun nor even authentically an Orthodox Christian, her martyrdom meaningless because she died for protecting Jews, Communists, and Resistance members. Alexander Men's assassin will never be found.

Yet each of these transcended the opposition and condemnations in their own lifetimes, many being fully vindicated only after their deaths. The possibilities and realities of evil are not intruders but everpresent members of the community of faith, of the life in search of God. The line between evil and good, Bulgakov said, echoing an ancient saying, runs down through the center of our being. It is not some line demarcating the wicked from ourselves. "Of sinners, I am the first," goes the precommunion prayer of the Byzantine liturgy, quoting St. Paul. *Simul justus et peccator,* in Martin Luther's phrasing, Ambrose of Milan long before him (as well as St. Paul) concurring that we are at once redeemed yet erring. More than this, the central motif emerges, from death to life, as one sees in Barbara Brown Taylor's and Nora Gallagher's and Darcey Steinke's memoirs. Death comes in so many forms, in this life, as these accounts demonstrate—but so does life.

More often, in daily life it is not a question of life and death. The tangle is less dramatic, not so ultimate. If I have heard a wise commentary on the experiences of what is bad about religion, about the damage that has been done by church leaders and people, all the while denying it and then trying to minimize scandal by covering it up, it is this. The reality of wrongdoing, followed by anger, fear, and other reactions, must be accepted as *real* and not dismissed as insubordination, a lack of trust or obedience, a failure of spirituality.

The presence of the Spirit in the church does not preclude the presence and action of weak, fallible humanity. But we are so tempted to spiritualize, to deny the toxicity, to blame the victim as much if not more than the perpetrator. Why is it that there is so much hostility toward retired archbishop Rembert Weakland's memoir when he admits his wrongdoing and errors in judgment? Some readers still are threatened by the honesty of Thomas Merton in his journals and by Mother Teresa's and Dorothy Day's accounts of their doubts and discouragement. The sagacious Matthew Kelty, a former missionary, hermit, and monk at Gethsemani Abbey and novice under Merton, is very helpful on this:

> Hostility, fear, rejection, indifference, seem to me normal responses to the presence of God. It is good to reflect on this and to be able to understand what happens.
>
> When we speak of God, when we reveal Him, it must not be thought at once that hostility, fear, rejection, or indifference indicate that we have not communicated well or that the reaction has been unacceptable. We may have communicated very well, the hearers may know exactly

what we mean, and they may not be able to cope with it. So, they become hostile or frightened. They reject what we offer or fall asleep or something similar.

In dealing with the human heart, God may find the same scenario. If you look into your own heart's life, I daresay you have, as I have, answered God now in one way, now in another, but in some cases negatively. This is not because we have failed to understand Him, or that we did not want to respond, but by being overwhelmed we were simply not capable of anything else.

In which case, what does God do? He waits and comes back later. He is not easily discouraged. He will keep this up for a lifetime if need be. He never gives up. Hostility, fear, rejection, and indifference are not rare at all in our relationship to God. They are common. . . . The point is, I think, not to deny hostility, fear, rejection and indifference, but rather to recognize what is going on. Hostility need not indicate disagreement or conflict at all. Nor need fear mean that one cannot trust, but only that one cannot do so at the moment. Rejection is not rejection. It is a way of getting rid of someone at the door you are not willing, able, or ready to admit. Indifference is perhaps a more subtle approach, but indicates anything but indifference.

All of this explains why we are at such pains to make God predictable, manageable, someone with whom we can deal. An unpredictable, unmanageable God is far more than we can live with. We like structure, routine, rubric, regularity, and order in our lives. We expect God to arrive in that way. Let Him come in sacrament and worship, let Him arrive on time, in proper context, in good order.[17]

## Jesus Freak: Sara Miles's Further Adventures

It is not just to save face—our own and that of others in our community—that we often deny the destructive, poisonous side of the church, of the ordained ministry, even of spirituality. It is also because we would rather have God being and acting in our own image and likeness. The search for God also entails a search for ourselves. Every one of the accounts here witnesses to that, from Patricia Hampl's to Matthew Kelty's and all those in between. Father Matthew devoted a number of essays to examining his own spiritual journey, collected in the volume *Flute Solo,* and reminiscences crop up in his homilies and other talks. To find yourself is to find God—this has been a dictum from the earliest desert mothers and fathers down to our own time. It is there, as we shall see, in Lauren Winner's exodus from Judaism to Christianity, in Diana Butler Bass's journey as well as her pilgrimage through many communities of faith. It is not possible to tell a story of one's search for God without chapters of disappointment, disgust at what passes for faith in the institutional church or religious life. But in the end, these need not be walls. They also need not force us out and away from the search and the holy life. There is joy to be found, where God and one's own self are to be found.

Now, several years after Sara's discovery of the bread of life and the community and the many works of love that come with being fed Christ, she has become an integral part of the parish of St. Gregory of Nyssa. The title of her newest book is what she has become: *Jesus Freak.* It is not the whole sweep of her life from childhood on that we travel. Rather the story now is of her daily grind, doing outreach from St. Gregory, the colorful account of a job that pays little, that regularly sticks your nose in other people's miseries and complaints and stench. It is comforting and comfortable religion thrown out the door.

> It might be comforting, to those Christians who doubt the current indwelling of the Holy Spirit in our damaged, compromised selves, to tell ourselves our failures are because Jesus is now far, far away.
>
> It might be reassuring, to those tired of dealing with our violent, scary or just unpleasant neighbors, to think that we can worship God by turning our backs on them. That we can't do much anymore about our lives, or the lives of other people, except gaze at the sky and pray to a disembodied spirit. That Jesus was alive once, and we remember him fondly, but now we're left with nothing more powerful than plastic crosses, Christian rock bands, and church committees. With Jesus safely tucked away in heaven, we're off the hook.
>
> But he's still breathing in us.[18]

Miles lets us in on some colorful yet very difficult experiences of hers as a kind of deacon or chaplain in the neighborhoods around her church. What Sara does better than most writers is to relate honestly and in detail the hard, difficult, ugly sides of a life with God. Sensitive to the people she serves and the difficulties in their lives, she does not shortchange us on her own doubts and fear, and what brings her peace.

> Like most people, I have an ambivalent relationship to power. I want it and I'm scared of it. I think I couldn't possibly use it well, and I know others can't. Why should humans receive the power of the Spirit? Isn't that what God's for?
>
> But Jesus is right here with me and the crazy guy: the lowly and unprepared, as the prophets foretold. Among the weak, faithless, and doubting, as his disciples proved, then and now. He doesn't look for the most "religious," the most doctrinally correct, or, for that matter, the smartest of his beloved people to build his Kingdom, but hands over authority to anyone willing to suspend self-doubt and simply trust Jesus' faith in us.
>
> There is no other authority on earth we have to wait for, no permission we need in order to act on his words. All it takes to be a Jesus freak is to follow him.[19]

And follow Jesus she does throughout her neighborhood, as we read. I think of the lines in the Gospel where Jesus assures us that there will be conflict—family member versus family member, friend against friend, yes even Christian against Christian!—but sadly this we know all too well. While not at all embarrassed about showing us Christianity's humanly nasty sides, Sara also takes us along when she runs empty and then is shown a well, a spring of delicious, cold water—of life. Visiting a fifteen-year-old boy charged with felonies at Juvenile Hall, she recalls meeting him first years earlier when still a child, eager to be at church, full of life.

> I sat there on the waiting room benches and all I could think about was the "hard wood of the cross," as Christians say. It is *really* hard. It's hard to have to hold the ways we hurt and fail each other. It's hard to hold betrayal, and loss, and the violence and emotional pain that people inflict on their families and strangers. It's hard to bear the weight of the princi-

palities and powers that bind our lives: the crushing, unfair justice system, the courts, the "machine," as this boy's mother said to me. "It's like he's going slowly down into the mouth of a machine that's going to swallow him up." The cross is just plain hard. As is the good news of Jesus, which tells us that suffering is real, but joy comes in the morning. That the humiliation and pain of the cross—of watching a disturbed child suffer, of having a kid in jail, of wishing but being unable to stop violence—is always, everywhere, redeemed by love. . . . God knows our lives are hard, and God knows we make them harder all the time through obdurate, vain, judgmental actions; through faithless reliance on Law, and through faithless refusal to participate with Jesus in mercy. But God's mercy remains everlasting. It's wide. It's profligate, encompassing devastated victims, ashamed parents, kids who've been hired to kill other kids, and adults who've been hired to handcuff and guard children. It encompasses me, with my prideful and inarticulate desire to make a difference; it encompasses the terrified neighborhood woman who failed to save a life; it encompasses the saintly math teacher and the angry gang leader. It holds the judge, the betrayer, the condemned criminal, and Mary, the criminal's mother, in perfect love.[20]

I could not put Sara in the category of writers who always find the "happy ending" or who can locate the silver lining amid treacherous weather. The life she has experienced, the cruelties she has witnessed children of God inflicting on one another and themselves has been too hard a teacher for her to gild what is grimy and grim. It was very painful for me, ordained almost thirty years, to follow her initiation, as an enthusiastic, idealistic new Christian, into the boring, detached, and destructive culture of the institutional church. The articulate but politically correct, always sensitive yet corporately savvy voices she had to listen to—of her own pastors as well as fellow parishioners and higher level church staff—are all too familiar to me, and depressing.

How the fiery words of Jesus captured in the Gospels can be tamed into trade talk reminiscent of human resources is both amazing and discouraging. That "church" for many means a zone of personal comfort, insulation from the suffering and escape from the ugly contentious disputes of our era, a bath of pious phrases and sweet images—is enough to want to follow the Jesus who Mother Maria Skobtsova described as trapped in a sentimental, ritualistic church building.[21] Herself a veteran of chasing down the homeless and addicted in Paris streets and foraging for food at the produce and meat stalls at Les Halles market, Mother Maria claimed, to the scandal of her clergy and lay fellow Russian Orthodox, that finding himself so imprisoned, Jesus would march out through the icon screen and down the nave, out the door of the church building and into the streets, where he would breath free again, with his own—all the riff-raff scurrying about there.[22]

> There seems to be an idea in the contemporary church that following Jesus requires . . . outfitting and preparation. Apparently, Christians can't feed people without a permit from the state, a certificate from the church insurance fund, and a resolution at a denominational convention. You can't teach without audiovisual aids and rooms full of approved Christian gear. You can't touch sick people without 125 hours of supervised clinical instruction and latex gloves. You can't proclaim repentance unless you've been to seminary—and even then it's a bit dicey. And God forbid you should claim authority to act in Jesus' name without a feasibility study, a mission statement, a capital outlay of ten thousand dollars and at least six months of committee meetings. But ordinary people still hope, suspect, and believe they can be Jesus. The formulas of religion may be so overfamiliar that people have a hard time acting as if this most surprising narrative is true. . . . They may, like me, be afraid because there's no way to be Jesus on your own private terms. . . . But Jesus is real, and so, praise God, are we. Every single thing the resurrected Jesus does on earth now he does through our bodies. You're fed, you're healed, you're forgiven, you're pronounced clean. You are loved, and you are raised from the dead. Go and do likewise.[23]

It is encouraging to hear that we can listen to Jesus, follow him by doing what he did and still does *despite* the structures, the traditions, the hierarchy—all the elements of institutionalized religion that get in the way. It is possible to recognize and then to repent of the errors, the wrongs of religion.

Don't idolize religion, Jesus reminds his disciples impatiently. Of course, all of us long for religion. In Jesus' time, every part of life—hygiene, food, sex, money, agriculture, economics, child rearing, health, ethics, marriage, death, and temple practice—was governed by a catalog of religious laws that attempted to shape human life to please the Divine. And though it's easy, at the distance of centuries, to mock a religion that specified exactly which fabrics were acceptable to God, we still share our forebears' desire to codify our lives in order to manage God. Religion is a set of ideas about God, purified and abstracted from ongoing relationship with God. And from religion springs sin: the attempt to separate ourselves from others, the failure to see everyone as an inseparable part of God's body. The feverish wish to practice correct religion with the right kind of people. The inability to comprehend that other human beings, not like me, are human beings. And that they hold, precisely because they are not like me, the key to my salvation.[24]

Miles proceeds to the encounter of Jesus with the Canaanite woman, someone completely outside the boundaries of his community of faith, as a place to see whether religion still rules in the Gospel (Mt 15:21–28). And not surprisingly in her reflection she sees this as Jesus' own healing, his own indictment of the sin of religion and his becoming the healing, the cure for religion. (In the verses just before this condemnation and cure begin: "Listen and understand," Jesus says, "it is not what goes into the mouth that defiles a person, but it is what comes out of the mouth that defiles" (Mt 15:10–11). His disciples quickly point out how offended the scribes and Pharisees already are at the apparent abandonment of religious requirements such as washing before eating (Mt 15:1–9). Jesus quotes the prophet Isaiah's invectives at them—they honor God with their prayers but their hearts are very far from God. They worship in vain because they have put human cultural precepts in the place of God's own words.

When I listen to Sara Miles—an admitted political and social Christian radical—and her riveting accounts of anointing a poor woman dying of cancer, of her struggles with church official and rules, I am reminded of the dozens of entries in the journal of someone rather different. He was a political and social conservative, a critic of

the waves of cultural change in the 1970s from the women's movement to the French left, from the passion for social justice to the ecumenical movement. I am thinking here of Alexander Schmemann.

As opposed as he and Sara Miles might appear on first compari-
son, how united they are in seeing everywhere the kingdom of God
open to us, the opportunities to love God and serve the neighbor
readily available but so often evaded in ordinary "religious" behavior.
Experiences of what is toxic and destructive in the church, in religion
more broadly, and in the search for God are not restricted to this
chapter or to these writers. They are to be found and listened to
throughout. I have some of my own in a later chapter. As divergent as
their perspectives and personalities may be, Sara Miles and Alexander
Schmemann nevertheless offer, I think, the strongest witness there is
to what so many detest in religion. What is most important is that
they make no attempt to excuse it or explain it away. Rather, they
name it, in excruciating detail to be sure, as do Barbara Brown Taylor,
Nora Gallagher, and Darcey Steinke and the rest. Further, they recognize it not only in others—rectors, bishops, committees, destructive
parish members—but also in themselves. They describe the personal
blindness or the self-righteous confidence and arrogance or the leth-
argy and sheer exhaustion, perhaps the depression that generates the
poison, that destroys hope and initiative. The chronicle that Lillian
Daniel and Martin Copenhaver have produced—often startlingly
honest reflections on themselves as pastors—also comes to mind here.
The brother or sister of the community is the "clergy killer," the an-
tagonist, the torturer. All too often, and in the name of God or of
God's law, the very shepherds or pastors, spiritual mothers or fathers
or fellow believers become spiritual terrorists. But also, as the famous
Walt Kelly Pogo cartoon strip put it: "We have met the enemy and he
is us." Each of us too, wittingly or not, contributes to what is pathological, but this is not spiritual retreat or denial of the toxicity of others. It is no use denying that around the sacred, within the institutional
structures of the church and religious life, there resides much that is
mean, cruel, pathological, and destructive.

Ourselves, others—there is plenty of guilt to share for what gives
religion a bad name. It comes from all sorts of sources too: respect,
love for tradition that has fossilized into fundamentalism, supersti-

tion, legalism, fear of getting something wrong. Sister Aloysius from *Doubt* again comes to mind—consumed with certainty, willing to run over anyone in her way to the "truth," indifferent to the collateral damage done to people. The believers who make religion deadly come in an infinite variety of costumes and personalities, with all sorts of justifications and aims—and they include ourselves. Yet what Schmemann and Miles show is that within the faith and the life with God for which we search is the reality that there is One who has vanquished what is destructive and toxic and pathological. Matthew Kelty urged that we not ignore the miserable and repulsive.

> Hostility, fear, rejection, and indifference are not rare at all in our relationship to God. They are common. . . . The point is, I think, not to deny hostility, fear, rejection and indifference, but rather to recognize what is going on.[25]

Since we here have decided to remain within the Christian tradition, it is the risen Christ who blasts open the locked doors of hell to lead out Adam and Eve and all their children from death, in which we all float even while alive, to life. Whether it is Thomas Merton or Peter Berger, Sara Miles or Alexander Schmemann, what sustains them, what convicts them of their wrongs, what keeps them going, praying, working, is this Jesus.

# CHAPTER FOUR

# Holiness and the Search for Joy

In attempting to learn about experiences of the search for God and the attempt to live the life of holiness, we have already listened to contemporaries of ours in their spiritual journeys. What is more, we started with the more difficult experiences of the mess that we and our families and lives usually are. As if that were not enough of a reality check, we then proceeded to look in some detail, often painful to face, at just how bad, how destructive, how poisonous religion, the institutional church, our own versions of spirituality can be. Despite our looking for what is like God—what is good, beautiful, and true—given our human nature and condition, we cannot help but collide with the misery we often create ourselves, but which is also there in abundance, lurking where we least expect it: within the community of faith and even among ordained and other religious professionals.

However, real honesty before God and ourselves also demands that we hear about joy in the search for holiness. Here we will listen to accounts of significant time spent in formation and in service in the church. Later we will also hear some ordinary tales of searching for and finding God and joy.

### *A Long Time with the Jesuits: Andrew Krivak's* A Long Retreat

Andrew Krivak, a wonderful writer, published a beautiful spiritual memoir, a reflective and often colorful account of his eight years in formation in the Society of Jesus, the Jesuits.[1] He used for the title the thirty-day Ignatian spiritual exercise that is part of not just training but regular spiritual life for Jesuits, the "Long Retreat." Having spent slightly longer myself in formation and in a religious community, the Carmelites, from my teens till my early twenties, I was intrigued and eventually very moved by his account.

On the return from his father's funeral with his wife Amelia, amid a swirl of memories of the man, of their relationship, the shock of loss and his absence, Andrew decides that they will stay overnight at an inn on Lake Cazenovia near Syracuse and continue back to Boston for their flight home the next day. Stopping there put him very close to Le Moyne College, and on that campus was a brick building that had marked the start of a significant period in his life. He and Amelia visit the place, and thus begins a remarkable spiritual memoir, which at least one commentator has seen as a contemporary version of St. Augustine's *Confessions*. Krivak is a writer by education and trade and a very good one, and this pilgrimage back and through his Jesuit years must be read in its entirety, for the insight into religious life, into faith, and especially into one's own life and personality. Knowing that discussion and some excerpts cannot do it justice any more than previous looks at Barbara Brown Taylor, Nora Gallagher, and Sara Miles, Krivak's account is an important one to which to listen in this effort to look at the spiritual paths of ordinary people.

In late August 1990, after undergraduate work at St. John's College, Annapolis, graduate study, a degree from Columbia, and some work in sailing, twenty-seven-year-old Andrew Krivak entered the Jesuit novitiate of St. Andrew on the campus of Le Moyne College in Syracuse, New York. And so began what can only be called an adventure in every respect. Soon he has found his way into the *ordo*, the daily schedule of prayer both common and private, Eucharistic liturgy, study, and work that, with some variations, would be the pattern of the rest of his life in the "company." The Jesuits have by far the longest and most complex formation process. During a focused two years' novitiate of study, prayer, and some outreach work—assimilating into community life as well as the Jesuit "culture" of that

life—there are stints of supervised work. Jesuit formation involves
further study—in Andrew's case, time in the Dominican Republic,
Russia, and Slovakia, including language acquisition and experience
abroad, but also work in hospital chaplaincy. After this there is more
structured ministry assignment. In Andrew's case, given his academic
credentials, this was a year of undergraduate teaching. Further study
included the philosophy needed for ordination, this done by Andrew
at Fordham, and theological studies themselves, done at the Weston
School of Theology, relocated to Cambridge, Massachusetts, next
door to the Episcopal Divinity School.

> Regardless of what questions and convictions we had come to this house
> of novices with, what we all had in common, after our own personal pe-
> riods of discernment, was the determination to live the life of the Jesuit.
> Not inclined to try it, not waiting for when it got so hard we would cut
> and run. Most of us were college-educated. All of us had known work.
> Not one of us was younger than twenty-one. At the outset or in the
> midst of what should have been our "professional" lives (consultants,
> lawyers, professors, writers), we embraced becoming novices again, and
> not by picking up another trade. We had to reorder our lives so that to
> be poor, chaste, and obedient meant fulfillment rather than frustration.
> And that doesn't happen overnight, regardless of how long you've been
> a practicing Catholic. Gone—but not too long ago—was the harsh old
> theology of priests and nuns "dying to the world" when they entered
> the seminary or convent, taking new names, sleeping in cells on straw,
> wearing identical habits, and disappearing to family and friends. We
> didn't change our names or attach to one another's names the formal
> prefix "Brother." Our rooms in the house were simple but warm and
> spacious. . . . We wore the same clothes we were used to. . . . We received
> mail, were allotted a stipend for long-distance calls, and would be al-
> lowed to visit our families for two days after Christmas. What we gave
> up in its totality was what the world said we needed: credit cards, bank
> accounts, investments, awards, connections, independence, and "the
> genital expression of intimacy," also known as sex. It wasn't that these
> things were perceived of as evil. We believed that a less attached life was
> not only possible but desirable, a life in which a man could live on a dif-
> ferent kind of capital, a different kind of freedom, a different kind of

affect. In everyone's story there was the example of someone who showed that it could be done. And not through a tortured existence of self-hatred, hair shirts, and leg chains but through the ongoing journey to "Know Thyself." That's what you might call the real ideal. It didn't take long, though, for the struggles to appear, struggles we all brought with us no matter how light we traveled.[2]

For the next seven years, no matter the location or the exact terms of assignment and work, Andrew and his colleagues would wend their way through many different experiences and elements of the formation process to help them continue on in the Society. There were regular meetings with superiors charged with supervision of the novices or students. As Krivak shows, these interactions could be confrontational—challenges to patterns of action he displayed that were inappropriate or revealed resistance on his part to formation. One such clash occurred over the kind of bicycle Andrew wanted to get for commuting. Some encounters were deeply rewarding exchanges of experience, sometimes consoling, other times encouraging or revealing. There is a consistency to the Jesuit culture too, for no matter where he was, there was the rhythm of prayer, study, work, and the ongoing process of discernment, both personal and in conversation with his superior or counselor. This held true in the Bronx studying at Fordham or doing hospital work or in the overseas assignments doing language immersion or a crash course in the liturgy and life of the Eastern Church, the latter based on Andrew's Eastern European family roots and his interest in the Byzantine Rite.

Andrew with his classmates does the thirty-day long retreat designed by the founder of his community, St. Ignatius Loyola. The retreat of the spiritual exercises is rigorous and fairly well known. Thomas Merton tried to follow it, as he described in *The Seven Storey Mountain*. Each week has its own focus, such as encountering the reality of sin in the first week. Ignatius prescribes a system of meditation points in which a person puts himself into a location, then not only to think about but in every sense to experience what is there. Krivak describes in some detail the directions for this with regard to being in hell. The schedule is reduced to the minimum prayer services. Liturgy, meals, and a walk outside occur, but all in silence and with no distractions such as email, iPods, and Blackberries. It is demanding, yet the long retreat does help a person to go inside, to struggle with boredom and distraction, with apathy and one's attitudes to just about everyone and everything. Krivak is particularly insightful in describing his meditation on a passage in the Gospel of Luke during the long retreat: "Put out into deep water," Jesus' command to his disciples who were fishermen. It resonated with his time working in the sailing industry but also with the larger project that the years of formation were becoming. Both his regular conversations with Jesuit formation leaders and then with secular counselors did get him on the path of "going inside," seeing what his family had meant, what kind of impact his earlier education, friendships, and romantic relationships had on him.

In the course of the narrative Krivak discloses some details of his growing up, his devout parents, his relationship with a larger than life father, his involvement with a girl and its aftermath. He also describes a difficult tense relationship with another, older Jesuit who kept trying to establish some sort of friendship with him in unwanted and sometimes emotionally ambiguous ways. Andrew also comes face-to-face with more objective issues. He explores the Eastern Church, and he asks hard questions about the disease and suffering and death that he observes in his pastoral placements in hospitals. When his love for writing and graduate work in it keeps being pushed aside, he is frustrated about how much of who he is the Society can or should claim. The portraits he crafts of his superiors and fellow seminarians throughout are rich, engaging ones. Father Gerald J. Chojnacki, superior of Ciszek Hall, the students' residence at Fordham, stands out. He seems to get through and into Andrew's head like no other director had been able to do. His sessions peel up an edge on Andrew's restlessness and what turns out to be depression, which leads to counseling. Krivak later says that this priest saved his life in more ways than one.

Finally at Weston, after meeting Amelia Dunlop, there is a turn in direction for Andrew. After spending some time together, he pulls away, does not keep up contact with her (as his superiors had advised in such situations in the past and would again in this case.) Despite his coming to within a year of ordination to the priesthood as a Jesuit, and having gotten through what is the longest and the most varied and rigorous formation process in the church, Andrew realizes he is in very serious doubt about his future with the Society of Jesus. A meeting with the major superior, the provincial, and another formation leader is troubling. He tells them very honestly of his doubt, of his meeting Amelia and their mutual attraction. He is dealt with fairly but without much interest or compassion. They can give him another assignment away from Cambridge and Amelia. His ordination can be put off with no reflection on his candidacy.

Andrew Krivak does what he's been taught for almost a decade to do in such a situation. Going to a retreat house, he makes a private retreat with a Jesuit directing and speaking to him. In the course of the conversations and prayer, the director, Father Fury, identifies where Krivak is—he has made a decision to leave the Jesuits and is looking for confirmation of it. All of the smaller issues are really subordinate to this. Amelia is central, but by no means the only factor. With real skill, the priest suggests that Andrew use Psalm 139 to pray further.

> The next morning, an hour before the liturgy, the psalm floated about me like a voice: "Lord, you have probed me, you know me. . . . My travels and my rest you mark; with all my ways you are familiar." That Lord did in fact know enough about me not to be anxious with where I was going. So why should I? Then praying with the [retired] fathers—Jesuits of many years, wheeled in, hobbling in or walking of their own accord . . . all with the burning desire to be with their Lord, who knew them—made it plain to me what I would be leaving. Not a life of poverty, chastity, and obedience in decline but a community of men who, at the beginning and at the end of the day, expressed a singular longing. It is and always has been a pilgrim's journey, right from the days of Ignatius and his first companions. If the world is our house, why should I fear or mistrust the reach of any man? If it is of God, it cannot be withstood. And yet can't I also express a singular longing for another person? I took Father Fury's direction to heart. I began to say that I was leaving the Society of Jesus. In my prayer, I imagined saying it to others. . . . I told a fellow retreatant, "I came here looking for confirmation." Later, on a walk, I said to myself out loud in those woods, "This is what I have to do."[3]

As someone who once was in very much the same situation as Krivak, I found this last part of his memoir particularly striking and expressed with remarkable grace and clarity. Father Fury reminded Andrew that all who are baptized are called to the common priesthood. It was not a question of having a "call" to be a Jesuit or a priest or having no calling at all. Having studied a great deal of theology and at that point having spent almost eight years in Jesuit training, somehow it was as if this fundamental truth had escaped him. Neither ignorant nor rejecting of it, this basic reality simply was not on his radar. He tells us he reread chapters of both Augustine's *Confessions* and Merton's *The Seven Storey Mountain*, as well as Thoreau's conclusion to *Walden*. Merton's joy in leaving family, friends, marriage, a profession, at that early point in his monastic life—a perspective that was to radically change for him—no longer rang true for Andrew. I think this one last citation allows him to relate his decision himself.

> When I became a Jesuit, on the Long Retreat of the Spiritual Exercises, this became a desire to serve God, to imitate Christ in a priestly order of men, a desire that remained so until I felt the loss not of God but of who I was as a man. And now one question concerned me, one I always figured I could find in God while I kept it at bay from my fellow men and women searchers: Love. Pure and simple. Not some diffuse and vague feeling of warmth. Rather, *this:* How should a man love well? Without a life in search of that, I decided, I would find nothing, in service of no one. I would be a driftless and emptied community of . . . what? Certainly not a believer. The great mystery of Christianity is that God loves us *first.* If I doubted the possibility not of loving but of being loved, then I doubted everything.[4]

And in a few more pages, the long retreat is over, Andrew's things get packed and moved out, and soon he sits in his new apartment with a $1500 severance check, realizing it is time to get a job. He closes his memoir with the baptism of one of his sons by one of his Jesuit classmates, and online if one searches there is at least one photo of him, Amelia, and their two boys. If one were to sum up his beautiful account, it surely could be called one of both dying and rising, the end of one path and the start of another, sorrow and loss, but in the end joy. Andrew's journey is just one of those we have looked at here, a long, serious commitment to what he felt was a particular call to Christian life and service—that of a member of the Jesuit community and a priest.

In another era, it might have been said that all those years spent in Jesuit formation were a waste, that at the end of it all, Andrew Krivak was very nearly a "spoiled priest," one who left for a woman, for marriage and a family. We are usually not immediately aware that, as C. Wright Mills put it, history and biography do indeed intersect. Our tendency, perhaps the psychological perspective of the modern era, is to see everything as our own individual reality—my need to leave this empty, restrictive religion, my venture later on to reclaim my faith. But we are part of something much larger: a long religious tradition, the community of the church stretching across centuries and countries. Then there is the further reality that nothing remains the same. Despite the claims that our creeds, scriptures, doctrines, and liturgies are changeless, within a living tradition, things do change, at the very least, how we understand and practice them.

So yes, I remember the time when well-meaning church people did think and talk that way. It was a tragedy, even a scandal to leave a seminary or religious house. In fact, I experienced this reaction from colleagues I'd known for years, who had worked hard to prepare me for the calling I would leave. There was a higher value placed on the priesthood and religious life than on marriage and parenthood. I know, I heard talks and sermons of that sort. But then many things changed. Good Pope John XXIII opened the windows and doors, the Second Vatican Council seemed to be "discerning the signs of the times." The documents of that council spoke in strong, fresh terms of the church as the "people of God," saw the church as responding to the needs of the modern world. Religious freedom was for the first time explicitly recognized, and the Roman Catholic Church finally admitted that those outside her boundaries were also Christians. Despite divisions, a new ecumenical awareness was seen as right, aiming toward Christ's own vision of unity, put forward in the high priestly prayer at the last supper.

Many things changed, and later these transformations would be attacked as a near abandonment of the faith. Several of the most extreme traditionalist groups in the Catholic Church to this day refuse to recognize Vatican II's reforms and renewal. All of what Andrew Krivak described was on the other side of Vatican II, and the effects of change are evident in his formation experience. To be able to see that one is called to follow Christ, to live the gospel in whatever state of life or work, as Father Fury indicated to Andrew—this is one of the many fruits of transformation in vision and understanding of the church.

## Odd and Wondrous Callings

Andrew Krivak's experience was within the Jesuit tradition and the Roman Catholic Church. The next one I will relate was in another community within the Catholic communion, so there is the nagging question of celibacy, not to mention obedience and community life in both our accounts. Many others have different and often even more complicated experiences that involve spouses and children. A number of the writers we are listening to fall into this category. But two in particular have recently offered remarkably revealing views of the ups and downs of ordained service in the church and are worth hearing.

Lillian Daniel and Martin Copenhaver are both pastors in the United Church of Christ. Between them, they have almost forty years of pastoral service in the church. Both are married and have children. Both went through the seminary process, internships, ordination, and service in several congregations. Both are gifted preachers and writers. You find them featured at many preaching and other theological conferences as well as frequently in the pages of periodicals such as *The Christian Century*. Their recently coauthored collection of essays about experiences in pastoral work is a marvelously honest, touching, and often very funny narrative about the life of the ordained.[5] The essays are about both the private and public sides of their lives as ministers. They are startling in their honesty as they talk about their finances, their spouses, their kids as PKs. They tell of mistakes they have made with parishioners and what they dread in their vocations as well as what brings them great joy.

Lillian Daniel describes her failure to enter the candidacy process in the Episcopal Church in which she was raised. She also tells of what a young woman seminarian and then pastor experiences—being questioned as to whether she really is a pastor; that she looks so "cute" up there in the pulpit in her ministerial robe; the feeling when she's told, "I was looking for the pastor but you'll do"; as well as being told she's simply too young for the position (something I warrant she's outgrown by now). I am one who has spent all the years since my ordination as an assistant or associate, and her memories of being in those positions ring true. She notes the effect of the senior pastor adding a homily at the end of announcements on the Sundays you preach, or saying "Thanks, Lillian" at the end of a sermon or a service when you have presided. Daniel also describes the complexity of being a pastor with a spouse who is supportive but not himself ordained, and the struggle to survive as a family.

> In the preaching moment each week, clergy are given the privilege and the challenge of engaging money through the eyes of the One who provides for us in more ultimate ways. I believe our work as clergy actually shapes us, and makes it impossible for us to believe the simple theories and easy answers. We cannot help but wrestle with money in complex ways, given a typical workweek. One Sunday we preach about Jesus saying, "Woe to you Pharisees! For you tithe mint and rue and herbs of all kinds, and neglect justice and the love of God" (Luke 11:42). Then we go home to unpaid bills, and prepare the next Monday morning for the upcoming pledge drive. . . . Yet there is no denying that as clergy we often find ourselves living in economic disconnect with our neighbors and parishioners. Sometimes the clergy are the poorest members in a wealthy community, allowed to live there geographically by virtue of their position, but not really able to live like others. Our children may associate with the wealthy, but they cannot afford to go on the same ski trips, drive the same cars, or attend the same colleges that many of their friends do. . . . In other words, they are in the community of wealth and privilege but not of it. This is a tricky place from which to proclaim good news to the poor. In other communities, the minister may be one of the wealthiest members of a financially strapped congregation, able to have a nice car when others do not.[6]

She raises many of the issues that connect to money in the Christian community and life and work of the pastor, underscoring the difficulty of cutting so very close to the bone for most people when money is mentioned. Yet she reveals her own family's debt as well as the imperative to be faithful to the Gospel and not take the easy way out when it comes to money—what a parish does with it, how the pastor must confront this reality in all our lives. That she and her husband struggled with bills and patterns of spending shows the humanity of those who shepherd and lead the flock.

One of the most gripping of her narratives is the terrifying story of her inability to give her diabetic son an insulin shot, instead hitting a muscle and causing even more pain by pulling it out. Obviously a skilled, highly educated, and self-confident person, her inability to meet his medical needs was crushing, and she shares it in the context of Palm Sunday and holy week, when this occurred. Daniel also brings us into a parish council meeting just after she has visited an elderly cerebral palsy victim, dying in the ICU. The council is discussing their twice a year turn preparing and serving a meal at the local homeless shelter. The dish decided upon is chili mac, a casserole combing macaroni and cheese with canned chili. Every imaginable detail is pondered, debated—large or small cans of chili, bought from the local supermarket or a big box store, do we buy grated cheese or grate it ourselves and do we have graters enough to do this—on and on this goes, including the critical question of whether the concoction should be vegetarian, which provokes the comment, "How can you be homeless and a vegetarian?"

> Now it's been fifty minutes. On chili mac. This moment is eternity. I am losing my religion. I have lost my eschatology. Fifty-one minutes. I find myself dreaming of the past. I remember feeling a call to preach having never once laid eyes on a woman minister until I set off for divinity school. . . . I think of the papers I wrote, staying up all night on fire for God and the theology of one person or another. . . . I think of the prayers I said earlier that day at the hospital bedside, and wonder if the woman I prayed with is even still in this world. . . . We see God's possibilities even in the midst of grated cheese or broken bodies, because in the end they are not so different. They both point to the fragility of life, the desperate delicacy with which we try to live with order, balance, and meaning in a chaotic world. . . . It is God who prepares us for what might be out there. God will not leave us orphaned. Christ crucified and

resurrected prepares us to find majesty in the ordinary, mystery in the concrete, love in the midst of feuding, a ministry of tending to the details in the midst of grated cheese.[7]

When a council member blurts out that he'd hate to be homeless on a bitterly cold, blowing night such as the one in which the meeting was being held, there was a momentary pause. You could hear from the breathing who had a cold, who was in good shape or not, who was choked up at the thought of being out on the street with no place to go. Grace had broken in, Daniel writes, carrying the council on into minute fifty-four.

Like Lillian Daniel, Martin Copenhaver inhabits the complicated, often messy pastoral world. He writes about the complexity of having a spouse who is a nonbeliever, with whom he shares a life and children, but not what is deepest in his own heart.[8] He describes the humbling experience of having to be taken care of and ministered to as he experiences a health crisis. So often the one to visit and console and pray with a sick person, a cardiac scare turns him most uncomfortably into the one who now is prayed for, who is counseled about life style and stress, and who must return to the sanctuary acknowledging his human frailty.[9] He shares what it is like to have had a father who was a pastor and to then eventually lose him in death.[10] Head of a large, affluent congregation he admits he wants and needs words of praise and dreads criticism and indifference. But in the ministry, one experiences both, often, as he calls them, as "twin impostors."[11]

In one of several reflections on how to best describe pastoral ministry he challenges the idea of the pastor as parent, whether we call the pastor "Father" or "Mother or not or envision the role as bringing spiritual life to birth and nurturing it.

It is simply too exhausting to think of oneself as a parent to a congregation. The challenge of parenting my own two children is demanding enough without adopting the hundreds of parishioners who are part of my congregation. Instead, I have come to view my role as more like that of a mid-wife, someone who is trained to assist in the birthing process . . . sometimes by coaching the parents and other times by providing direct assistance, and often, when little needs to be done, simply standing by in wonder and awe. . . . We are not the center of the action, or even key players in the drama. . . . Our role can be quite important, but it is limited nonetheless. We perform our role in a variety of ways— for instance, by teaching, leading worship, and visiting the sick. We tell the Christian story, coach and encourage, listen and pray. What unites all these roles and activities is that each provides an opportunity to encounter God. It is a joy to be present at a birth. It is something even more—a real privilege—to play a role, however small or incidental, in that birth. Actually, in my work as a pastor, often I am not aware that anything so momentous is taking place. But then someone will report, fresh from a kind of birth, that a particular worship service helped her experience Jesus Christ as a living presence, as if for the first time. . . . I am very aware that I did not make anything happen. . . . Nevertheless, something I did not provide, something clearly beyond me, that "something" called the presence of God, was at work. On such occasions I feel like a wick that is in awe that it can be used by a flame. So, much of the time, I feel like an invited guest to special places where wondrous things happen. I am not invited because I am a special person, or because I have a particular set of skills, or because I have greater faith than anyone else does. Nevertheless, I am invited to those places in people's lives because I have accepted God's call to do this holy work.[12]

Now this is a remarkable reflection of ordination and the life and work of a pastor. Both Copenhaver and Daniel provide plenty of instances of being humbled, even humiliated in seminary training, in their early years in the ministry, or being the recipients of real revelations of holiness in their parishioners, as well as visionaries who see flashes of the presence of God in bleak situations to which they minister.

Heard along with Barbara Brown Taylor, Nora Gallagher, and others, one might be tempted to protest that Daniel and Copenhaver write of what is awe-inspiring, beautiful, and upbuilding in church life, and that, in so doing, perhaps unwittingly, they minimize what is ugly and painful in pastoral ministry, in church life, in the search for God. Given studies that track the many reasons why pastors leave the ministry, one can ask why, when one in four of new clergy have moved out of parish work within five years of ordination, is this pair of pastor-writers sentimentally basking in the moments of joy, the epiphanies of God's omnipresence and power and love for us?[13]

Hardly. As noted, they ruthlessly bare their own failures and faults, the pains inherent in following the call to lead and care for the people of God. Just as to overlook the toxic and pathological in the spiritual life would be wrong, as well as damaging, likewise it would also be distorting to ignore the voices and experiences of women and men who have gone through suffering, death, and resurrection in their lives of faith as did their Christ. And it is telling that even those who provide us hard stories of how destructive religious communities and leaders can be also furnish evidence of their own rising through these experiences.

# CHAPTER FIVE

# "You want to be *happy?*"

*My Carmelite Years*

Interspersed with a memoir of my own experience in religious life is the rule of the Carmelites, the order to which I belonged. It is the shortest of the rules of religious communities, but its brevity does not obscure the balance of life among prayer, study, and work that I was gifted with in these Carmelite years.[1] So, the rule, though ancient, has a great deal to do with how I did learn how to be happy, not just in my Carmelite days but throughout the rest of my life—something Father Vincent McDonald, as you will hear, was concerned for me to understand and make my own.

[1]
Albert, called by God's favor to be patriarch of the church of Jerusalem, bids health in the Lord and the blessing of the Holy Spirit to his beloved sons in Christ, B. and the other hermits under obedience to him, who live near the spring on Mount Carmel.

[2]
Many and varied are the ways in which our saintly forefathers laid down how everyone, whatever his station or the kind of religious observance he has chosen, should live a life in allegiance to Jesus Christ— how, pure in heart and stout in conscience, he must be unswerving in the service of the Master.

[3]
It is to me, however, that you have come for a rule of life in keeping
with your avowed purpose, a rule you may hold fast to henceforward;
and therefore:

[4]
The first thing I require is for you to have a prior, one of yourselves,
who is to be chosen for the office by common consent, or that of the
greater and more mature part of you; each of the others must promise
him obedience—of which, once promised, he must try to make his
deeds the true reflection—and also chastity and the renunciation of
ownership.

*The Rule of St. Albert*[2]


*Following a "Vocation"*


Like many of my age, in the late 1950s and early 1960s I was encouraged to pursue "a vocation." Later, the Second Vatican Council, with
its rediscovery of the priesthood of all the baptized and of the church
as "the people of God," made it clear that *every* person had, through
baptism, a vocation to serve God and the neighbor. But in those days,
though, "vocations" were to the ordained ministry and, in churches
that had it, the religious life of brothers and sisters. The churches
needed such "vocations." Then, it was difficult to imagine other professions or careers that measured up to the sacrifice and good that
these servants of the church could do. Thus families were usually
strong in support of a son or daughter who felt so called.

Even in the rigorous Trappist observance, Thomas Merton wrote
of the flooding of Gethsemani Monastery with applicants in the post–
World War II years. There were so many aspiring to monastic life that
several new monasteries were established within a decade to disperse
the influx of all these candidates. Once his first infatuation for monasticism faded, Merton saw many areas in which reform and renewal
were necessary. He saw the flood of candidates as unsustainable. He
was right on both counts. Religious life had become insulated and
isolated from the rest of the church and the world. Rigorous intellec-

tual development needed to return, as well as a more humane style of life. Those pursuing the life of the vows should be able to mature not only through studies but also human relationships, in community life. Often what passed for community was a formal schedule of events done in common. The atmosphere was one of many rules and authoritarian oversight.[3]

By the end of the 1960s, though, the trend of increased application for entrance to religious life had stopped. The number of applicants dropped, and many in religious life discerned it was not a life commitment for them and left. Eventually the ranks of the religious communities and the priesthood were dramatically reduced. As I look at a photo of my graduation class from the Carmelite minor seminary I attended, of the nineteen pictured there, eleven completed the year of novitiate that followed, but no one remained in the Carmelites, though two are priests and one a deacon.

My favorite priest and teacher at St. Albert's minor seminary was Father Albert Daly. He had been a rising star in the order, had been principal of Mount Carmel High School in Los Angeles, the master of students at the International House of Studies in Rome, and a member of the executive committee of our province in the order. He was urbane, fluent in several languages, well read, and humane. We called him "the Cos," for cosmopolitan. I remember the French cuffs he always wore beneath the Carmelite habit, as well as his reverent liturgical celebration and his masterful teaching of Latin (until 1965, all the services were in Latin). I accompanied him several times to New Hampton Farms and the Annex, two juvenile correctional facilities near Middletown, New York, where St. Albert's was located. Father Albert was the Catholic chaplain at both, the Annex being a maximum security institution. In an old vocations booklet I have, there is a wonderful picture of him in his habit in the huge "yard" at New Hampton, talking to a resident whose back is to the camera.

What I learned many years after I left the Carmelites in 1971 was that in the midst of his "rise," Father Albert's alcoholism threatened not only his career but his priesthood. What we saw, both in his being our teacher at St. Albert's and later one of the three priests who staffed the novitiate in Williamstown, Massachusetts, was the other side of his career. I recall him reminding us that he was good to students on their "way up," so that they'd be good to him on his "way down," when he was old and dependent. Father Albert, even well after his retirement, continued as a volunteer chaplain at a skilled nursing home. When I saw him again, a married person with a couple of kids, at the one reunion I attended at St. Albert's, he echoed to me the same thought that I'd heard from another Carmelite I ran into later in life. No matter what we became, whatever work or situation in life in which we ended up, our training in the Carmelites, he thought, would always prove to be a good foundation and useful. And whatever we were doing in life could be a vocation, a way of serving God and our neighbor. Father Albert, along with Father Vincent, about whom I'll say more below, are two of the strong links that bind together my memories and thought about my time in the Carmelites.

*Joining an Order*

I recall being interested in a number of different religious orders while growing up in Yonkers, New York, and attending St. John the Baptist Elementary School. My family on both sides originally belonged to the Ukrainian Greek Catholic Church, having immigrated here from the province of Galicia in the Austro-Hungarian Empire in the first decade of the twentieth century. Three of my four grandparents were from the small village of Burkaniew, in the county of Ternopil in what is now western Ukraine, a couple hours southwest of L'viv. On both sides of the family there were Poles and Ruthenians, later called "Ukrainians," and my grandparents all came through Ellis Island. I have been able to locate their travel and immigration records. They settled first on the lower east side of New York City, both couples marrying in St. George's Ukrainian Greek Catholic Church on 7th Street, still an active parish. My father's folks relocated to the coal region of eastern Pennsylvania, Nanticoke, my mother's to West Haven, Connecticut, both towns having Galician communities. A great-grandfather of mine, on my mother's side, was the cantor of the Burkaniew parish church, and one of my father's brothers, Msgr. Miron Plekon, served for over fifty years as a priest in the dioceses of Philadelphia and Stamford. All of my grandparents as well as my parents were regular churchgoers. Grace before meals, prayers before bedtime, attendance at Mass every Sunday and feastday, crosses and icons on the walls—this was the home in which I grew up.

It was no surprise that in the late 1950s I should be encouraged by family, teachers, and parish clergy to pursue a vocation. At that time this meant doing high school in a "preparatory" or "minor" seminary. I somehow chose that of the New York province of the Carmelites, St. Albert's, in Middletown, New York. I had been interested in becoming a priest, more specifically in a religious order. I am still not sure what in particular attracted me to the Carmelites, but after contacting their director of vocations, I attended a summer vocation camp there after both seventh and eighth grades. Staffed by Carmelite priests and brothers, I thus got to know the friars and the school. So at the age of thirteen, in September 1961, my parents drove the almost two hours up to St. Albert's to drop me off. I was one of an entering class of close to fifty, very likely the largest ever enrolled.

I have many memories of the four years there, much like New England prep schools but without the prestige and resources.[4] Some are good, humorous, yet others are painful. In addition to those four years, I spent another one in novitiate, four in undergraduate studies, and one teaching high school—all told, a decade of formation with the Carmelites, from the age of thirteen to twenty-three. It was not all church services and pious reading though. I remember, in senior year, slugging a classmate, Bill McCormick, giving him a black eye. I don't remember why I did that but we were assigned by Father Paschal Greco to work together every afternoon for the next month. We did not remain enemies very long, and were laughing about the imposed togetherness very quickly. Often, punishments were really very helpful opportunities to reflect, to see your own motivations, sometimes to change and do otherwise. Sometimes, though, they were just punishments, "penances" to be endured. This was the quixotic character of religious life, I would later come to realize. The rhetoric was always that superiors knew best, and that obeying made you better. However, as it turned out—and it was bound to so turn out—superiors were not always right or even in their right minds!

I have some photographs from these years. So many guys in white shirts, black suits and ties, short hair, and nerdy glasses! They tend to cluster around a play we put on or the baseball team on which I played or class trips. Recently several other St. Albert's alumni have posted their photos from those years on a Facebook page. We played varsity baseball and basketball against other minor seminarians within reasonable driving distance: the Oblates, the Franciscans, and the Salesians. Other sports, such as soccer and football, were intramural. When the lakes froze there was skating and pick-up hockey games. We fished in the lakes, lifted weights, hiked—it was a very "muscular" Christianity that our master of students, Father William Rogers, promoted.

The academic program was high caliber, with small classes, and excellent Carmelite instructors. Every day there was a recited Mass in Latin along with morning and evening prayers. We were taught the Gregorian chant used for the services of great feasts and Sunday Mass, followed the New York State Board of Regents curriculum, took the infamous Regents' exams in geometry, biology, chemistry, physics, history, English, and various languages such as Latin, French, Spanish. In addition to the standard range of high school subjects we also had courses in theology, the scriptures, church history, and the Carmelite Order's history and spirituality.

The chapel was the center, but the classroom was the other most significant element of our life at St. Albert's. Other important ingredients were sports, as mentioned, but also cultural events such as plays, musicals, and, lastly, work—manual labor. All of the grounds maintenance, dishwashing, and cleaning of dorm rooms and classrooms was done by us students. There was at least an hour of worktime every day, plus regular schedules for dishwashing and table set-up. On Saturdays another hour or so was added to work on seasonal things such as leaf raking, grass mowing, painting, waxing of floors. The patterns of these poles of life—prayer, study, work, time for recreation, and fellowship—would remain later in the novitiate and while in undergraduate studies.

The traditional name for minor seminarians in the Carmelite tradition was *Mariani,* literally "Mary's boys." Devotion to the Mother of God was central, the official canonical name of the community being *Ordo fratrum beatae Mariae virginis de Monte Carmelo,* "the order of the brothers of the Blessed Virgin Mary of Mount Carmel."

Thus in the liturgical year the feasts of the Mother of God were special days, though the most important ones in the order, namely, that of Our Lady of Mount Carmel, July 16, and the Assumption, August 15, took place while we were home on summer vacation.

Our families could come to Middletown—if they lived within reasonable distance—and visit us on the first Sunday of the month. We went home at Thanksgiving, Christmas, and for the summer, from late June until early September. One could obtain permission for leave for funerals, weddings, and other important family events though throughout the school year. We had access to newspapers and magazines in a decent library. A bit of TV time was allowed on Sunday evenings and feast days. We were for the most part restricted to campus. As minor seminarians we went on some field trips, but, compared to our peers in high school, we did not get out much. There was no opportunity for meeting girls or dating, and both were strongly discouraged over summer break, given that celibacy would be part of both Carmelite religious life and the priesthood. Looking back, for students preparing to be pastors, we were denied contact with families, children, women, and the elderly, and for the next decade or more would be confined to an all male and clerical culture. No wonder the explosions later to occur.

Yet my photos and memories remind me in many ways we were not much different, other than the lack of contact with girls, from any other adolescents. We were probably hardly distinguishable from any other adolescent of the early 1960s at an all boys' high school. Like other less religiously focused prep schools, there were various "initiations" and ceremonies of ritual degradation for freshmen perpetrated by upper classmen, from having your head stuck in a urinal or toilet as it was flushed, to being doused with Ajax or Pine Oil or other liquids while in a shower, to having your bed "creamed," that is, the sheets lathered with Vaseline or Vicks or toothpaste or shaving cream for you to slide into at bedtime. I recall that we were also forced to "walk the ice," that is, cross one of the very shallow ponds when the winter ice was just forming, guaranteeing a dunk in fairly cold water but with no danger of drowning. As at West Point, we had to obey all upperclassmen, sometimes do chores for them, and often this obedience would be further ritualized into having to stand on your chair in the dining room and sing a song or repeat some lines fed you by upperclassmen. I do not recall any of these "initiation rites" that were physically or psychologically damaging, but I do remember that when a new principal and prior took over in my sophomore year, Father Bartholomew Parsons, not only was the academic side ramped up, but all of the initiation activities were banned under pain of suspension and, on a second offense, expulsion from the school.

These were years of long hours in the classroom, with work periods and sports in the afternoon and then two to three hours of study hall before dinner. After dinner we had a brief free time until lights out at 10:30 pm. Each dormitory floor had a Carmelite priest resident along with several fifth-year proctors who rang a bell to announce lights out. Evening prayers, a shortened, simplified version of the office of Compline we would later chant, concluded with the singing of the hymn to Our Lady, *Salve Regina*—"Hail holy Queen." After a night's sleep, the day began as the proctors came round knocking on each door: *Benedicamus Domino!* "Let us bless the Lord," to which one responded, *Deo gratias!* "Thanks be to God!"

Each year some classmates would leave, or be asked to leave, both during the school year or over the summer. By our graduation, we were nineteen remaining out of fifty who started, a dramatic decrease but still a sizeable class to enter novitiate. Having described much of what our life was like (with more to come) how did all of this affect me? Where was I in these years—what was I thinking, feeling, anticipating, fearing?

*Becoming a Seminarian: Living in the Culture of Religious Life*

I do remember a real mix of emotions and experiences, happy and complicated, from these years. My daughter found that my first effort in writing my remembrances was very good at the details of services, clothing, daily activities, but rather short on feelings and experiences. "There was not enough of *you* in it," Hannah told me. Little did she realize that she was on to something. Emotional reserve, the distancing of oneself from others and from one's own feelings, having little to say about one's own thoughts, less even about one's personality—all

Peter L. Berger.
Photo courtesy of
the Institute on Culture,
Religion, and
World Affairs,
Boston University.

Barbara Brown Taylor.
Photo by and used with
permission of Studio
Chambers.

Sergei Bulgakov.
Sketch by Sister
Joanna Reitlinger,
courtesy of Nikita
and Maria Struve.
Photo of sketch used
with permission of
Christopher Mark,
Christ the Saviour
Monastic Trust,
Sussex, England.

Diana Butler Bass.
Photo by
Richard Bass.

Father Alexander Schmemann. Photo from the collection of and used with permission of the Very Reverend Victor Sokolov.

Darcey Steinke
Photo by Maude
Schuyler Clay.

Frater Simon, O.Carm. (that is, Michael Plekon), in Carmelite habit at the occasion of his first profession, September 8, 1966. Photo used with permission of the author.

Novitiate class from Williamstown, Massachusetts, September 8, 1966. Michael Plekon is second from the left. Photo used with permission of the author.

Top: St. Albert's Junior Seminary, Middletown, New York, where the author spent four years of high school. The buildings and grounds are still actively used by the Carmelite order. Bottom: Mt. Carmel Novitiate, Williamstown, Massachusetts, where the author spent a year as a novice. Photos used with permission of the author.

Martin Copenhaver

Lillian Daniel

Nora Gallagher

Patricia Hampl. Photo by Barry Goldstein.

Father Matthew Kelty. Photo by and used with permission of Peter Jordan Photography, ©www.peterjordanphoto.com.

Andrew Krivak. Photo by and used with permission of Marzena Pogorzaly.

Father Vincent McDonald (left) and Michael Plekon in June 2010.
Photo used with permission of the author.

Thomas Merton. Photo by John Howard Griffin, used with permission of the Merton Legacy Trust and the Thomas Merton Center at Bellarmine University.

Sara Miles

Kathleen Norris. Photo by Garry Yamamoto.

Lauren Winner. Photo by and used with permission of Jen Fariello
Photography.

of this was to some extent acquired in the formation I experienced in the Carmelites. But to tell the truth, I was never formed satisfactorily, as my superiors discovered and tried to correct many times, with little success. I could not stifle my likes and dislikes. I came clean when I should have been less forthcoming. I resisted being shaped in ways I disagreed with. That I have found this consistently to be how I am, no matter the stage in life, the churchly location, or the others around me, tells me it is for real. I obey the rules, fulfill my obligations, possess the requisite skills, even "exceed expectations," but never exactly according to the prevailing institutional culture. I have never been able to make myself fit in or be a "company man." I surely remember, especially back in the Carmelite days, the constant pressure to do so, the warnings and sanctions for not conforming, at least externally. I may have been able to conform outwardly, most of the time, but internally, I was at odds with the culture and the system.

Like most freshmen at St. Albert's, I was homesick the first few weeks of fall term, despite the time away at summer camps there. The highly regimented environment, the pressure of obeying the rules lest one be dismissed, the virtually all-male atmosphere were different from anything I had ever experienced, including eight years with the nuns in parochial school. There was also a very monotonous quality that was part and parcel of religious life, even in these high school years before we formally entered the Carmelite Order.

Yet seminary or not, there was also a wild, often reckless side to adolescent males living together in a nearly female-free environment. Going on summer vacation back to the real world that had mothers, grandmothers, aunts, sisters, and girls was both a thrill and yet, given the clerical culture of the time, girls were to be avoided if you were going to vow chastity and be ordained to a celibate priesthood. I do remember rather quickly becoming self-reliant, not only "responsible" in the appropriate sense our teachers stressed, but a kind of streetwise, "watch-your-back" awareness. This was one of the truly valuable skills I learned. Other traits pounded into us were more dysfunctional, even damaging in the long run—particularly complete submission to authority and the stifling of your own thinking. In a not so obvious way, you were on your own at St. Albert's and thereafter. Despite all the rules and services, the superiors and others in your class, and those above or below you, you were alone. This I now realize was a built-in contradiction: that despite a communal existence, one could be and very often was alone—on your own, and at times, lonely.

Why was this the case—alone, among so many others your own age? This was the time period in which in religious institutions any close "particular friendships" were regularly warned against. If you were seen palling around too much with another classmate, you'd be told to branch out and not focus attention and friendship on any one person. The net effect of this was a stifling of feelings, a dampening of the urge to share what was most terrifying or exciting with another. To be sure, I did make friends. I did listen to others, and with a very few reveal my thoughts, fears, frustrations. I was then and remain today outgoing and sociable. Yet as I long ago realized, my defense mechanism was to resist being formed into something I felt was alien. Although I was repeatedly taught the importance of it, the periods of enforced silence throughout the Carmelite years were difficult for me. And not just back then. Just a few years ago, my participation in a supposedly silent retreat was excruciating. I am not proud (nor really am I ashamed) that I helped dismantle the silence component of it. In fact, the imposed silence directly contradicted the focus of the retreat—suffering and how to pastorally deal with it. Opportunities for discussion and sharing of experiences were appropriate, along with silence. My resistance, insubordinate as it was, had a reason, and it made exchange about this central human experience possible. Here, as in some other small things, I realize that despite the Carmelite effort at my disciplined "formation," meaning obedience of a blind sort, a resistance still lives in me, a resistance that is healthy.

At St. Albert's and then afterwards, close or particular friendships were taboo. In effect we were to shun intimacy of any kind. In retrospect, the fear of what such relationships could lead to—homosexual relations or, for that matter, heterosexual ones—was exaggerated and misplaced. What kind of personality, what kind of life could one expect to have with no friendships, no intimacy? Those who have studied the history of monastic life know better, having recognized the close mentor-student relationships among the desert fathers and mothers, the authentic meaning of being "brother" or "sister" to the others in community. Merton echoes this in his journals, having lived through years of Trappist "signs" and then a more open culture of communication at Gethsemani Abbey.

After years of this ethos and the discipline accompanying it at St. Albert's and elsewhere in houses of formation, it is no surprise that many of us, myself included, became guarded, uneasy at sharing important things, keeping personal feelings both positive and negative to ourselves. Even though my own personality runs very much counter to this reserve, decades later I still feel the restraints. I think my resistance to artificially imposed restrictions and rules is the part of me that has remained consistent, the voice that echoes back from saying "No" both to myself and regularly aloud—to my teachers, my novice master, and later on to professors and colleagues.

We were as crazy and edgy as adolescents and young adults ordinarily were, but a lot of emotional interiority was simply shut down, starved off, repressed. As I grew older, this was the emptiness, the sad loneliness, the emotional distance I saw in fellow Carmelites. Later on, this culture of life without relationships made the entire project bizarre and pointless, particularly when I left the cocoon of the formation houses to attend Catholic University with the rest of the undergraduates. Probably more than anything else, the loneliness and desire for some kind of companionship and friendship, not only sexual expression, propelled most of my class out of the order in the years after novitiate. The same exodus occurred with a number of younger priests a decade or so later, as they left the formation period's isolation and were placed into parishes and high schools and chaplaincies. I remember one early evening thinking to myself over drinks that I did not want to end up lonely and drunk every night—as I saw a significant number of older confreres.

But this is to fast-forward too far ahead from the St. Albert's days. Was there a lot of acting out—sexual or otherwise—as a result of all the repression in those days? My memory says that there was no more than what I have heard from others who attended high schools where I had grown up in lower Westchester. The period from 1961 to 1965 was still rather a nerdy, conformist time, despite the "British invasion" of the Beatles, Gerry and the Pacemakers, the Stones, and others; the space race; and American Bandstand. The recent, meticulously detailed ABC-TV series "American Dreams" often provided a startlingly accurate vision of growing up in those years, trailing off further into the Vietnam era. Because the novitiate followed directly after high school and, for my class, the first two years of college being at the order internal house of studies, Mt. Carmel College in Niagara Falls, Ontario, our exposure to the cultural and social changes of the later 1960s was somewhat postponed.

[5]
If the prior and the brothers see fit, you may have foundations in solitary places, or where you are given a site suitable and convenient for the observance proper to your Order.

[6]
Next, each one of you is to have a separate cell, situated as the lie of the land you propose to occupy may dictate, and allotted by disposition of the prior with the agreement of the other brothers, or the more mature among them.

[7]
However, you are to eat whatever may have been given you in a common refectory, listening together meanwhile to a reading from Holy Scripture where that can be done without difficulty.

[8]
None of the brothers is to occupy a cell other than that allotted to him or to exchange cells with another, without leave of whoever is prior at the time.

[9]
The prior's cell should stand near the entrance to your property, so that he may be the first to meet those who approach, and whatever has to be done in consequence may all be carried out as he may decide and order.

[10]
Each one of you is to stay in his own cell or nearby, pondering the Lord's law day and night and keeping watch at his prayers unless attending to some other duty.

*The Rule of St. Albert*

*Why the Carmelites?*

I did not have personal contact with the Carmelites until I contacted their vocations director and attended a summer vocations camp in 1959. The Carmelites were one of the smallest orders in the New York City area in which I grew up, with parishes in the Bronx, Manhattan, and one in Tarrytown, New York, not far from Yonkers, my hometown. This province, or part of the order, had been invited to the chaplaincy of Bellevue Hospital in 1889 by Cardinal Corrigan, who knew of their ministry in Dublin hospitals and in secondary schools as well as parishes. The Irish leadership and significant population of the New York archdiocese and the Carmelites of the Irish province were good matches. Later on the New York Carmelites would establish mission work in what is today Zimbabwe, as well as high schools in upstate Auburn, New York, as well as Los Angeles and Encino, California.

When I entered, and for centuries previous, the Carmelites had become primarily a clerical order, most of the members ordained priests involved in a variety of ministries.[5] Their early-thirteenth-century origins lay in Palestine. Those who petitioned the Latin patriarch of Jerusalem were western European Crusaders who remained there living essentially a hermit life in the spirit of the prophets Elijah and Elisha. During the later Middle Ages an elaborate mythology of their spiritual roots in the prophetic brotherhoods was crafted. As the friars came west, their eremetical pattern disappeared and they became active in university teaching and parish and chaplaincy work in England, Wales, Ireland, and several Scandinavian countries, Denmark producing in the fifteenth century one of their leading writers, Paul Heliae. They also settled at the university of Paris and in Toulouse and other locations in France, as well as many houses in Spain — later the site of the reforms of John of the Cross and Teresa of Avila — with houses also in Italy and in Poland, among other places. In addition to the great Spanish reformers, Thérèse of Lisieux is one of the best known of Carmelite saints.

I don't think that anything that I read about the Carmelites attracted me more than the Carmelites I met at St. Albert's in the summer camps — Fathers Albert Daly, Matthias DesLauiers, and John

Howe; the Donohue brothers, Francis and Timothy; Brothers Aquinas Stack and Bernard Godfrey; the vocation director Father Raymond Dolan. As I look at a few of the pieces of vocation literature I somehow saved, full of photos of St. Albert's students in class, in chapel services, on the athletic fields, at work in the kitchen or fields, I see the dormitory and classroom buildings now demolished and gone at Middletown, though the chapel remains and what was our study hall and dining and recreation rooms are now a retirement wing. The distinctive brown, everyday habits are there, the emphasis on the basics of the Carmelite life already in place for high school seminarians in the early 1960s. There had been one or another formation process there at Middletown since the property was acquired in 1917. The novitiate had been there, as well as the minor seminary and a place for summer assignments for work for student friars, which I would experience myself.

But it is not just the buildings that are gone. The entire concept of beginning formation in high school, proceeding directly into the novitiate, and entering the order in one's late teens—all this has long been gone, at least twenty-five or more years now. Candidates must now complete undergraduate work before they are accepted as postulants and then novices.

## Becoming a Friar

In my day, you arrived at the novitiate house a few weeks before being received into the order as a novice. During this time of retreat, in our case, from the feast of the Assumption of Our Lady, August 15, until the eve of the feast of Our Lady's birth, September 8, we were called "postulants"—those "seeking" entrance into the order. We wore the brown tunic and scapular of the habit, but not the *capuche,* or cowl. The Carmelites were called "Whitefriars" in the Middle Ages because of the white outer cape and cowl they wore. But we wore this only in church and on festive occasions. The everyday habit—tunic, scapular, and cowl—were brown. The habit was worn except for manual labor and sleeping.

We did not as yet have our new religious name or the title of *frater,* Latin for "brother," from which "friar" comes. In those days one submitted three possible new names for oneself in religious life to the novice master and prior, literally the "first one" or superior of the house. Later on many would return to their own original baptismal names. I was given one of the three I proposed, "Simon" (I no longer remember the others). I received the name of St. Simon Stock, the thirteenth-century head of the order in England and prior of the house at Aylesford, in Kent. The novitiate back then was a year of intense religious formation with no visits home and no contact with our families or friends whatsoever. Each of us became "Frater" Simon, or Gregory, or Alexis, and so on. And as a group we were referred to as "frats," though hardly resembling the members of Greek societies at undergraduate schools.

The novitiate house I entered was a property outside the village of Williamstown, site of Williams College, which had been author Sinclair Lewis's estate. The main house sat up on a bluff, with concrete block additions for the chapel and the rest of the novitiate space. The buildings faced Mt. Greylock, a beautiful mountain miles away across the valley. A great lawn and fields swept down to the town road. Hundreds of acres of woods were in back with trails leading up Mt. Berlin. Down at the entrance carved on a stone marker was the estate's former name, "Thorvale"—Thunder Valley.

Despite the location in a college town and in the resort area of the Berkshires, and due to the requirement in those days for the novices to be strictly isolated or cloistered not only from the rest of the order's members but from just about everyone and everything else, we had no contact with Williams College, the Clark Art Institute, the local parishes, anything. Not once did we even visit the Clark or attend a lecture at the college. Twice during the entire year were we permitted a trip, one a day trip to West Point, the other a visit to St. Joseph's priory, the house of studies in Washington DC.

That novitiate year remains vivid for me probably due to our isolation and the utter starkness of the novitiate schedule and house—the grey unpainted cinderblock interior of the large addition where was located the chapel, the refectory, the classroom, and our individual rooms, or "cells." Everything was hard—the block walls, the linoleum-tiled corridors. There was not one carpet or soft chair in the entire building, only in a parlor in the old house and the priests' rooms. The year was rigorous but not as hard as the observance of the

Trappists, which Merton describes in *The Seven Storey Mountain*. It was unrelenting in its sameness, with rare breaks from the routine. In retrospect, the full rigor of the observance of the rule was imposed on us only in that novitiate year. Life for the professed and ordained in the various Carmelite houses was nowhere near as strict in observance—all of which makes me wonder what the rationale was for the rigor. Did the superiors really believe that one hard year would form you for the rest of your life, even when the office and other key elements of the rule were dispensed with due to demands of pastoral work?

Novitiate was an unremitting round of daily prayer, work, study, and an hour for recreation, which mostly meant conversation because there were no papers or magazines, no record player or TV. There was a chess set, also checkers and some board games. This *horarium* or daily schedule would never be lived again in such rigor, since a vocation in the order meant ordination to the priesthood and then placement in some ministry such as chaplaincy, education, or parish work. Even later in undergraduate student days one would be permitted a beer on occasion. Television, radio, records, papers, and periodicals were available in the student houses when we were undergraduates.

[11]
Those who know how to say the canonical hours with those in orders should do so, in the way those holy forefathers of ours laid down, and according to the Church's approved custom. Those who do not know the hours must say twenty-five Our Fathers for the night office, except on Sundays and solemnities when that number is to be doubled so that the Our Father is said fifty times; the same prayer must be said seven times in the morning in place of Lauds, and seven times too for each of the other hours, except for Vespers when it must be said fifteen times.

[12]
None of the brothers must lay claim to anything as his own, but you are to possess everything in common; and each is to receive from the prior—that is from the brother he appoints for the purpose—whatever befits his age and needs.

[13]
You may have as many asses and mules as you need, however, and may keep a certain amount of livestock or poultry.

[14]
An oratory should be built as conveniently as possible among the cells, where, if it can be done without difficulty, you are to gather each morning to hear Mass.

*The Rule of St. Albert*

From novitiate year I remember many hours every day in the chapel. I can still hear the few chords we were taught to play on the electric organ to support the chanting of the Psalms of the office in Latin. I still have a set of the breviaries or office books we used. Every day there were seven different parts of the office. At 5:00 each evening we chanted vespers or evening prayer and then the matins or morning prayer of the next day in anticipation. This took between an hour and an hour and a half on ordinary days. At a major feast the readings, hymns, and the Psalms were longer. At vespers there would be several Psalms appointed for that day, a brief reading and hymn, the *Magnificat* (or the song of Mary from Luke), and several collects or prayers. Matins was three parts or "nocturns," with three Psalms and a short reading from scripture and the fathers for each nocturn. After dinner at 7:30 pm, we returned for the last office of the day, *Completorium*, or compline, which was unchanging in content for the most part, though there was a more solemn version with more elaborate chant for great feasts and Sunday evenings. And at the end of compline, a hymn to the Virgin was sung, *Salve, Regina.* In the morning we had to be in chapel by 5:45 am when another morning office, *Laudes* or "the praises" was sung, several Psalms, a short scripture reading, the song of Zechariah, the *Benedictus,* and concluding prayers. This was followed by forty-five minutes of silent prayer. You could remain in the chapel—deadly, a strong invitation to fall asleep whether kneeling or sitting—or you could return to your room, discouraged due to the even more sure drifting off to sleep. Or you could in good weather walk outdoors, which was my preference unless rainy or too cold. Since we received at first no instruction whatsoever on how to spend the period of silent prayer, some would read from the scriptures, a theological text, or a book on spirituality. It was a monumental struggle not to fall asleep during this time, the house bathed in silence. Later in our class we were exposed to extremely structured forms and approaches to "mental prayer," most of which resembled the Jesuit method Andrew Krivak was taught and used.

When the period of silent prayer was ended, the first office of the day, *Prima*, or "Prime," was chanted. Then Mass was celebrated, a "low Mass" in Latin for the first half of the year, then after Advent the readings and some parts in English, though we continued to use the Latin chants when the Mass was sung on Sundays and feast days, and recited on ordinary weekdays. There was a time for thanksgiving after receiving communion after the Mass, then the third office of the day was sung, *Tertia*, or "Tierce."

Services and prayer time in the chapel were not always serious. I remember, on the hot humid feast of Our Lady of Mount Carmel on July 16, several colleagues fainting under the heavy white mantle and hood. The sight of falling bodies—they were caught and injuries avoided—should not have been funny, but somehow it was. There was the loud snoring of another classmate during meditation early in the morning. Some of the sermons given were unintentionally hilarious, with our laughter only minimally stifled. One morning early in the year, not yet used to the habit, I found myself trapped in my choir seat, the scapular, or apron-like part, having gotten lodged where the seat back folded up. Desperately trying to free myself, I finally gave up, remaining kneeling in apparently deep contemplation when the others left the chapel for breakfast. I had a laughing fit while taking off the hood and scapular and wriggling the stuck portion out of the seat without tearing it. Another time, later in the student house in Washington, a classmate read a lesson from the Hebrew Bible about being conceived in sin and worthy of being thrown on a dunghill, and, given this classmate's dramatic personality and often maudlin behavior, the words of scripture simply turned the chapel into a howling, laughing mess. Once laughing began for me in chapel, it was the end. I recall having to leave temporarily, for what others would have thought a restroom visit, in order to not disturb the service with my laughing.

Breakfast in silence followed morning services, except on Sundays when there might be pancakes or eggs if we were not in a fasting season. All the other meals were simple and eaten in silence while one of us read from a spiritual text. On a feastday there would be some minutes of talk allowed after reading. I remember that any eating between meals was forbidden as was taking any food whatsoever from the refectory, and the kitchen was off limits unless you were assigned to work there.

After breakfast the novice master met with us briefly, this gathering called "chapter," but he was the only one talking, outlining the day's activities and sharing with us any news he felt appropriate from the world or the country or the church. Most of all I recall this morning chapter as his podium for making criticism of the behavior of those of us he found lacking or problematic, never identifying the culprit(s) by name, but describing in fastidious detail the offenses and warning us to avoid these infractions and stay in line. His military past echoed in these briefings. I will never forget his daily admonition when dismissing us to clean our rooms and then get to class. "No foostering!" he would exclaim in conclusion, after warning us not to complain or criticize or have any useless conversations with each other. I am still unsure of what precisely the word meant. We all interpreted it to mean anything the novice master didn't like. And since Father Brendan was singularly noncommunicative, his many talks and harangues notwithstanding, one never really knew if the line was being crossed. One day you would be scolded for walking too slowly in the corridor, the next for walking too quickly. In retrospect it resembled the nonrational, sometimes absurdist challenges my father once described from officers' training school. The bottom line was obedience!

The prior, a retired former parish pastor, somewhat dotty and forgetful, would also feel compelled to join in the sport of haranguing us for infractions of the rule. Unlike Father Brendan's controlled but occasionally raging ferocity, Father John Wholley's rants often were more comedic for their blustery pronouncements about those not-to-be-named misbehavers who thought they were getting away with things. He often lost track of what he was ranting about, which deflated the rage considerably. The net effect was comedy, and, given his defective hearing, when he turned around to the altar, he could neither see nor hear the giggles and smirks. Irreverent, disrespectful behavior on the part of us novices, but commensurate with Father John's rambling, incoherent, and empty complaining about vague infractions by unnamed individuals among us! What was truly comical is that the real rule-breaking events were never discovered, or, if they were, they were ignored. Looking back, I am glad our class had several genuine comics, whose ability to make light of the overly serious formation process kept us all sane.

Even though allowed now to talk the rest of the day until the end of Compline, we were encouraged to maintain silence as much as possible, especially in the chapel, our rooms, and the corridor joining them all. The other priest assigned to the house, with no special title or responsibility, was Father Albert Daly. Father Albert, beloved from our high school days, never engaged in the harangues. If there was something serious, he would confront the novice, but privately and without all the raving. Father Brendan did most of the teaching, with the exception of Father Albert subbing once in a while and the occasional visiting priest who would offer us a class and who would be available as external confessor, such as Fathers Daniel Lynch and Vincent McDonald. This was not to be primarily an academic year. The library holdings were meager, and the focus of the class was limited to the history and spirituality of the order, some booklets of Joachim Smet, the order's Directory by John of the Cross Brenninger, and the old-fashioned text of de Guibert.

More than anything in the novitiate, I remember my having the nerve or the insanity of talking back in private to Father Brendan Hourihan, the novice master. He was an Irish immigrant, retaining a thick brogue in his speech. He had worked on the docks and served in the U.S. Army, and was as much a drill sergeant as a priest. When I told him what I thought of how a classmate had been treated or what I thought of how he treated us—I truly thought he was either going to explode or get off his chair and deck me, so infuriated did he become. Each of us novices were supposed to meet once a month with the master, first listening to all his criticism of our behavior and attitude, then confiding in him—seriously, this was what we were told—anything on our mind or heart. It was totally absurd. The man had no soft side, was always scowling, constantly tearing us apart with comments, warning us we could be out and on the bus home before we knew it. It was impossible for him to treat us with anything resembling humor or understanding, so rigid was his idea of his status and role as novice master. Thankfully, the other resident priests were much more approachable, though they deferred to the novice master in any dispute. Given what I earlier described as our warnings about intimacy, friendship, individuality, or opinions, why would any of us want to confide anything crucial, important, or painful with him? To register a complaint or criticism was, as I learned, a recipe for disaster. My "arrogance and temper," he told me, would be broken and fixed by him.

For my talking back, actually my challenging of him, I spent the next several months shining every inch of stainless steel in the novitiate kitchen during work periods. I must have been extremely mouthy because I also recall, after another monthly meeting, having to strip and then wax every stair in every staircase in the novitiate building over and over again for what seemed like a month. Suffice it to say that after a couple of these month-long solitary work periods, I learned to shut up, to go through the motions, telling him how everything was fine in the monthly meetings, how much I looked forward to making first vows and going on to undergraduate studies. It was not so much that I learned to dissemble but that I learned how to do what was necessary to get by, to survive. Externally I followed the rules, including "the" Carmelite Rule. Internally, I thought my own thoughts but kept them to myself.

But I also remember hanging my habit on a tree and quite illegally climbing Berlin, the mountain behind the novitiate, with classmates and some visiting student friars at night, a place where it was safe to smoke a forbidden cigarette. The town dump was another such location. The trip to the dump also presented opportunities to look at the papers and magazines in the supermarket, and a classmate's visit home for a funeral provided some change for a candy bar and a soda and pack of cigarettes—all illegal. In retrospect I would have to say we weren't even very good at breaking rules that year, if these secretive smokes, snacks, and reading events were any indication.

There was either outdoor or indoor work in the early afternoon, some sports later on—much the same pattern as in high school years in the minor seminary. The food was decent, much better than what we had at Middletown in minor seminary, because a woman from town cooked for the fifteen or so of us and felt sorry for such young boys being away from the families, working so hard. During holy week and Easter the student friars from the house of studies in DC came up to celebrate this holiest time of the liturgical year with us. I still vividly recall that one of them, a musician, had composed music with English texts for all the services of the great Three Days including the paschal vigil and Easter in nontraditional jazz and folk genres. By the time we started undergraduate work the next year, at Mount Carmel College, the western province's house of studies in Niagara Falls, Ontario, all of the daily prayer services and the Mass were in English.

[15]
On Sundays too, or other days if necessary, you should discuss matters of discipline and your spiritual welfare; and on this occasion the indiscretions and failings of the brothers, if any be found at fault, should be lovingly corrected.

[16]
You are to fast every day, except Sundays, from the feast of the Exaltation of the Holy Cross until Easter Day, unless bodily sickness or feebleness, or some other good reason, demand a dispensation from the fast; for necessity overrides every law.

[17]
You are to abstain from meat, except as a remedy for sickness or feebleness. But as, when you are on a journey, you more often than not have to beg your way; outside your own houses you may eat foodstuffs that have been cooked with meat, so as to avoid giving trouble to your hosts. At sea, however, meat may be eaten.

[18]
Since man's life on earth is a time of trial, and all who would live devotedly in Christ must undergo persecution, and the devil your foe is on the prowl like a roaring lion looking for prey to devour, you must use every care to clothe yourselves in God's armor so that you may be ready to withstand the enemy's ambush.

[19]
Your loins are to be girt with chastity, your breast fortified by holy meditations, for as Scripture has it, holy meditation will save you. Put on holiness as your breastplate, and it will enable you to love the Lord your God with all your heart and soul and strength, and your neighbor as yourself. Faith must be your shield on all occasions, and with it you will be able to quench all the flaming missiles of the wicked one: there can be no pleasing God without faith; and the victory lies in this—your faith. On your head set the helmet of salvation, and so be sure of deliverance by our only Savior, who sets his own free from their sins. The sword of the spirit, the word of God, must abound in your mouths and hearts. Let all you do have the Lord's word for accompaniment.

[20]
You must give yourselves to work of some kind, so that the devil may always find you busy; no idleness on your part must give him a chance to pierce the defenses of your souls. In this respect you have both the teaching and the example of Saint Paul the Apostle, into whose mouth Christ put his own words. God made him preacher and teacher of faith and truth to the nations: with him as your leader you cannot go astray. We lived among you, he said, laboring and weary, toiling night and day so as not to be a burden to any of you; not because we had no power to do otherwise but so as to give you, in your own selves, an example you might imitate. For the charge we gave you when we were with you was this: that whoever is not willing to work should not be allowed to eat either. For we have heard that there are certain restless idlers among you. We charge people of this kind, and implore them in the name of our Lord Jesus Christ, that they earn their own bread by silent toil. This is the way of holiness and goodness: see that you follow it.

[21]
The Apostle would have us keep silence, for in silence he tells us to work. As the Prophet also makes known to us: Silence is the way to foster holiness. Elsewhere he says: Your strength will lie in silence and hope. For this reason I lay down that you are to keep silence from after Compline until after Prime the next day. At other times, although you need not keep silence so strictly, be careful not to indulge in a great

deal of talk, for as Scripture has it—and experience teaches us no less—
sin will not be wanting where there is much talk, and he who is careless
in speech will come to harm; and elsewhere: The use of many words
brings harm to the speaker's soul. And our Lord says in the Gospel:
Every rash word uttered will have to be accounted for on judgment
day. Make a balance then, each of you, to weigh his words in; keep a
tight rein on your mouths, lest you should stumble and fall in speech,
and your fall be irreparable and prove mortal. Like the Prophet, watch
your step lest your tongue give offence, and employ every care in
keeping silent, which is the way to foster holiness.

*The Rule of St. Albert*

## Life and Work and Return to the World

The Carmelite Rule assumes that not just for monastics but for all
Christians, fasting, prayer, the sacraments, and the scriptures will be
weapons in a struggle, a conflict against the power of evil in the world
around us, but also a personal combat against that which wars against
God in ourselves. The wisdom of the ancient literature of the desert
fathers and mothers, of the Rules of Augustine and Pachomius, of the
Master and of Basil the Great, among others, is still recognized today.
New or renewing communities such as that of the monks and nuns
of New Skete, of Bose and Taizé, of the community of Jerusalem, of
Sant'Egidio all cite these classic texts. They recognize that in a world
of Blackberrys and laptops, iPods and CDs, we still struggle but that
the life these rules serve to direct and support—the life of the gospel—
can still be lived.

In remembering my Carmelite years, I cannot simply present
everything as good, beautiful, and true. Some of what I experienced
was questionable, even wrong, ugly, and false. The idea that religious
life was contrary to a full human life, that human relationships were
always suspect and dangerous, that unquestioning obedience was an
absolute virtue, that there could be no change, when eventually change
was both inevitable and necessary—I have tried to show how I experienced some of these, and I will continue to do so in what follows.
But my reminiscence echoes what has been heard from many other of

the voices in this book. The life of the Spirit is powerful, healing what is broken and ailing. The life in and with God teaches us to be like God—forgiving, free, life-giving. But given that it is fallible, weak, selfish, proud human beings who constitute the community of faith, there can be much that is destructive and toxic. We can be our own worst enemies.

The classical monastic ideal of prayer, study, and work in community life, of course with the modifications that the Carmelites and other friar orders made, made for a remarkably fine work ethic and a balanced Christian life. Much like the Rule of St. Benedict, everything was there despite some of the contradictory elements I have described—fellowship, hospitality, the cycle of the liturgical services, time for spiritual reading and contemplative prayer, as well as the sharing of all this in outreach, in ministries of all sorts in the church. My Carmelite experience sustained me through my graduate education and has continued to do so for over thirty years in university teaching, research, and writing, and the same in ordained service. I cannot exhaust the gifts the experience of life in the Carmelite tradition and order gave me: a love for liturgy and daily prayer, a strong work ethic, all the more because everything is prayer, not just the daily office and liturgy but classes, reading, house cleaning, cooking.

All through the years of my Carmelite formation, work was a staple of our lives. Even when we were full-time students there were house keeping chores and even outside jobs. Each summer student friars were sent to do summer camps or building repair and grounds maintenance at some house of the order. All of my years I had the regular framework of community life, daily prayer and meals in common, along with either full-time studies or work. From a Carmelite a couple of classes below me who has remained in the order until today, I learned that the Catholic clergy shortage and dramatic decrease in candidates to the order destroyed much of this framework. Perhaps several Carmelites would indeed live under the same roof, but their differing day jobs—from teaching to counseling or parish administration—left only a token community possible. During the week a high school teacher and all weekend a liturgical/sacramental machine, my former colleague feels that little of the life he entered and wanted is left.

My bucolic, rigorous, ancient rhythm of the novitiate gave way to a very different undergraduate experience. At every level, from secondary school through undergraduate, we received a stellar education. Between the time at Mt. Carmel College, where I began undergraduate work, and the last years at Catholic University in Washington DC, I had enough credits for not only a BA, but had they been graduate courses, for an MA as well. I easily had a double major, close to a triple. At Catholic University, a candidate for ordination needed a philosophy minor at least, and we paired that with a theology minor and, in my case, a major in sociology.

The tents from Resurrection City were still up on the Mall in Washington DC when we arrived in the summer of 1967 to complete undergraduate work at Catholic University. Far more striking were the burned-out streets that would remain from the rioting after Dr. King's assassination in April 1968. In those years until we graduated and left in early summer of 1970, I attended numerous protest gatherings, most notably the series of antiwar Moratorium events downtown in the federal district. I sniffed tear gas and ran as protestors were routed from around downtown federal buildings. When David Dellinger stumbled on the names of all the groups that had to be announced as participants in the Moratorium, we knew the end of these large demonstrations was near. The morning after the publication of the encyclical *Humanae vitae,* still wearing clerical clothes, I was stopped as I headed to class on the Catholic University by none other than Daniel Schorr, then a CBS correspondent, and was asked to comment on this statement condemning any kind of birth control for Catholics. My nuanced, too lengthy answer did not make the evening news.

It was a fresh, exciting atmosphere, the "little Rome" of the Catholic University campus in those days, named for the many religious houses that surrounded the university and sent their sisters and brothers and priests to school there. The Second Vatican Council's reforms were really still in the process of being implemented. Many student sisters and brothers not to mention faculty such as Charles Curran and Daniel Maguire were questioning the traditions that a few years earlier had been so formidable, unchangeable. (Curran and Maguire would be forced from the school for their questioning of the encyclical.) During my years in DC, the Washington Theological

Consortium was established, pooling both the faculties and students of what previously had been small theological schools, also opening theological studies to lay people, not just seminarians and members of religious communities. The Vatican II vision of preparation for the ordained ministry translated into the closing of many small houses of theology that functioned as quasimonastic enclosures. Those who would be serving in pastoral ministry in the larger society, in parishes, chaplaincies, or schools should have a more open process of education and formation. Very often this resulted in the merging of theological school and the creation of a consortium or union, such as in those in Washington, Chicago, and Berkeley, as well as interseminary programs elsewhere.

It was a time of experimentation and reform, of ferment, inquiry, debate, dissent. Religious habits were dispensed with—such was the eventual practice for us—except for church services. I am sure my own life-long impetus to question, challenge, and dissent was most importantly shaped in these years, despite heavy-handed authoritarianism within our house, St. Joseph's priory in Washington, and more broadly in the New York province. In the early 1960s, when it was yet the custom and culture most everywhere, the demand for unquestioning obedience, as well as regular ridicule and "testing" of students for the priesthood and religious life, were accepted. This was indeed necessary, for signs of rebellion or individuality would first be the matter of warning, then punishment, and eventually expulsion. Conformity was paramount. Obedience as well as the other vows and virtues had become not means to living the Christian life, but ends, even obsessions, in and of themselves. The severity of the rebellion of so many sisters, brothers, and priests, the exodus of so many of them in the years to follow was not, as traditionalists have claimed, because of permissiveness and secularism, worldliness and promiscuity. As others of my generation who entered religious life at that time demonstrate, it was the reaction to a great deal of deprivation and dehumanizing conditions. The thoroughgoing changes introduced since, with dramatically reduced numbers of religious, I say witnesses to the truth of this claim.

In DC we did weekend work assisting and teaching in parishes. Even before the Metro system made travel easier, DC was a rich feast of culture and ecumenical religious experience. The newly opened

Washington Theological Consortium brought together students from many religious communities and dioceses in the area. On our stretch of Harewood Road alone were the Ukrainian Greek Catholics, Capuchin Franciscans, Oblates, Atonement friars, Augustinians, and Marianists. Not far away were many more: Paulists, Dominicans, Redemptorists, Benedictines, and many others of the Franciscan family. Over time, the religious habit was left to use in chapel and at the house of studies, and either a clerical shirt or just ordinary clothes became what we wore to class.

More than being in the nation's capital, more even than the protests and rallies against the war, the biggest change for me and the rest of us was that we were back with ordinary people—our professors and women and men our own age who were our classmates. We studied not only theology but the natural and social sciences and the humanities. We had no special status but were undergraduates like everyone else in our courses and on the CUA campus. Looking back on it now, it was the most constructive, healthiest thing that happened to us. No longer isolated in a seminary, we were part of college life just as other students. When of legal age, we experienced the Rathskellar's excellent on-tap beers. We knew where you could get unlimited coffee refills, where the cheapest food was to be found—on Monroe Street. We were invited to other students' dorms for pizza and conversation. I recall very early one morning coasting a beat-up car down the driveway to the house of studies, several of us having stayed all night at classmates' dorms talking, singing, arguing, and, yes, having a few beers. I took the bus downtown to a part-time job at a sandwich shop just down Pennsylvania Avenue from the White House, on the campus of George Washington University. During the summer we cut grass, painted rooms, and refinished floors at the Carmelites' retreat houses and other facilities in repayment for the education we received during the school year.

[22]
You, brother B., and whoever may succeed you as prior, must always keep in mind and put into practice what our Lord said in the Gospel: Whoever has a mind to become a leader among you must make himself servant to the rest, and whichever of you would be first must become your bondsman.

[23]
You other brothers too, hold your prior in humble reverence, your minds not on him but on Christ who has placed him over you, and who, to those who rule the Churches, addressed these words: Whoever pays you heed pays heed to me, and whoever treats you with dishonor dishonors me; if you remain so minded you will not be found guilty of contempt, but will merit life eternal as fit reward for your obedience.

[24]
Here then are a few points I have written down to provide you with a standard of conduct to live up to; but our Lord, at his second coming, will reward anyone who does more than he is obliged to do. See that the bounds of common sense are not exceeded, however, for common sense is the guide of the virtues.

*The Rule of St. Albert*

By the time I graduated in May 1970, I had survived two years with a superior at the house of studies who was tyrannical, vindictive, and unpredictable. A former missionary in what is now Zimbabwe, Charles Haggerty had no previous experience in formation, only a high-school teaching stint. Later, despite his failure as the head of a formation house and his addiction and emotional sickness, he was nevertheless elected superior, or prior provincial—head of the St. Elias province. He was well connected in the province. Despite his pathologies, even after his terms as provincial ended he was named pastor of one of the province's largest parishes. His condition however did not improve.

At the house of studies in Washington, he was determined to keep the student friars in line and under his thumb in the turbulent late 1960s. He routinely put some of us on trial before a selected group of senior student friars and resident priests. I once was interrogated for hours for having stopped off to visit my family on the way back from summer work at St. Albert's. Having confided my uncertainty about continuing in the order with the superior, I found this action made me a constant suspect. Several other classmates were told upon arrival home from classes in the late afternoon they had to be out of the house and the order by noon the next day. Usually money for a bus home was provided, but that was all. It did not make any difference if

you were in the middle of a semester or not. The superior would no-
tify the university that the individual was no longer with the Carmelites and that from that point on all tuition and fees were his own
responsibility. I recall several colleagues obtaining loans from family
and staying with fellow students until they could locate housing.

It is not my intent to simply savage or ridicule here all those years
in remembering them—the classmates, teachers, the order of prayer,
study and work we lived, or even the "culture" that inevitably devel-
ops in all-male religious communities. As rich, as good as the Carmelite experience was for me, it also had another side. It was my experience that the religious community's culture was unable to process or
confront realities of life such as loneliness, the need and desire for intimacy, affection, privacy, one's own hopes for professional training
and work. In Andrew Krivak's account, occurring twenty years after
my own experience, much had changed in the formation process—
and for the better. Yet there too I noted at some points the same difficulty of formation leaders to comprehend the person in the process.
Andrew's meeting with the formation director and his provincial superior about his real and growing affection for Amelia was one such
instance for me. Yet in my earlier time, there were to be individual
Carmelites who could understand and discern these rather ordinary,
normal feelings and pulls in a young person's life.

The last year in the house of studies in Washington was the worst
part of the ten years for me, though there were other difficult times.
For me this period culminated in a three-way meeting with Father
Charles and the head of the province, Father Lawrence Mooney.
Within a few minutes, Father Charles' assault on my character, mo-
tives, and behavior made a conversation impossible. He wanted me
thrown out. Having also shared my vocational doubts with the provincial head, he asked what I thought should be done with me. I asked
to be allowed to go out and work, still as a member of the order, much
like those in Jesuit formation and other programs. I even suggested
the house in Pottsville, Pennsylvania. My salary from teaching there
would cover my room and board even though technically I was entitled to this as a professed Carmelite. When Father Charles rejected
anything except further punishment under his control in Washington
or immediate ejection, the provincial, Father Lawrence, ended the

conversation. He thought this was an extreme position and had found my proposal of the year of discernment teaching in a Carmelite community acceptable, even appropriate, given my situation. Such external formation years had been customary in some communities such as the Jesuits, and in time would become standard parts of the formation process, occurring either before one was ordained deacon or priest or thereafter.

Father Lawrence said, because the request seemed reasonable, that he would contact the community and superior there to see if the proposal was workable. I asked that we meet perhaps once during the year and then close to the end so I could tell him what the discernment process seemed to be telling me, adding that I would ask the counsel of the other members of the Pottsville community, the superior of which had been a teacher of mine at St. Albert's. Later in the summer everything fell into place and I embarked on the beginning of my teaching career.

From every aspect it was a good year. Two of the community members were younger priests who had been a few years ahead of me in the formation process, James Goulding and Robert Hulse. The prior I knew as a teacher in high school—Romaeus Cooney—and Brocard Conners had also been a teacher at St. Albert's for a year and had been one of my summer work supervisors. He was a deeply spiritual man who had wanted to live in the eremitical house of the order but whose graduate degrees and teaching experience were deemed too necessary to "waste" on purely contemplative existence. All of us were faculty members at the local Catholic high school, and, on the weekends, the others—all priests—did "supply" work in local parishes, that is, they heard confessions and celebrated the liturgy as well as other pastoral activities as needed. The Pottsville house of friars thus supported itself through the stipends from the weekend pastoral work and the faculty salaries, much lower than public school levels and even lower for celibate clergy and members of religious communities like ourselves.

Except for the brown habit I wore, I was any other rookie secondary school teacher. I taught both an advanced class and one of the lowest ranked ones, had a home room. I chaperoned school dances, went to a lot of games: football was biggest there in the coal region, basketball second, my own sport, baseball, after that. I accompanied the priests to their Sunday supply locations. All did at least two masses on Sundays and one on Saturday night. They knew that for me this was a year of internship but also of discernment about my future, and, while I did talk to most all of them, it did not become an obsessive topic. Only Father Romaeus, the prior, was consistently distant and noncommunicative. He was most uncomfortable with me seeking to discern my vocation. My recollection is that he said to talk to him later on, when I'd come to a decision. While the fact that I was in vocational doubt and discernment was troubling to him, he treated me as I expected, given my familiarity of him for four years in high school. He was civil but distant, probably also because I was not yet a priest. As noted, the internal caste system was formidable, the one dividing the nonordained from the ordained.

Toward the end of the academic year, perhaps a month before classes would end, I met with the provincial superior, Father Lawrence, as we had agreed. I told him it had been a year different from all the others when I had always been a student of one sort or another, but it had been a very good year, quite possibly the best. I had a full taste of what community life might be like after my education, in the teaching profession as a Carmelite. It was in every way a very good year of discernment. As never before I experienced how beloved to the community priests and religious were. Pottsville was predominantly Roman Catholic, and those with the titles of father, brother, or sister were respected, befriended, loved.

My year as a friar teaching high school in Pottsville was one of the best I had in the Carmelites. The coal region kids had a great time with my strange New York accent. The section I had with lowest academic achievement were the most affectionate. One class, I eventually realized that a chalkboard presentation by one of them was a skillful parody of my teaching style, gestures, even vocabulary. I felt at home with other young teachers there, when I could went out for a beer with them, much to the disapproval of Father Romaeus. But then he never approved of anything, never recognized anything I did, was really never happy. The other Carmelites treated me as a peer though, for the first time in the order, as an actual adult. It was a wonderful year.

It also enabled me to see that it was not the Carmelite Rule or way of life that was the problem. Rather it was that after ten years I was no longer capable of committing myself to it for the rest of my life. I had come to want to be married and have a family. I still wanted to do graduate work and teach at the college level, and I also wanted to do priestly work—but as the provincial said, "That's not possible in this church." He respected my decision, and, as promised a year earlier, said he would take care of the necessary paperwork that would be needed for me to ask dispensation from my vows in leaving the order. He wished me the best, said he thought I'd do well whatever it was I chose to pursue. I asked his blessing and that was that. When I went to the prior of the house, I could see from his face that the provincial had already informed him. He looked at the calendar, noted the last day of class, asked how long I would need to read and grade the students' exams and papers. I thought the weekend after the last day of exams on Friday would suffice. So he pointed to Monday and said that I would leave that morning. He said that I should say nothing to any of the administration or other teachers or any of the students at school. I honored that request.

So in a few weeks' the end of the term arrived. I finished my grading. With all the other members of the house busy with Sunday supply, and some of them heading off that Monday, I was offered a ride by Bob Hulse, who could drop me off at my parents on the way home to his north of where I was raised. The superior was not at breakfast the morning I was to go, so I stopped at his room, knocked on the door. He extended me an envelope and said "Bye." There was never any discussion. I did get to say goodbye to the rest, and warmly, personally.

And with $100, home I went after a decade in the Carmelites. It all ended as abruptly as that.

## The Need and the Burden of Remembering

There are different kinds of memoirs. In reading for this book, I worked my way through some of the very angry and painful ones. Francine du Plessix Gray's memoir of her parents, *Them*, comes to mind. Also there is Patricia Hampl's exquisite one of her mother and father, *The Florist's Daughter*, and Frank Schaeffer's account of growing up under the evangelical gurus Francis and Edith Schaeffer in the L'Abri community over which they presided, *Crazy for God*. I earlier mentioned the three by Mary Karr. Mary Gordon's *Circling My Mother* and *The Shadow Man* are poignant, sometimes very difficult too. There is Honor Moore's account of her own life in relationship to her father, Bishop Paul Moore's life, marriages, and deeper identity, *The Bishop's Daughter*. I think too of the journals of Thomas Merton, Dorothy Day, and Alexander Schmemann, and the memoirs of Rembert Weakland, Stanley Hauerwas, and Eugene Peterson—all incredibly rich, painful, yet beautiful. There are so many different keys registered in this genre. Yet, as the other chapters here I hope indicate, remembering is a very effective way to track the journey to and with God.

I was not really successful in remembering at first. I did not realize how difficult it would be to put out my own experiences for others to read. For reasons I have mentioned, speaking out, especially critically, within the Carmelites was something I was taught not to do. But as I also have said, there was a part of me that never was properly "formed" or socialized in religious or broader church life. And now, more than forty years later, I am at least to some extent a different person. The experience of graduate school and many years teaching in a university that is diverse surely taught me to be critical, to express myself. So did marriage and parenthood and thirty years of ordained ministry. This book as well as others and numerous articles and papers have been my work of reflection and growth.

Nevertheless, in returning to the Carmelite years I was convinced to be more analytical, first by my daughter and then by several others in conversation. One was with a Carmelite colleague from my years who has remained in the order. Other conversations were with classmates and former Carmelite seminarians several years behind me. They filled me in on people we knew and events that occurred after my departure, and provided impressions of what I had written here compared with their own experience. Still another was with a former teacher who had eventually left the order and priesthood. Coincidentally, photos of my class were posted on a Facebook page, and I was able to identify them all from lists I kept in an old address book. All of this sent me rummaging through a box or two of old photos, programs of plays and graduations, even the booklet of the profession service in which the vows were taken. All of this gathered up together fragments of feelings and memories, a few aggravations that lingered, but mostly very beautiful people and experiences for which I am grateful. It is to say the least jolting to see your face at the age of eighteen again, not to mention viewing the faces of classmates and then comparing them to their Facebook profile photos, one of whom appears with silver hair and beard holding a grandchild. Quite a journey from a collection of still teenaged "Whitefriars" posed on the day of the first profession of vows, as in the photo in the gallery.

Now, decades later, when I think about the reaction of the community to those of us who left, my reaction is more nuanced. I can begin to see it not only from my perspective back then but from their point of view as well. Having crossed into middle age myself, I can now understand why the priests who had taught us were resentful over our being so different from them and, more importantly, at our leaving the order. After all, they had invested a great deal of time and attention to us. Despite the emotional distance that prevailed in this male world, there was some kind of bond with us. But then we, the future of the community, who had raised such a stink about the need for reform and renewal in the order, in how we lived—we were leaving. I admit feeling very angry when I read an online piece by a Carmelite I never had as a teacher or colleague about student friars in the time after Vatican II. Otherwise an always competent administrator and teacher, a historian by trade, in just a few words he wrote off all of us in the late 1960s as spoiled brats, ill-prepared for religious life, unable to remain in it and thus good for nothing. We were too much of that time, too rebellious, too interested in change. The latter characterization is true, for me at least, and has remained so into middle age. In retrospect, it was a clash of generations and outlooks, of those senior to us in the late 1960s and early 1970s who had grown up in the late 1940s and early 1950s, a time of greater certainty and less debate. In time, I also came to learn, as I have said, about the emotional pain some of them experienced, the overwork and isolation and loneliness, and the ease with which the bottle became a consolation.

But it is one thing to understand, it is another to forgive without discerning. The truth is that we were very young, impressionable, idealistic, and, given the culture of obedience and conformity, our urge to want to resist, reject, reform was a major break from how we were formed. It was difficult and costly to stand up against authority, not in general—in the nation of that time, Nixon, the Vietnam War, and all the rest of it—but against this one superior. Not a few with whom I shared those years in the Carmelite Order left all institutional religion because of what they encountered there. I do not mean sexual abuse, but I would say abuse—psychological more than anything else, but also disregard for us on emotional, intellectual, personal, and, yes, spiritual dimensions. That so many of us in the house of studies on Harewood Road in Washington DC were harassed, ridiculed, taunted, and in most cases ejected by one sick man—with no intervention of other senior friars from that community or from the prior provincial or the provincial committee—this was inexcusable. He was the superior, perhaps convinced he was "cleaning house" to rid the order of misfits and malcontents. We were decades younger and dependent on his will even to remain in the house. The absence of responsible oversight of students in that era cost the Carmelites too. Not only did many students leave, eventually there were others who did so, not so much due to this poor treatment but because they too faced the failure of the various local communities to have any real common life in which to anchor one's identity and work. One colleague guessed that those who stayed did so either because they could not imagine another life or because pastoral ministry somehow became what gave them meaning and a sense of belonging.

*Wanting to Be Happy*

A figure from these years was Father Vincent McDonald, a round-faced, ebullient man who had spent years as a parish priest and chaplain. He had also been director of the Third Order lay Carmelites. My contact with him, and a most memorable one, was during the novitiate year at Williamstown. He was one of the "external" or visiting priests who came several times a year so that the novices could go to confession and have time for conversation, even counseling, with someone from outside the novitiate community. Canonically novices were to have access to a confessor other than their novice master. For me at least, and I suspect for most in my class, this was welcome.

But back to Father Vincent. He was no sentimental figure. From Queens, he had not only the proverbial accent of that borough but a truly resonant, high-pitched voice, reminiscent of W. C. Fields. I remember him actually spending recreation time with us—the priests sat at their own table in the dining room and only "mixed" with us once during the year, on Christmas morning, after the Mass, for coffee and cake. Father Vincent was particularly good when the year had grown long, in the interminable Massachusetts winter. He would tell stories from his chaplain experiences. I also think he may have done some police and fire department work in that vein. But the incident I remember best was when I went to him on one of these visits and after a fairly brief and formal confession, he asked me how I was doing. I made the mistake, but a good one as it happened, to blurt out what I really felt.

It wasn't homesickness—I'd been a boarding student at St. Albert's from the age of thirteen, for four years. It wasn't yet a vocational crisis—although almost half my class left that year. I suspect it was hitting the wall of a daily schedule in which there was little variation, no diversions. There were lots of services every day, dishes to wash, grass to cut, weeds to pull, snow to shovel, leaves to rake, dusting, mopping, painting—remember my stints with the stairs and the stainless steel, for a couple hours each afternoon, by myself.

So it is not confession, but in the classroom/library where Father Vincent and I are meeting. He was an outsider to the novitiate, a different face, someone sent up there to listen.

So I told Vinnie (as we called him), "I'm not happy."

His theater of a face went blank, then he scrunched up his brow and squinted his eyes at me, and muttered softly, "What?"

"I . . . I'm not happy."

"Your health is good?" he asked.

"Yes, of course."

"You get along with the rest, with the novice master?"

"Yeah, well, occasionally no but for the most part, yeah, sure."

"You hear from your folks, everything OK at home?"

"Yes, they miss me but they're fine."

"HAPPY?" The Queens air-raid siren of a voice went full volume. "HAPPY?" Vinnie went on to give me a brief but powerful reflection I have never forgotten.

Everyone *wants* to be happy, of course, this is human nature, normal, universal. As I write, the *New York Times* has an ongoing series of articles on what happiness means, this in the midst of the severe recession, high unemployment, monumental losses for most people in their investments and retirement funds—a grim time all around.

Vinnie went on to remind me that on any given day, men and women had to get up, ready their kids for school, go off to their jobs, deal with all kinds of demands, insults, abuse, and worries financial, health, familial. No one, he said, is ever happy all the time. He was most concrete in what he said: "A mother up all night with a sick child, a man working overtime when he's exhausted, to support his family . . . and YOU . . . YOU want to be happy all the time?"

I use this as the title for this chapter because of the wisdom and the compassion of Father Vincent, both in his stance toward life and the world, and toward the naïve, selfish, eighteen-year-old I was that day. This exchange, his words have burned themselves into my identity, my vision, my life. While many faces and names, details and events have become blurred from those Carmelite days, this man and these words remain in great clarity, truly vivid images for me. And this is so because they transcend the monotony of those years, the smallness, my own petty obsessions as well as those of my classmates, also the sometimes cold, remote teachers and priests who were responsible for our formation as friars and eventually priests.

Remembering Father Vincent and Father Albert has made me also remember other really luminous individuals in the Carmelites who even in little ways made us students feel welcome and pointed us in positive directions. Much ridiculed for his love of the liturgy was Father Gregory Smith, a wonderful preacher, who donated the best liturgical vestments and other appointments to the seminary houses and who never gave up encouraging us that the liturgy was truly the "primary theology," the meeting place with the Lord. Regarded as a romantic, a dreamer, Father Gregory had been years ahead of the rest of the church in trying to open up the liturgy to the assembly, in urging scripturally based preaching, in holding up liturgy not as rubrics or fascination with sacred art but as the most important link in the chain of "living tradition" from the ancient church down through the Middles Ages and the rest of its history to our own time. Many of the student friars resonated with his enthusiasm and, looking back, for me he is another real light in those years.

There were several other then-young Carmelite priests, themselves recently ordained and finished with graduate work, who put the documents of the Second Vatican Council and other good texts on reading lists for us. David Kearns, John Ryan, and Damian Sheehan were among them, also Edward Murphy and Richard Champigny. Over forty years ago they opened up for me a more ancient understanding of the church as the people of God, as a community of faith, of the church across time and space as "communion." This "return to the sources" in the sacraments, liturgy, and ecclesiology has informed all of my writing on holy people and the life of holiness and the basic reality of the priesthood of all the baptized. These real messengers of *aggiornamento* urged us to reach out into our communities, to identify with social justice issues. Romaeus Cooney was a very positive influence on us high school seminarians on the way in. He directed us in Gilbert and Sullivan's *Mikado*, in *The Importance of Being Earnest* of Oscar Wilde, and several other plays. He taught us new music for the liturgy including the Mass based on spiritual and gospel hymns by Clarence Rivers, the Psalms and canticles using Hebrew chant models of Joseph Gelineau, the "return to the sources" liturgical pieces of Lucien Deiss, himself both a musician and liturgical historian. When today the miserable music post–Vatican II is condemned, it is not this excellent repertoire that a man himself devoted to Gregorian chant nevertheless taught and had us sing in the chapel at St. Albert's minor seminary.

There were yet others. We were given excellent French language instruction by Father Pius Gagnon, whose officially serious front covered a true intellectual's encouragement to us to be thinking persons. Decades later my ability to read and translate enabled me to bring a number of Paul Evdokimov's and Elisabeth Behr-Sigel's writings into publication. Later he became a temporary adversary of mine in my last year in the order, thinking I was chasing after several student nuns at his retreat house where I was doing my summer work assignment. Years later he contacted me after himself having left the order and marrying. When I look at my own scholarly work, Pius's teaching, along with that of others, gave me, gave us, so much. Father Nicholas Canning came to teach only during our senior year. He was perhaps the most psychologically complex and intellectually intense teacher or priest we had encountered to that point. In retrospect, I think he must have been working out some things in his own life, but he was a relentless teacher of literature and writing. He told us after viewing our first samples that none of us could write, or for that matter read or think, so poor were our products. He stuck our faces into poetry and fiction, challenged us to speak not only from the head but from the heart. He likewise told us we would never be real adults or good priests unless we came to know ourselves, every inch, the good as well as the disgusting. Compared to the distance and reserve experienced with many others, even later on in our training, his presence was electric.

When we were sent for the first two years of undergraduate work to the other province's house of studies, Mt. Carmel College, we were thrown together with our peers from that group and became part of probably the largest community I ever lived in, almost a hundred student friars, with a most diverse faculty. Keith Egan, the prior, had studied with David Knowles at Cambridge, and was rigorous at 8:00 am with ancient Christian texts. One of the first priest-psychologists, Jeremiah Mahoney, administered a then-new battery of tests and profiles for seminarians and gave us an appreciation for what psychology could do for us both personally and professionally. Joachim Smet showed us how crucial historical research was, not just to religious life but to wider life in our society. Having spent most of his life in work on the oldest texts of the order's history, he conveyed the respect for where a text came from, when it was produced, what it said then and to us in our own situation. Among the lay brothers who usually directed grounds work I remember the simplicity and good humor of Brother Bernard Godfrey, a man from County Kerry (who made sure you knew this!) and former New York City transit worker, and Brother Augustine Sidoti, whose patience with mechanical klutzes and compassion were boundless. And there were so many more like these.

Many of the Carmelites I have named here have passed into the kingdom. When I visit the cemetery at St. Albert's in Middletown, I walk through several rows of their gravestones, and the names propel me back decades to so many happy days there, right across the road, in the chapel, classrooms, and the rest of the seminary. Only a few remain, and as the photo of us together in the gallery witnesses, one was Vinnie, still alert at almost ninety, when the picture was taken. But now he too is there in that cemetary. Father Vincent died on January 4, 2012, having been a Carmelite for seventy-three years and a priest for sixty-five. I remember Father Vincent's words because they rang true to everything I knew from the Bible and liturgy, the core of Christian faith. They proclaimed, if obliquely, that our lives are a series of deaths and resurrections, fallings and risings.

What he said was more than a spiritual Advil for a mopey novice friar. His words were attested by his own way of always treating us students with kindness, with respect. His eyes, no, his entire face lit up with real joy, though surely as chaplain and parish priest he had heard and seen much misery. In my personal collection of "living icons," Father Vincent, along with Father Albert, have important places. Having myself now come along in life as far as they had when I knew them, I better understand and even more profoundly appreciate their discernment for us, much younger and so different from themselves. I value greatly their compassion and patience for us too. Though unknown outside the small community to which they belonged, Fathers Vincent and Albert and most of those I have mentioned surely put the gospel into words, into acts of lovingkindness for me. Moreover, they planted in me a great deal of what has come up good in my life—a love for learning and teaching, for the liturgy and the saints, a sense that, in the old saying of the friar orders, actually Dominican in origin, "to give away what one has received spiritually" (*aliis contemplate tradere*) is truly the way to be happy.

*Looking back on Religious Life*

It was not permissible for members of the Carmelite community to have any contact with those who had left during my years and for a good decade or more afterwards. Other former members have confirmed this. But changes called forth even more changes. Members leaving made for the closing of larger houses and led as well to different kinds of recruiting as well as different kinds of ministries for religious communities. Among the Carmelites it took some time, but the exodus of not only student friars but ordained members began to reduce the size of what had always been a small community in the case of my province of St. Elias. No one from my class remained, nor from the classes immediately before or after mine. Today, province newsletters report most new members of the order are from Vietnam or the Caribbean. Longstanding locations of Carmelite work were given up due to decreased numbers and in some cases were simply taken away. When the Bellevue Hospital expansion led to the closing and demolition of the nearby Carmelite parish, they were given another eastside parish in which to continue their presence and work, until just a few years ago when this parish was without warning taken back by the archdiocese along with the Bellevue chaplaincy, ending over a century of service there. Long involved also in Catholic high schools, this ministry too has continued to shrink, the Carmelites of both American provinces giving up many of their own schools, and even withdrawing from teaching and pastoral ministries at many others, such as Pottsville, where I had worked.

In time, a more welcoming attitude toward former members emerged. In the early 1980s a "St. Albert's alumni" group was formed by a number of former Carmelites, and this endeavor was accepted and encouraged by the provincial leadership. My class was invited back for a reunion at which ten or more participated. The few priests I knew who attended were warm and welcoming, Father Albert Daly in particular. As with all alumni activities, participation is varied. My rare visits to the site of the former minor seminary—now a pilgrimage center, provincial headquarters, and residence for retired Carmelites—were made more meaningful by the presence of a former colleague who had remained. We remembered each other and since reconnecting have regularly communicated and visited, with much to discuss not only from the past but on our present work, he in retreats and parish supervision while remaining in the order yet living apart from any Carmelite houses. Reports of the state of things vary. I have heard not only from my former colleague but from others in various communities that active common prayer and life are exceedingly rare.

While members live under the same roof, their various ministries and jobs put them on individual schedules that make common activities the exception rather than the norm. While this might be taken as the simple further erosion of religious life, it may in fact be the response and adaptation to dramatically reduced numbers of friars or sisters. The experiments in returning to simpler, small communities by the Benedictines of Weston Priory in Vermont, Mount Savior monastery in Elmira, New York, and the New Skete communities now face the same situation as all other communities—dwindling numbers of candidates and aging members.

Given so much feeling both positive and negative, progressive and traditionalist about why religious life seems to have diminished and how it can be "revived," a few words are necessary. In sharing experiences with a number of friends who have remained in religious life—sisters and brothers at New Skete, members of the Trappist and other communities—there is among those of us who experienced this life, the so-called "good old days" before Vatican II, scant nostalgia or desire to see those times and the culture of that religious life return. Even while, like myself, there is much good remembered and retained, there was much that was toxic, destructive, inhumane even in denial of basic human realities and needs for privacy, continued education, affection, and friendship. Every brother, sister, or religious priest I know who remained has in one way or another found some degree of freedom, independence, companionship, peace, and respect. It is easy to ridicule the unruly behavior and rebelliousness of us post–Vatican II junior religious. We thought differently, behaved badly, and left. But the reality is that many senior to us, ordained and experienced Carmelites, eventually also left to marry and have other kinds of Christian vocations. Among my friends among the sisters and brothers at New Skete, the most important realization of their communities' now forty-plus years is that the religious life is real in its own right as a lay institution. Ordained priesthood is always there but is not the monastic or religious vocation. As I noted, for orders and communities that had been predominantly clericalized, with most members eventually functioning in priestly service, this pattern has remained. Candidates enter to be ordained in the future. The Carmelites, for example, remain essentially a priestly order, as do the Dominicans, Augustinians, and Jesuits, though the Franciscans less so.

Not so with such communities as the Benedictines, the Trappists, and Eastern Church monasteries, where lay monks have once again come to outnumber the few priests ordained for service to those communities.

## After the Carmelites

It is always best to overcome doubt and misfortunes, not by evading them or brushing them aside, but by passing through them.[6]

But the state of religious life—past, present, or future—is not my major concern here. Nor was my intent to write a full memoir of my life in the church or, better, churches. A lot has happened since I left the Carmelite Order in 1971. Frater Simon may no longer exist, but Michael Plekon surely does. I met Jeanne Berggreen and fell in love with her immediately. We married and raised a son and a daughter. I completed graduate studies and found a faculty position at Baruch College of the City University of New York. I got ordained eventually. Along the way there were hundreds of students to teach, many articles and chapters to write, not to mention many communions and homilies, weddings, baptisms, and funerals. I have experienced the church both East and West—Lutheran, Greek Catholic, Roman Catholic, and Eastern Orthodox. I learned some very important and positive things from my journey, but a narrative of all that will have to come some other time.

Recently in extensive cleaning of the house in which I grew up, one of my brothers and I rescued boxes and boxes of family photographs, none of them cataloged or book-mounted, most still in the envelopes from the developing service. Among them were several dozen of me in these Carmelite years, a pudgy minor seminarian or a thin, idealistic novice and student friar, as well as many classmates and other comrades from those years. My family still has a hard time recognizing me in them, but I know that is not unusual. Staring hard, I scarcely can believe that was me either. Remembering, writing, getting feedback from some of the old friends, digging harder and deeper into my memories and feelings, has been disturbing and provocative and good for me. Not only am I better able to recognize myself and what I experienced in those days. I think it has helped me to better see who I am, what I have become now.

I learned something of what it is to be happy, as Father Vincent had long ago put it. He was right. So is Father Elchaninov. It is better not to run from disappointment and failure but to face them, own them, and live through them. Not just because I picked them for this, but pretty much all of the writers listened to here, despite some pain, some damage, some loss, have done likewise.

Andrew Krivak's recollections as well as mine and those of Lillian Daniel, Martin Copenhaver, and many of the others here were presented to make a point about religion and life. Despite the often destructive aspects of the institutional church and religious life, the search for God can bring great joy. A careful reader of this chapter challenged me on this. The writer's task is to show, not tell, to reveal rather than preach or teach. Would not a further and fuller narrative of my life after the Carmelites better enable a reader to judge whether this had all been worthwhile, whether it did in fact lead to joy? Perhaps, but this is not the place for such an extended effort. Much of what I experienced in the Carmelites was good and to me remains so. It shaped me, gave me realizations as well as skills that still sustain me—that everything can be prayer, that one can indeed share what is given in prayer, in study, that before God one is always alone, that to know and love God you have to open yourself, your heart—this holds for any other person as well. Yet I also experienced what power in the wrong hands can do. I experienced how destructive can be the desire to make impressionable young people conform—by drumming into them the idea that they should have no thoughts, certainly not critical ones, of their own. The contradiction between rigorous observance and the reality of the Carmelites' lives later on has remained. I wish I could see it as other than naiveté or hypocrisy or simply delusion, but I cannot. And I have seen it replicated in other church contexts thereafter. I am glad that I learned to look critically at those in authority over me but also to scrutinize myself.

# CHAPTER SIX

# Conversion and Community

*Searching for Love in All the Wrong Places and*
*Finding It Nonetheless*

So far, we have been looking at some of the experiences of women and men looking for God, trying to live the life of holiness—in ordinary ways: "saints as they really are." And this has led us to turn from saints on pedestals, on walls, in icons to some who have tried to express something of the journey, the pilgrimage that holiness is. One collection of experiences has to do with the reality that we are imperfect souls, all of us, that our lives are messy, our vision often distorted, our relationships sometimes not right.

We have seen how religion can be toxic, the church and various vocations and life within can be obsessive, introverted, exclusive, and destructive. Yet the search for God is both a looking for and a finding of joy, of peace, of beauty, no matter the twists and turns the paths take us on. We also have seen how this searching takes place amid losing and loss. We mistake the finite for the infinite, means for ends, the structure for the Spirit, law or rules for grace and freedom. We confuse feelings with faith, and there are many places to fall or become distracted. This happens to us all. But as we listened to a number of wonderful descriptions of the mess, the loss, the toxicity, we also learned of the joy.

## Patricia Hampl's Memoir: A Pilgrimage

In many of the beautiful books about searching for God and remembering one's spiritual life, the question of "conversion" occurs. One of the most striking is Sara Miles's *Take This Bread.* Another is a very different kind, really a narrative of return interwoven with a number of fascinating pilgrimages, all lyrically and gorgeously narrated by Patricia Hampl. I mean here *Virgin Time: In Search of the Contemplative Life.* A constant figure is a Poor Clare, a cloistered Franciscan nun, Sister Madonna or "Donnie," who became Hampl's spiritual director. Living in San Damiano Monastery outside Minneapolis, she is a most discerning, often hilarious respondent to Patricia's questions and issues, much as Sister Leslie was to Darcey Steinke in *Easter Everywhere.*

Patricia Hampl is a master of the memoir. She has written a poignant account of her parents, their lives and her relationship to them, *The Florist's Daughter.* She also penned *A Romantic Education,* an account of her time in Prague, from which her father and his family came, her experience of growing up in the late '50s and early '60s, the tumult of her university years, and the beginning of her career as a writer. All this is crowned by her travel and experiences in Prague, a city to which she regularly returns to teach.

In her account of her own return to faith and to the practice of the spiritual life, Hampl brings us more than her own memories of growing up Catholic in St. Paul in the 1950s and, prominent in this experience, her years of interactions with the sisters at the Catholic convent school she attended. All the bittersweet aspects are present—the talent and dedication of these religious women, their passing on of skills in French, but also their narrowness. That Hampl chose to enter the wild, open world of the University of Minnesota (with all those non-Catholics) for her undergraduate education was both shock and insult to the nuns, one of whom assured her that she would lose her faith there.

## In Search of the Life of Holiness: Francis, Clare, and the Franciscans

Well, indeed, she seems to have lost it, announcing to her father one Sunday morning that she was done with going to Mass. But after a lot of life, Hampl seems to have rediscovered not that conformist Catholicism but a far more diverse, deeper faith. Much of this appears to have come about through meetings with a Poor Clare, a cloistered Franciscan "Donnie," to whom she goes for spiritual direction. In turn, a travel grant enables her to settle herself in the center of all existence for Franciscans: Assisi. Hampl first spends time in Annunciation Monastery of the Poor Clares, keeping pretty much to herself. But she does visit with a transplanted American woman who, having once tried the Poor Clares and left, had once more entered the community in Assisi. For Patricia Hampl, this encounter with a nun is the beginning of a rich, often hilarious tour of Assisi with a collection of Franciscan friars and sisters, there to "do" the holy city and sights of their beloved founders and family members, Francis and Clare. One, Sister Francine, a retired teacher of literature, observes in jest that their entourage might be as diverse and interesting as that of the band of pilgrims we all know from Chaucer's *Canterbury Tales*. (By this point Hampl has already riffed on the same *Tales* in describing her companions in a walking tour through Umbria.)

But the colorful, ragtag team of Franciscans, perhaps unwittingly, provides Patricia with some truly insightful accounts. The first is of Francis and Clare as individuals, as "living icons" of holiness. Then we learn of the historical context of Francis's break with his father, with his family's early capitalist wealth and his radical embrace of the lepers—excluded from church and society by the Third Lateran Council in 1179. Hampl gives one of the finest portraits one can find of Francis's distinctive gifts and personality. She underscores his radical embrace of the lepers and the poor, who are always social and ecclesial outcasts. He even weds himself to "Lady Poverty," and in his primitive, largely uneducated radicalism returns to the simplicity of Jesus of Nazareth in Palestine of the first century of the common era. He undergoes an utter break with the institutional church and its titles, ranks, and strictures, as well as its piety. It is a striking destination in life for a former mercenary and ladies' man.

In pondering Francis, the Franciscans on the tour were not on a historic quest. Rather, they touched the two gushing sources of contemporary psychology: the family and the self. In Francis they encountered the self held in the communal embrace of family and Church, *and* the individual mind desperately seeking free flight from that very clutch, seeking the Godhead, where all divisions are lost, where self, family, you, me, cease to exist and everything becomes It.

His father wasn't the saint's only trouble. Francis's vision of Christian poverty was so radical (or so nuts, as one of the friars on the tour said cheerfully) that the Brothers of his own order took control of the community before he died; he was relegated to the sidelines of the very family he founded.

Francis was drawn to create the family, the community, but his temperament was mystic, anarchic—individual. It sustained visions, not a social structure. His was no patriarchy. . . . The Franciscans read Francis and Clare not for stories but for signals. They read them as moderns who had performed a miracle: from the bloody family battlefield to have plucked the unbruised rose of individual self-consciousness, and to have found in this flower not isolation and self-absorption but full union with God and the world. . . . It was a reclamation of the radical Christian idea: a *People* could be forged by the miracle of the imagination, what Keats much later called "the holiness of the heart's affections." The most basic act—eat this, drink this—became the way to union, a tribe for all seeking the All.

Nor was the Franciscan vision pietistic or lost in interior moments untranslatable to the world. Francis ran first to find the lepers. He didn't run howling into the woods to *help* them. He simply went to join them, to *be* with them. He wasn't a do-gooder, not a missionary in the convert-the-heathen sort of way. He was a joyous mystic who *needed* to suffer the great pain of his age, because not to suffer, especially to miss out on the suffering of the world, was not to live. If he was the first modern man, discovering the self, he recognized the self as an instrument, not a thing unto itself. . . . His miracle retained its capacity to endure, which meant that two thirteenth-century saints were not dead but uncannily alive not only in Assisi but in the lives of the American Franciscans who had made this trip to find them.[1]

Francis becomes a conduit for getting back to the very basics of Christian faith and living. His life is a bridge from the Middle Ages to the present. We do not forget that he is a citizen of the city-states of his time, but, as Hampl deftly shows, his moves in following Christ and living out the gospel are stunning in their resonance with our twenty-first-century demands for authenticity. Francis and his blonde and beautiful companion, Clare, are not saints on pedestals, not trapped in the frescoes by Cimabue and Giotto that give us accurate images of their faces. They are family for the pilgrim Franciscan friars and sisters in whose company Patricia finds herself. What is most original here is the almost Greek chorus these sisters and friars form, a real collection of personalities admirable and laughable, in which burns the love for God, the searching for communion with God and with all of the world. Hampl sketches for us what saints really look like, with all their particularities and their eccentricities, their strengths and their weaknesses: the dotty Sister Antoinette who can't keep from being sold too many religious medals; the dysfunctional Third Order lay Franciscan Ray; the apparently cynical but actually discerning Father Felix, in transition to being the paid chaplain of a well-off group in Hawaii; the retired schoolteachers Brothers Philip and Sylvan; Sister Bridget who has worked over thirty-five years in health care in Malayasia; bumbling Father Thaddeus, the New Yorker's New Yorker from the 34th Street Franciscan Church with the food pantry; and finally Patricia's roommate, a most unhappy, chain-smoking, abandoned-by-her-miserable-husband charismatic Elsie Pickett.

It is also important, both for Patricia Hampl and for me, that for Francis and Clare as well as their contemporary sisters and brothers, that most difficult of realities—the church—is also dealt with. Hampl starts with Fr. Felix.

There was no dogma to Felix, no rigidity, just the constant feints and lunges of a man observing the day tirelessly, and living it absolutely as prayer.

Existence was prayer. The *day* was prayer, and he was in the day, therefore in prayer. That was the feeling he and Donnie and Bridget—and even Thaddeus—all gave off. Prayer was not effort, not just something they did. It was something they were in, as obviously as they were in the world.

The Church, the order—these constituted the tradition they had inherited, a huge heap of an ancestral home in which they lived rent-free. They stayed in this house because they were born in it, a wreck of a place full of priceless pieces and a lot of junk—but theirs as indelibly as their blood types. The house might be falling down around their ears and have a questionable history, a structure impossible to repair, but it was home, the setting for all they did and all that mattered.

Finally, however, the Church was just a place, not life itself. Life was prayer. And that was to be found in every second of every minute of all the days of their lives. In a sense, they lived in the old beat-up house precisely because it had become automatic, unnoticeable. The life of the gaze—that's what they were after, a way of life that trained attention beyond the physical, beyond will and desire. Such a life made possible the concentration that was the real point of their vow of poverty.[2]

For all their imperfections, maybe in some cases a lack of advanced education, these sisters and brothers nevertheless teach a subtle and important lesson about organized religion, whether their own Franciscan Order or the institutional church. They do not reject or leave these quite fallible institutions, but neither do they confuse them with the reality of God, with the actual living out of the gospel. They come to terms with the disorder, the clericalism and hyper-piety, the legalism and ritualism and moral obsessiveness because they recognize that the church is human and a means to an end, not the end itself. Patricia Hampl had to wend her own way through to this too.

So Felix and Bridget, Thaddeus and Francine, and all the rest of the pilgrim-tourists, even those less obviously spiritual folks Patricia was with before Assisi, they all become books for her, expressions of searching, other models of what she herself was doing—seeking herself, seeking God, and some kind of relationship.

*Lourdes and the Redwoods Monastery: Ordinary Miracles*

Patricia Hampl continues on from Assisi to Lourdes—the famous shrine where Our Lady appeared, the miraculous spring, the candles, the basilica, the singing, and all the sick, hoping for a cure. All "beezness," a waiter at a restaurant tells her, "Bad, everything beezness," referring to the souvenir shops, the bottled Lourdes water, the whole commercialized pilgrim scene. But she has several epiphanic moments, one of a crippled man lovingly fed supper by his wife, another of the young waiter, young enough to be her son, who flirts with her, asks if she believes. "Yes, I believe," she blurts, but she hears her fellow pilgrims—Donnie from back home at the monastery and the Franciscan friar Thaddeus's way of saying it: "Hey, man, it was a divine discontent got me."[3] But this pilgrimage spot is another step on her deep journey.

As night truly fell and the Rosary droned on in the endless whirling way it is meant to, losing sense to silence, the candles began to come on, more and more candles, until the whole great public space was a vibrating carpet of light. It was not something to have an opinion about. A shock of reverence passed into me and lodged there.

I understood, vaguely, that the awe was for *all this,* the human this, the marvel—not altogether beautiful, but extraordinary—of this communal moment. But that distinction, between the human this and the divine that, suddenly struck me as puny, laughable. What had Donnie said when I asked her how she squared divine revelation in the Bible with—well, with reality?

"Oh," she said, as if she'd assumed all along that I understood the point of the sacred, "it's the whole intelligence, heart, mind, soul, history, *everything,* of a people." A People, the eternal presence of ourselves—and yet not ourselves, the beyond-ourselves of every urge and hope, every fear and fragment of desire we are destined to live and die. That was what Scripture exposed, she said. The fact that we are a People.[4]

The last stop on Patricia's journey is nowhere famous abroad, but rather a Cistercian women's monastery in northern California recommended by Donnie. Thomas Merton himself had visited it, in his search for a more remote hermitage site. It was a community of nine unusually independent nuns and a chaplain-monk-priest. The monastery's setting close to the redwoods forests—from which the monastery took its name—was almost magical in its beauty, something that comes across in Hampl's lines. The design of its buildings is utter simplicity, the pattern of its daily round of silence, prayer in common, meals, and work most ordinary but at the same time exquisite. The chapel and most of the monastery's design was spare and minimalist, even by spartan Cistercian tradition. And the nuns adapted the traditional monastic customs to the present. They donned the white cowl for church but otherwise wore simple clothes appropriate for work or dinner. Aside from some few but articulate comments from the visiting brother who organized the summer vegetable garden and a brief encounter with the chaplain, the retreat week she spent there was without striking personalities or happenings. The words of the Psalms, the wildflowers of the fields, the towering cathedral of redwoods, and the silence, however, penetrated her, and when the morning service was held out close to where redwoods were being cut—a terrible thing—Hampl receives the experience, the conversion moment, the *point vierge* she hoped for, maybe wanted, expected, or perhaps did not think could come. It was so many things converging—her parents, her Catholic upbringing, the product of the convent school she attended. It was her effort to break from it all—from Mass, the conformist behavior, the well-defined morality of being a "good Catholic girl," but also from the retreat, the distance she herself had traveled from all that in her youth.

I wanted to betray it all, wanted to join that real world where no good girls are allowed, except as decorative touches here and there. *Catholic? Well, I was brought up Catholic but of course . . .* I wanted to radiate not this ridiculous girlish light but the dark fire of ordeals and events, episodes and affairs. I was terrified I was missing out on Life, that thing called "experience," all because I'd been held in the cooing Catholic embrace too long and was forever marked. But marked by what? The indelible brand of innocence, which is to be marked by an absence, a vacancy. By nothing at all.

Now all these years later, to stand on a hill at sunrise with a bunch of nuns who don't look like nuns, everybody wearing sweatshirts and big sweaters, my girlish fury burned, the embers still glowing, joining our light to the new sun of midsummer, mid-life: to find a use for innocence, after all. Tears spiked my eyes. *I can't help it, it's how I am.* Like the hot metal of a Linotype, these ordinary words cast themselves across my mind. The words could have been "Lord have mercy," or "Forgive me, for I have sinned." They *were* those words, in fact, those prayerful words of old, but neatly camouflaged in my modern voice that can't resist ripping the religious art off the walls. I can't help it, it's how I am. Finally, prayer. After all my running away from it . . . and then running after it to Assisi and Lourdes.

Standing in a circle of prayer, shivering in the morning cold, with all these strangers. It was another of those moments of oddity carried forward from childhood—the world is so funny, I used to think, lying in my flower-papered bedroom. How funny prayer turned out to be. At that moment of saying the words, feeling them course through me like electrical impulses as unbidden as the synapses of my brain, I understood prayer is, after all, a plain statement of fact. An admission of existence. That's all. A surrender of self to the All of history and oblivion. Surrender of intention into the truth of a life. You don't get to live Life—that thing I feared I was missing. You just live a life. This one. Was I crying because the sun was rising? . . . This was the immaculate moment we had climbed into, drenched by the long dewy grasses, achieving the high meadow by 6 a.m., where we turned east, instinctively toward the first rays of summer which we had come to meet. Here I met myself, here I said my first prayer. *I can't help it, it's how I am.*[5]

Patricia Hampl's encounters with all those other tourist-pilgrims, with the Franciscans, with Sisters Cecile and Jeanine, Brother Thomas the gardener and Father Andre the chaplain, with her fellow retreatants and the rest of the community at the Redwoods monastery—these took place years ago, before *Virgin Time* first appeared in 1992. Yet I have to believe that the search she documents here remains beautiful and instructive today. Surely it will always be part of her memory and living. But it is one of the most instructive sources for anyone seeking the life of holiness, trying to understand what this life means, what it does to your life.

Hampl learned a great deal about formal, liturgical prayer from the sisters of the convent school of her childhood. But she continued to learn through the years beyond that, even when she was not particularly "active" or "observant." And as far as I can see, from not only *Virgin Time* but from all of her books and essays, she has never stopped searching for the life of the Spirit, of holiness, or learning how to pray. I felt very much at home with that mixed bag of Franciscans with whom she "did" Assisi. They were family, much like many I have known, back in the Carmelite days and thereafter. No, she never became a nun or took theology courses or got involved in any official way ecclesiastically, to the best of my knowledge. However it is not about such official or professional paths after all, prayer, I mean.

I take her writing to be simply exquisite prayer. It is also prayer that is most expressive, prayer that could not be more personal, prayer that not only brings her to terms with her own past but also gives us a great deal for our own lives. Her writing/prayer reaches back into the past of her home and parents, into her own evolution as a woman in America in the 1960s and beyond—this is a story rich in its own right. But she also journeys back into her efforts to become a writer, as well as forward into the present of the things that matter to her. And, as I noted earlier, this *Virgin Time* is but one of the books in which she shares her journey of memory and contemplation. "Virgin time," the title, comes from Thomas Merton's attempt to describe the contemplative life, that of holiness.

> The contemplative life must provide an area, a space of liberty, of silence, in which possibilities are allowed to surface and new choices—beyond routine choice—become manifest. It should create a new experience of time, not as stopgap stillness, but as "temps vierge"—not a blank to be filled or an untouched space to be conquered and violated, but a space which can enjoy its own potentialities and hopes—and its own presence to itself. One's own time. But not dominated by one's own ego and its demands. Hence open to others—compassionate time, rooted in the sense of common illusion and in criticism of it.[6]

As we examine that part of the life of holiness that is searching and finding, Patricia Hampl surely has taken us into a space of her own. We have been her fellow travelers—along with some other interesting tourists—to a number of places of pilgrimage. And yet, as with all such journeys, we come home and we learn that prayer and God are there too.

## The Winner Girl Meets God

> Sometimes, lately, I feel a sort of sinking staleness, and it feels familiar, and it scares me. I felt it the other day sitting in class. All of a sudden I

felt, *This isn't working. I don't believe this Christian thing anymore, this is just some crazy fix I've been on, and now I've reached my toleration level, and it's not working.* I thought about how Lamaze teachers tell you to breathe through your pain. I breathed. The feelings passed. But they'll come back. They are familiar. They are what I felt when I started to stop Judaism. So I come home from the library, or I come home from class, or I come home from work, wherever I am when the staleness comes over me, and I think about what I've learned, and I think about how to do it differently, how to ride out the staleness this time, instead of switching religions when it all gets too stale. . . . My glue to Christianity will have to come from somewhere other than my dreams of salvation. It will have to come from God's place of faithfulness, not from some pot of faithfulness all my own. Fidelity to prayerbooks, never mind to the people who've taught me to pray with them, is not my strong suit.

Sometimes, some relative or friend asks me what religion I'll pick next; they ask when I'll convert to Buddhism. "You used to believe Orthodox Judaism was true," they say. "Now you believe Christianity is true. Maybe next week you'll believe something else is true." But I feel there will be no conversions to Buddhism next week or next month or next year—for several reasons. First, Judaism and Christianity have something to do with each other. Judaism and Christianity make a path. They make a path through the Bible, and through history. Christianity and Buddhism don't make the same path.

Second, I'm not seventeen anymore. I watch the Christian teenagers I know and I am awed at the way God fires up our faith when we are teens. I think about the impassioned letters I wrote my Orthodox cousin, Jane. I think about the earnestness and fervor of my reaching for Orthodoxy, and I am transfixed by the fervor, and relieved, a little, that I'm no longer seventeen. I am not sure that I have the passion to fall in love with a religion again. How to fall in love is not, now, what I need to learn. What I need to learn, maybe what God wants me to learn, is the long grind after you've landed.

But the most important reason is this: I want to stay in Christ. I want to live in this Christian grammar as surely as I live in my apartment. I want God to give me grace to stick with this, to stay here. And I believe He will.

My friend Meredith will be confirmed next week. She is terrified. She thinks she may run away. . . . She says she is not having new doubts, just the same ones she has every Sunday, only magnified. "Every time I stand up to say the Creed, I wonder if I can say I believe these things," she says. . . . I tell her there is a Hasidic story. A student goes to his teacher and says, "Rabbi, how can I say 'I believe' when I pray, if I am not sure that I believe?"

His rabbi has an answer: "'I believe' is a prayer meaning, 'Oh, that I may believe!'"[7]

In this passage from the end of her memoir, we hear a different voice with a somewhat different story than most we have listened to here. The tone is that of a twenty-something. It is quick, the ideas zip by, but there is sharp introspective insight. There is also a healthy self-criticism and a wonderful sense of humor. We have here a best selling author.[8]

But while we have encountered individuals who have experienced many changes in their path to God, even conversions, there is no one who comes close to the still very young Lauren Winner. Now on the faculty at Duke Divinity School, she is no longer the zealous teenager who leaps into Orthodox Judaism after a childhood of relative non-observance. And this was some leap, as the deep imprint of the practice of Judaism remains in her, from her formal studies to dress to the details of the observance of the Sabbath and the holy days to the very language and "culture" of that *frum* (pious, strict) observance. As she recounts it both in *Girl Meets God* and *Mudhouse Sabbath,* she uses the liturgical calendars of both Christianity and Judaism to mark the days, weeks, months, and year: Pentecost/Shavuot, Easter/Pesach.

As she writes above, it is an understatement to say that Judaism and Christianity have something to do with each other! What she offers, seldom to be found, is an observant Jew's insider view of the Christian tradition. And if this were not enough, she provides something just as, or maybe even more rare—a Christian insider's view of Orthodox Judaism. Further, her own profound experience is of both these traditions not in some distant historical period, but as devoted Jews and Christians attempt, in community life, in liturgy and study, even in their meals and conversations and friendships, to sustain these sacred ways now, in the wild, always changing twenty-first century, in a diverse, somewhat secular but also very passionately observant American society. If anyone worries about the alleged immorality and secularity, the doubting or nonbelieving aspects of young people in America, they should devour all of Lauren's books and her many articles both online and hardcopy. (She was book editor of Beliefnet .com and contributor to a number of online journals.)

I suppose that one might also consult other autobiographical accounts such as Veronica Chater, on growing up in an extreme traditional Catholic milieu.[9] There is also Susan Campbell, remembering growing up in a fundamentalist church.[10] Jon M. Sweeney and Christine Rosen offer similar accounts.[11] One of the most controversial religious memoirs is Frank Schaeffer's massive settling up with his father and mother, evangelical theologian Francis Schaeffer and the religious right.[12] There is also a noteworthy anthology of spiritual memoirs, all of these in addition to the ones featured here.[13] The number of spiritual or religious memoirs, not those by celebrity figures but by thoughtful individuals, is formidable and growing. I think this says much, contra the perspectives of Dawkins, Hitchens, and others about religion as solely toxic, clearly a point of view this book (and those of mine before it) tries to challenge. The memoirs just mentioned are only a few of those I deliberately did not choose to include in this book because of the at times dramatic confrontation with one's past, one's parents and faith, delivered in them. It is not that I wanted to avoid the hard edges of such accounts. Rather what I was more interested in was the recovery or rediscovery of a life of faith, of searching for God, which is the hallmark of the writers we are listening to here and less so a feature of some other spiritual memoirs.

But back to Lauren Winner. The chapters of *Girl Meets God,* arranged according to the liturgical calendar (as was Nora Gallagher's), is mostly about the journey from a not terribly religious childhood headlong into strictly observant Orthodox Judaism at age seventeen and then, gradually, out of this toward Christianity, baptism at Cambridge University, and belonging to All Angels Church on the upper West Side of New York City. Woven in, around, and through her account of entering the church is a rich narrative of Jewish life and belief, Torah and Talmud study, and what one eats to break the Yom

Kippur fast and how to make *challah* from scratch. Because her mother was not Jewish, though her father was, Lauren does indeed have to formally convert to enter Orthodox Judaism. The *bet din,* or rabbinical court, meets with her, one rabbi in particular specifying the credo of Maimonides, the *Ani Ma'amin* recited at the end of morning prayer. She does indeed "sign on" to it, answers acceptably about the charity laws of *tzedakah* and then is plunged completely naked for purification into a ritual bath, or *mikvah,* a block from 79th Street, on the upper West Side, where women go for purification after the mid-point of their periods.

All the other details of observant life—the long skirts, learning Hebrew and Aramaic for prayer and for study, the hats, the long sleeves, even the observant boyfriend—this is a fascinating look into the actual practice of Orthodox Judaism in our time, one of the in-valuable gifts Winner brings. But this will not be the last initiation and washing for her. She leads us along the unpredictable path—given her enormous attraction to Orthodoxy and zeal for observance—out of it. Lauren had chosen to attend Columbia on the upper West Side of New York City precisely because of the strong Orthodox presence there, all of which made an observant life possible. But Manhattan also had the Cloisters museum of medieval art—all of it intensely Christian, even Catholic, liturgical, Virgin Marys and saints galore, not to mention the crucifixes. Then there was Winner's interest, as a Southerner, in Southern religion and history and literature. The Or-thodox boyfriend introduced to her by her rabbi begins to find alarm-ing her hanging out at the Cloisters, her reading of Flannery O'Con-nor, her papers about the Great Awakening. There is a dream about being saved as a mermaid by a man she cannot identify. A former high school teacher who was a devout Christian insists it was Jesus. There is also a kind of staleness.

> But gradually, my Judaism broke. I couldn't remember why I was keep-ing Shabbat, why I was praying in Hebrew, why I was spending Friday nights and Saturday afternoons at long Sabbath meals, full of singing and wine, with people I loved. I called Rabbi M. and said I was having a spiritual dry spell. He said, *This is the beauty of Judaism. Even when you doubt, even when it doesn't feel like anything is happening, even*

*when it seems like God is not around, you keep doing the mitzvot. You keep saying the prayers, you keep rinsing your hands every morning, you keep decorating the sukkah with fruit, and lighting the Sabbath candles, and making latkes at Hanukkah. The action will get you through the dry spells. Eventually the feeling that God is hovering in between your shoulder blades will come back.* So I kept praying, and decorating the *sukkah* with fruit, and lighting the Sabbath candles.[14]

But the spell did not dissipate. Gradually, furtively at first by attendance at vespers at an Episcopal church and reading Teresa of Avila, doing more papers on the Great Awakening, Lauren was drifting away from Judaism and toward the way of the carpenter. A Presbyterian pastor urges her not to divorce herself from her Judaism. But before long she is enrolled in an inquirer's class and does a hilarious send-up of it and its content at a very liberal Episcopal parish. Only when doing graduate work at Cambridge does the second washing, her baptism, take place at Clare College chapel.

Looking back on what she too came to see was a divorce from the Judaism she married, naked in the *mikvah*, Lauren does a respectful but honest assessment of both the tradition as observed as well as her own practice. As with other writers we have listened to, she points to examples of where there were, for her at least, real breakdowns in the supposedly seamless wrap of all of life in Orthodoxy. She found rather quickly and painfully that as a convert (remember her mother was not Jewish) she was indeed a second-class citizen. When it came to thinking about marriage she learned the sad truth that she was not marriage material as such. She had not grown up in Judaism, had not attended all the right schools, and, despite her acquisition of Hebrew, her praying and practicing was just not right, plus how could her husband's parents ever dance with her own, divorced parents at the wedding?

She further came to see the highly limited place and roles for women, despite education and despite the progressive character of the Orthodoxy to which she belonged, often referred to as "Modern Orthodoxy." Since her writing, voices within the Modern Orthodox communities have turned more conservative, have wondered whether despite so many opportunities for observance attending a school like Columbia or Harvard or the University of Chicago is really right

for Orthodox Jewish men. Perhaps Yeshiva University and the Stern
College for Women are preferable for maintaining distance from those
outside Jewish law and belonging.

Lauren also notices the intrusion of wealth and status into the
outlook of the people she meets. Then there is her own inability to
practice the faith, maintain the observances without lapses and infractions. I found fascinating the juxtaposition of these accounts of her
falling from Orthodoxy with a brief assessment of what really defines
Christian fundamentalism—Lauren will admit to being an evangelical
but not a fundamentalist. She intertwines descriptions of Ash Wednesday worship and its significance and a suggestion from her priest to
give up reading in Lent with details of Sabbath prohibitions and then
kosher restrictions. She pairs the drama of Holy Week services with
the Passover Seder meals. Like others we have heard, Lauren cannot
but let the human side of religious faith and practice show itself—
from the desire of her Jewish "family" away from home in New York
City to give her a true sense of a "home," to all the very nontheologi-
cal aspects of the Eucharist that draw her to it, just as the human side
of Southern Christianity drew her to not only Southern writers but to
the historical research she would later do on customs, foods, and celebrations in Southern Christian practice in early times. This became
the focus of her doctoral dissertation.

There is one chapter in the Holy Week section that is really a
tour de force on the many different sides of the central sacrament and
liturgical action in the Christian tradition, the Eucharist. We get some
biblical foundations, but also anthropological and psychological an-
gles. Various theological interpretations over the centuries are trotted
out, and of course Anglicans hold all or some or none of them, Lauren
informs us. She even finds room for the appreciation of the Eucharist
by kids in a Sunday school class, really innovative ideas about the sacrament: "The priest is pouring God into the cup for us to drink." But
at the end of this brief nine-page reflection she manages to admit that
one doesn't always like one's fellow communicants, one's cobelievers.
She remembers that she really disliked most of the congregation at the
Clare College chapel at which she was baptized, save the priest and a
couple others. Lauren the bitch is in fact in generous display through-

out the memoir, not only deliberately but many times unwittingly, though by now I expect readers have made her aware of this.

Like Barbara Brown Taylor and Nora Gallagher, Lauren Winner lets us in on her difficulties with prayer, both in the Orthodox Jewish and Christian traditions. Once more we hear that for all the learning, all the good intentions and emotional desire, the actual performance of a religious tradition is really hard. Even if done with great attention and care, it is often imperfect, lacking in one or another aspect, at least when compared to the ideals in the lives of holy people or in texts.

Almost as if complying with a suggestion of the great Rabbi Hillel: "Do not separate from the community," Lauren embroiders into her memoir a great many people from her parents and a few other relatives and very close friends to those she has encountered along her journeys both in Orthodox Judaism and Christianity. The evangelical couple Hannah and Jim come back several times for appearances, as do a number of Episcopal priests Winner seeks out for confession, advice, spiritual direction, and instruction. She has a favorite among the rabbis, Rabbi M., and there is the Orthodox boyfriend Dov, his mother, as well as Benjamin and Randi and Opal. Father Peter, the Episcopal priest two hours upstate, is a composite and like others in the narrative likely given a fictional name to protect identity and privacy.

In her account of confession with him, Lauren gives a sensitive, discerning view into how this sacrament is traditionally conducted among Anglicans, Catholics, and Eastern Orthodox Christians. But she does not leave it there, choosing to be ruthlessly honest about the state of her own life, her sexual behavior, and what the ideas are on confession and asking forgiveness both in Christian and Jewish understandings. Father Peter tears up the six legal page list of sins Lauren has meticulously produced. Lauren is nothing if not dramatic in all her religious identities! Later, the sexual side would turn up in her book about sex in Christian teaching and in practice.

One unusual aspect, at least at the time that Winner was documenting her religious adventures, was her willingness to engage in, in fact mastermind, at least a couple of combined Jewish-Christian rites. One was not so unusual, a Christian *seder,* something done among a number of Protestant denominations. The other was a *leil tikkun*

*Shavuot*—literally a set order of study or vigil the night before the Jewish feast fifty days after Passover, *Shavuot,* commemorating the gift of the Torah, the teaching or law, by God to the people of Israel on Sinai. In the Torah the Israelites were overcome with sleep and Moses had to awaken them in the morning when God was to reveal himself and give the law. Hence there is the custom of spending the entire night in study and prayer. Lauren's Pentecost version is accompanied by numerous pots of tea, cheese blintzes, cheese and crackers, and a cheesecake. What they teach is to me an astounding weaving together again of the two traditions—the bringing together of the Torah-giving, God's voice, "Quiet, this is my decree," the memory of the martyred Rabbi Akiva, and the Pentecost descent of the Holy Spirit, described in the Acts of the Apostles, with the fire, windstorm, and shaking of the house and the ability to understand each other despite the foreigners gathered and their different languages.

Immediately following, Winner gives us a moving, again multidimensional reflection on the Book of Ruth, traditionally read on *Shavuot.* This is a story of deep human tragedy—death, impoverishment, loyalty, clinging to another. Of course the book ends with the marriage of Ruth and Boaz and the birth of their son, Obed, whose son was Jesse, whose son was David the king. And Lauren is off—into the New Testament genealogies in which Ruth as a number of other righteous and not so righteous women figure not just prominently but are necessary in being ancestors of Jesus the Messiah. These chapters really must be read to do them justice. And seemingly out of nowhere, Winner the historian introduces us to the art of papercutting and the images thus made which became popular in the seventeenth and eighteenth centuries particularly to decorate the Book of Esther and wedding contracts. Lauren ends up purchasing from contemporary artists a papercut of the lament of Naomi from the beginning of the Book of Ruth.

As if this is still not enough, she connects the Book of Ruth's focus on loss and recovery, on death and new life with the Gospel of Luke and Mary's song of praise, deliberately modeled on that of the righteous Hannah in the First Book of Samuel. And for good measure, she throws in an excursus, appropriate for the consideration of *Shavuot*/Pentecost, of *glossolalia,* the speaking in tongues resulting from "Spirit-baptism"' that came back into Christian practice in a small church on Azusa Street in Los Angeles just over a century ago.

*Complicated but Rich Travels*

Lauren Winner's story is without doubt the most complex of those we have encountered here, particularly in terms of the religious traditions of belonging through which she passed. Many of the writers to whom we have listened have done some traveling. Some have journeyed through career changes, others through marital and extremely difficult personal pilgrimages of sickness and death of loved ones. Some have traveled through a number of Christian denominations. Diana Butler Bass, for example, as we will see, moved from a childhood in the Methodist Church to be deeply influenced by evangelical Christianity, to end up finally in the Anglican tradition, in the Episcopal Church in the United States.

Others have emphasized not just the symbolism of pilgrimage but its deeper, archetypal significance in the Christian life.[15] The church and every member pass each year through the "great sea" of Lent, as an Eastern Church hymn describes, to end up at the harbor and haven of *Pascha*, Easter, the "feast of feasts" of the Lord's Resurrection, the festival that determines the rest of the liturgical year's calendar. Really, like Jewish sisters and brothers we cycle through the same feasts and fasts every year, no matter which calendar we adhere to, just as we cycle our way through the scriptures, no matter which lectionary we follow.

Even the chapters of this book, both as I originally planned them, and then as they have turned out in the writing and revising, comprise a journey. It seems to me that remembering, crafting a memoir of any kind, demands traveling—not just back in time but also out in different directions, to all the places and people to which one's life has led. Or perhaps to put it more accurately, all the individual journeys writers have shared here remind us there is only one pilgrimage— from birth to death, from life to life. The preface in the liturgy of burial in the western rite says *vita mutatur, non tollitur*—"life is not taken away, but changed."

Could it also be that in setting out—as the children of Israel, as Tobias and the angel Raphael, as Elijah into the wilderness, Mary, Joseph and the child Jesus to Egypt, the apostles and other innumerable pilgrims—we discover that the One we seek is always with us, is everywhere?

# CHAPTER SEVEN

# God Is Everywhere

*Merton and the Resurrection*

The only ultimate reality is God. God lives and dwells in us. We are not justified by any action of our own, but we are called by the voice of God . . . to pierce through the irrelevance of our life, while accepting and admitting that our life is totally irrelevant, in order to find relevance in Him. And this relevance in Him is not something we can grasp or possess. It is something that can only be received as a gift. Consequently, the kind of life that I represent is a life that is openness to gift; gift from God and gift from others.[1]

Poet Ron Seitz quoted Thomas Merton as saying that the spiritual life could be summarized in three words: "now, here, this." I can imagine Merton thinking this, even saying it in a talk. In audiotapes and transcripts of presentations he gave in the last years of his life, not to mention entries in his journals, Merton had gotten more precise, sharper, more urgent. Sitting on a stone wall near his hermitage, Merton spoke very lucidly and without any theological jargon about what was the core of his faith. Seitz scribbled it down shortly afterwards. Merton insisted that despite all the nonsense that passed for religion, it was only a living Christ that mattered. "Christ must be INCARNATE in all men, all women, each and every one of us chosen as the body named Jesus."[2]

In what would be the last months of his life, Merton was able to travel in Asia before participating in a monastic conference in Bangkok. He visited many teachers and monks of the Asian traditions, met the Dalai Lama—a remarkable photo and his journal entries document their profound encounter and understanding of each other. Merton's published Asian journal is filled with the many photos he took himself on the journey. There are the faces of rimpoches—spiritual masters—but also of ordinary people and children.

He stood transfixed before the statues at Polonnaruwa, especially that of the reclining, dying Buddha in Sri Lanka. It was a moment of real awakening and realization for him, an epiphany, not only of the Buddhist tradition but his own Christian one as well.

> I am able to approach the Buddhas barefoot and undisturbed, my feet in wet grass, wet sand. Then the silence of the extraordinary faces. The great smiles. Huge and yet subtle. Filled with every possibility, questioning nothing, knowing everything, rejecting nothing, the peace not of emotional resignation but of Madhyamika [the "Middle Path"], of sunyata [emptiness], that has seen through every question without trying to discredit anyone or anything—without refutation, without establishing some other argument. . . . Looking at these figures I was suddenly, almost forcibly, jerked clean out of the habitual, half-tied vision of things, and an inner clearness, clarity, as if exploding from the rocks themselves, became evident and obvious.[3]

Merton closes the entry by saying he knows and has seen what he was obscurely looking for in this Asian pilgrimage.

In the very last talk at the monastic conference in Bangkok, one hears the articulate, serious, and very direct perspective Merton had come to later in his life. It appears, for example, in the line "From now on brother, everybody stands on his own feet."[4] One can also hear this simplicity in the notes for a talk and an informal talk actually given at the First Spiritual Summit Conference in Calcutta and most poignantly in the prayer he composed for that conference.[5] Speaking to an interfaith group meeting, he cut to the heart of monastic life, trying to explain that this life was what he was bringing to them.

In the prayer he was asked to offer at the end of this conference, he first observed that a new language of prayer was necessary, given the interfaith nature of the group, something that "transcends all our traditions and comes from the immediacy of love." Not having written anything out, he counted on the reality that all were "creatures of love" who were to join hands in prayer. The prayer that he spontaneously offered reminds me of the distillation of the whole of the tradition, the scriptures, sacraments, asceticism, that in the end it is all about love—the realization of Paul, Augustine, Gregory of Nyssa, Aquinas, John of the Cross, Teresa of Avila, Seraphim of Sarov, Mother Maria Skobtsova, and Dorothy Day.

> Oh God, we are one with You. You have made us one with You. You have taught us that if we are open to one another, You dwell in us. Help us to preserve this openness and to fight for it with all our hearts. Help us to realize that there can be no understanding where there is mutual rejection. Oh God, in accepting one another wholeheartedly, fully, completely, we accept You, and we thank You, and we adore You, and we love You with our whole being, because our being is in Your being, our spirit is rooted in Your spirit. Fill us then with love, and let us be bound together with love as we go our diverse ways, united in this one spirit which makes You present in the world, and which makes You witness to the ultimate reality that is love. Love has overcome. Love is victorious. Amen.[6]

These simple yet frank statements are the products of years of reflection, study, and prayer on Merton's part. It was not just his immersion in Buddhism and its mindfulness, surely not a politically correct ecumenical diplomacy—this was long before that came into vogue. In a retreat given to heads of women's religious communities in 1967 he was just as direct to the point of being blunt, and painfully so, for the overly optimistic and hopeful.

He is often criticized for his activism, his commitment to the civil rights movement, the anti–Vietnam War movement, the anti-nuclear movement, as well as the Vatican II–inspired movement to renew church and monastic life, but reading Merton in the extended expanse of his journals and these retreat talks can be startling. He comes down very hard on what we now realize as the silliness and self-obsessive pleasures of the rebellious sixties. He calls the "huge effervescence of sex" that was going on not just immoral but a lie, "a bad piece of goods," an "empty box." "All the talk about growth and joy means nothing. They just have a big box of death."[7] Now, to be accurate, Merton said this at the end of a second retreat in which he was equally merciless with the fossilized culture within the church and within religious communities. He refused to excuse those in leadership— bishops, pastors, heads of communities—as well as rank and file members too set in comfortable ways, threatened by needed change, unwilling to open themselves to God and the world around them.

> This brings us to the real problem of the world of our time. It seems to me the issue is this: From a certain point of view, secular Christianity is saying, "OK. God has turned us loose, and left us to go along and make it by ourselves. But still, it is God who is doing it. So it's just fine to get along without a lot of religious activity and without all that religious superstructure. We're on our own." But it doesn't work like that. It often turns into exactly the opposite. We do have a problem in the New Testament with this whole secular structure, because there is more to it than just God and the world. There's a professional liar involved in it somewhere. What happens is the making of a whole structure of lies. It is not just a question of a good God and a neutral world which can be made good simply by referring it to God. In between is a structure of mendacity, of lies and false meaning.[8]

The belief that simply leaving the culture and structures of tradition would automatically make for peace, for personal fulfillment, for a more open church was not true. In his journey to Asia in the last months of his life, shortly after the last retreat with the sisters, Merton would experience the authentic struggles of monastics and ordinary people in Nepal, India, and Thailand. The monastic conference that was the formal purpose of the trip was disappointing. The then Benedictine abbot general Rembert Weakland grudgingly admitted this in an interview for Paul Wilkes's documentary on Merton. Many of the Asian Christian monastics were not able to connect with either Merton's or his friend the Benedictine monk and scholar Jean Leclercq's commitment to reform and renewal. The talk Merton gave on monastic life, its connections with Marxist communitarian ideals, and the need for personal responsibility sounded strange, ending abruptly with the midday break for lunch. Merton never returned for questions, answers, and a final statement. After lunch, his life ended suddenly when he touched a shorted out fan. But I think the unstated perspective is to be found at the very end of the sisters' retreat, after his perhaps unwelcome dose of realism on the achievements of the sixties, the ever present and potent "professional liar" and the necessity of standing on one's own.

> The only real answer to all this is the Resurrection. The only affirmation that makes sense to commit yourself to is the affirmation of the risen Christ. There is no other. Any Christian who gets involved in a whole series of answers that end up in another undertaker's parlor is simply being a fool. A person like that has no understanding of what Christian faith is really about. This awareness is central to us because we are witnesses to life in the Resurrection. We're witnesses to God's truth, not because it is something that we figured out and not because it's something implicit in the structure of living organisms. . . . It's based on a promise. God said it. You either believe it or you don't.[9]

Merton maintains this very immediate, classic stance through to the end of the retreat, bringing it to bear on the tangible matters of the manipulation of power in the church, the misuse of authority in religious communities, the resistance to change, as well as institutional inertia. Despite it all, Merton insists, "It's a question of the reality of a tradition that is alive. It's a matter of Christ actually being and living here and now in us."[10] It is exactly what Seitz quoted Merton as saying and believing: that God was everywhere, immediate, in every experience and thought we have, in every communication and relationship.

We keep thinking that *we* are the ones looking for God when all along God's already found us, is in and with us—so the New Testament says in many different ways. Jesus is God-with-us, Immanuel. God in the Incarnation has come to dwell, literally, to "pitch his tent," among us. The very first words of Jesus in the Gospel of Mark proclaim the presence: "The time is fulfilled, and the kingdom of God is at hand, repent and believe in the good news" (Mk 1:15). Matthew's Gospel ends with the same assurance: "Remember I am with you always, to the end of the age" (Mt 28:20). The Holy Spirit is said to "fill the whole earth." The prayer before all services in the Eastern Church says that the "Heavenly King, the Comforter, the Spirit of truth" is "everywhere, filling all things." Nonetheless the Spirit is called on to "come and abide in us." How many following Christ over the years say or paraphrase the claim of Augustine that God is closer to us than our own hearts, our own breathing, our own lives.

After so much listening to the spiritual ups and downs, the pilgrimages of people searching for God, for community, for joy and peace, finding life with God among the most diverse people and in unexpected places, it does not seem so strange to come to the conclusion that God is everywhere, in everything. But this is a realization that most of us have to come to only gradually, cumulatively, living through to it. Even then it may still be shocking: the idea that everything I was doing before—working, making meals, taking out the trash, watching the news, or going through websites online—that all of these are part of finding God, part of the life of holiness.

Many of us come to the conclusion that the search for God, for meaning and community, is not only spiritual but religious. With the emergence of the "I'm spiritual, but not very religious" expression, some take this as a challenge to rediscover and reclaim faith and tradition perhaps once left behind or never entered. We have heard much of this in the accounts of Nora Gallagher, Sara Miles, and Patricia Hampl. But in their journeys one of the realizations they came to was precisely that there is no place in life or in this world that God neglects or is absent from.

*Easter, God Everywhere: Darcey Steinke*

Darcey Steinke learned about God's being everywhere not just at the Sunday liturgy presided over by her pastor father and not just in Sunday church school. She seems to have absorbed it from all corners of her childhood home and experience, as she makes clear in *Easter Everywhere,* her memoir. She celebrated communion as a kid with friends to near disastrous consequences—the berry wine concocted for the "liturgy" was toxic! She baptized animals, and, despite the difficulties church life and her father's pastoral activities caused her mother and the rest of the family, her sense of the omnipresence of God is moving and genuine. No theological essay or spiritual reflection could craft such awareness of the sacred. In one of her most difficult stages she returns to the awareness of God.

I knew Thomas Merton believed that God gave man a nature that was ordered to the supernatural life: "He created man with a soul that was made not to bring itself to perfection in its own order, but to be perfected by him in an order infinitely beyond the reach of human powers." God was calling my name in restaurant bathrooms, on the Q train, from the water that streamed from the showerhead, and on the sidewalk along Flatbush Avenue.

In Mississippi I tried to contact God myself. Now I knew I needed some help. I thought about the elderly priest at the church in Brooklyn Heights. I'd gone to his rectory once and waited outside his office while he talked on the phone.[11]

She's directed to an Episcopal nun on the upper West Side.

Sister Leslie was diminutive under her black robe. Her small face jutted out of her wimple. She wore a wooden cross with a silver inlay of the seven-point star. I talked fast, running through my divorce, my stepmother leaving my father, my depression, my shaky state of mystification. I finished embarrassed and nearly out of breath. My cheeks burned and I knew my clavicle was getting spotty, as it always does when I feel humiliated.

"At the moment," I said, "I am kind of a mess."

Sister Leslie, her hands resting palms up, fingers curled beneath one another like a pink flesh flower, smiled.

"You were being smoothed," she said. "Now God is calling you to her."[12]

And so began a relationship in spiritual direction that is amazing to follow. But this same realization pops up all over her fiction. In her novel *Milk,* in addition to a former monk, we meet a troubled but perceptive priest named Walter and a young woman who's taken refuge in his rectory, fleeing an abusive marriage. She, Mary, is in a strange way a seeker, a mystic.

He understood what fueled her longing. It was unconscionable to live separated from God, like a cork held under water; the urge for union was often untenable. But what Mary wanted was technically impossible: to feel God's touch physically manifested.

"What you're saying is interesting, and I don't doubt what you suspect is true. If one believes in a divine presence that connects everything, a fine wed of interrelatedness, then inside any object, be it a squirrel or a refrigerator, resides particles of eternity. . . . And I can understand both your desire for unification with the Godhead and the hope that time might give way to infinity."

"So you don't think it's possible?" Mary said, looking into the fireplace filled with ash. Her face had clouded over.

He knew from reading saints' biographies that there was always a point of disassociation from reality, from the material world; there was, as doctors would say, the schizophrenic break that led either to the asylum or to greater knowledge. . . .

"That's not what I'm saying, "Walter said. "I'm saying that what you suspect is happening all the time. Just think about the crazy foliage God sends up in the spring, those green tulip tentacles coming out of the dead leaves, and what about snow?" He gestured to the window. "For God's sake, look at it." He held his hand high as if directing the tiny bits of crystallized ice. Flakes moved as they had all winter past the bay window in a gentle and glittering trajectory.

"See what I mean?"

"I guess," she said deflated. "You think I'm being too literal."

Walter shook his head. "No, I think you're not being literal enough. I mean religion insists on paradox. Everything is wonderful. Everything is terrible. Both at the same time. That's how it is with everything, degradation and divinity, the material and the corporeal, all unified so on one level a blade of grass is an everyday object, but in another way it's a supernatural thing."

Mary hung her head; she was clearly disappointed, and he could tell by the way she'd rested her hands, fingers spread, on her knees.

"I understand my soul is like a piece of God implanted in me, and while it's the same substance as God, it's much more cloudy because it's so hard to be human."

Walter stared at her. In her own way, he thought, Mary was spiritually advanced.[13]

For Darcey, the reality of God everywhere is bedrock and true, despite our inattention or doubt, despite even religious obsession or fanaticism. But what is equally strong in her vision is that the effort to be in communion with God does not require stereotypic sanctity, that of the stained-glass-window saints, those in the frescoes gaunt from fasting, able to be in two places at the same time. For Darcey, life with God is utterly of this world, of one's own body and the bodies of one's mate, one's child. Union with God, the living with and in holiness is not about heroic virtue or perfection. Quite the contrary. It is about being fully human, warts, wrinkles, infidelities, depression, and other issues and all. "A human being fully alive," said Irenaeus of Lyons almost two thousand years ago, "is the glory of God."

### The World as Altar: Barbara Brown Taylor

Earlier we tracked the journey Barbara Brown Taylor made in the ordained ministry, into and out of the parishes she served. It was a story of failure yet also success. In the end, she came face-to-face with herself, her strengths and her weaknesses. She looked long and honestly into what makes church toxic, what makes the ordained ministry destructive of the priest and the faithful. She did not blink as she opened the book of her own personality and life, her gifts and inadequacies in the preparation for and practice of the priesthood. This must have been a very difficult book to write, or perhaps better, I should say that the process that enabled it to be written must have been painful and demanding, just as the events that led up to it.

Barbara Brown Taylor is prolific. She has published several volumes of essays and sermons and has a very active schedule of conferences and lectures. But here I want to turn to what might be read as a sequel to, surely a companion to, *Leaving Church*. It is *An Altar in the World*. Subtitled *A Geography of Faith*, it is indeed another kind of pilgrimage through the terrain in which God can be found, but not the house of prayer, the church building, or even the community of the parish or denominational church. Rather she lays out for us a very worldly, material pilgrimage of faith, one that is also of the skin, about relationships, connections, the fact of being a body, with all that entails—eating, feeling, touching, suffering, being able to see and hear, and the absence of these senses.

> The physical boundaries of those houses [of worship] were clear. The communities in them were identified. *Here is the church; here is the steeple; open the doors and see all the people.* . . . We did things together in those sacred spaces that we did nowhere else in our lives: we named babies, we buried the dead, we sang psalms, we praised God for our lives. . . . We knew some things we could do to feel close to God inside the church, but after we stepped into the parking lot we lost that intimacy. The boundaries were not so clear out there. . . . That, at least, is how it looked to those of us who had forgotten that the whole world is the House of God. Somewhere along the line we bought—or were sold—the idea that God is chiefly interested in religion. We believed that God's home was the church, that God's people knew who they were, and that the world was a barren place full of lost souls in need of all the help they could get. . . . The problem is, many of the people in need of saving are in churches, and at least part of what they need saving from is the idea that God sees the world the same way as they do.[14]

Now if this passage sounds like the prelude to a polemical assault on churches, their tradition, worship, beliefs, structure, and the members in them, in the style of Richard Dawkins, Christopher Hitchens, or Sam Keen, this is most surely not the case. Barbara is not an angry former member of the clergy, now focused on spraying invective at organized religion in its every manifestation.

Rather, at the outset she wants to do what the Hebrew and Christian scriptures ought to be doing when we invariably listen to them in church, not only in the lessons read from them, but in all the other ways in which they suffuse what goes on in there: our hymns, all the prayers of the liturgy, the materials we use to be in communion with God and each other, bread, wine, water, oil. In the Bible people meet God everywhere—on mountains and in deserts, in the sky full of stars and in the city, in the fields where farmers toil, in the markets and homes of ordinary folk. While some of the action does take place in set-apart, sacred locations like the Tabernacle and then the Temple, and while there are minute descriptions of the priestly vestments and rites, most of the activity takes place without the clergy and outside of houses of worship. In the New Testament, this is especially true of the Gospels, but even in the Acts of the Apostles and the letters, with some exceptions, the reference is usually more to putting the good news to work in one's family life, work, in relationships not only with fellow believers but with all other citizens of the empire, the city, the village.

Barbara's suggestions of ways and places in which to encounter God do include traditional practices such as fasting and prayer, pilgrimage, and the works of mercy. But they go beyond or beneath these into the very mundane activities of everyday life that most often we would not see as having to do with God or the life of holiness—this is *our* myopia or blindness, though, not God's absence or the vulgar quality of something outside the liturgy or the church building.

> Or I can set a little altar, in the world or in my heart. I can stop what I am doing long enough to see where I am, who I am there with, and how awesome the place is. I can flag one more gate to heaven—one more patch of ordinary earth with ladder marks on it—where the divine traffic is heavy when I notice it and even when I do not. . . . Human beings may separate things into as many piles as we wish—separating spirit from flesh, sacred from secular, church from world. But we should not be surprised when God does not recognize the distinctions we make between the two. Earth is so thick with divine possibility that it is a wonder we can walk anywhere without cracking our shins on altars.[15]

The various practices Barbara examines are but a few of many others to which she alludes or cannot list. In our stimulus-crammed days (and nights), for all the information, images, and connections we now have at our disposal, there is not the clinical pathology but a more universal phenomenon of attention deficit. Hence it is not Ritalin or some other medication that is suggested, but rather mindfulness, being attentive to the person before us, to the action as significant or simple as it might be, from a phone call to see how a person is doing to making bread to completing a report. But it includes as well the natural world on which we so totally depend but which we take for granted. Nowadays, Michael Pollan's books and articles have awakened many of us to where the food that we cram into ourselves comes from—both to our disgust and to our delight.[16]

A bush on fire and its voice rivet Moses once and for all to God, who then appears in every detail of the universe, and whose *Torah*, whose words of teaching further insure that no aspect of human life will ever be seen as being outside God's presence and holiness. Julian of Norwich's beautiful vision sees it all from another angle, perhaps one could say, inside out. We can quickly become aware of the vastness of the universe, of the huge stretch of time and people before and around and in front of us in the future. But the crucified Jesus shows Julian something no bigger than a hazelnut in her hand. "It is everything which is made," he tells her, it is everything that God loves and it is everything that God cares for. What is the meaning of this cosmos-in-miniature?

"Know it well," Julian assures us, "love was his meaning. Who reveals it to you? Love. Why does he reveal it to you? For love. Remain in this and you will know more of the same. But you will never know different, without end."[17]

From consciousness, Brown Taylor turns to our bodies, to the practice of "being at home," as the saying goes, "in one's own skin." Our bodies do not lie. They tell us more about ourselves than our words ever can. This is clearly why all religious traditions involve more than the mind, more than cognitive assent to truth claims, involve eating, drinking, singing and dancing, touch and sight and hearing and smell—all of the senses. For Christians, the bodily base of faith is without equivocation: "And the Word became flesh and dwelt among us." Yet over the centuries, the Incarnation and the identity of Christ Jesus became the arena of the most profound conflict among those supposedly following Christ's way.

> When understanding finally came—not by reason but by faith—the first thing I understood was that it was not possible to trust that God loved all of me, including my body, without also trusting that God loved all bodies everywhere . . . hungry children and indentured women

along with the bodies of sleek athletes and cigar-smoking tycoons. . . . My body is what connects me to all of these other people. Wearing my skin is not a solitary practice but one that brings me into communion with all these other embodied souls. It is what we have most in common with one another. In Christian teaching, followers of Jesus are called to honor the bodies of our neighbors as we honor our own . . . leper bodies, possessed bodies, widow and orphan bodies, as well as foreign bodies and hostile bodies, none of which he shied away from. Read from the perspective of the body, his ministry was about encountering those whose flesh was discounted by the world in which they lived. What many of us miss, in our physical disease, is that our bodies remain God's best way of getting to us.[18]

And get to us God does, both in pleasure and in pain. The smell and feel of a loved one on returning home from being away, of sleep when exhausted, of the inability to sleep, of throbbing pain that even painkillers cannot completely remove, of the emptiness of loss when another has died, of the incomparable experience of holding a small child asleep in your arms. Christ puts spit and mud on the blind man's eyes, lays his hands on other sick people, on the baskets of a few barley loaves and fish. He removes his cloak, washes and dries his disciples' feet. He breaks the bread and passes around the cup of blessing. Perhaps we have so covered these actions with rubrics, so minimalized the food and drink into a crumb and a sip, the other gestures into ritualized daubs and sprinkles that the bodily engagement of Jesus with those around him has now been lost on us, whether in fear of ritualism or in obsession with correct performance of the same. Barbara invokes Stanley Hauerwas, Daniel Berrigan, and hymnwriter Brian Wren to underscore the intrinsic place of the body in Christianity, at the same time recounting a memorable exercise of not reciting but acting out, pantomiming the Beatitudes without words!

She stays with the body in describing the practice of walking, not just the moving experience of walking meditation in Buddhist performance but the walking of a labyrinth, a very old custom returning to use today. Also the one-foot-after-another process of making pilgrimage—to Jerusalem, Rome, Mecca, Compostela, Chartres, and numerous other holy sites. There are the many processions—those routinely in the liturgy of entrance, bringing the gifts, coming for communion, leaving, of Holy Week, as well as others at shrines of the Mother of God and saints. She reminds us of all the walking Jesus does in the Gospels, his usual form of transportation and a time for conversation, listening, and teaching.

> Sometimes we do not know what we know until it comes to us through the soles of our feet, the embrace of a tender lover, or the kindness of a stranger. Touching the truth with our minds alone is not enough. We are made to touch it with our bodies. I think this is why Christian tradition clings to the reality of resurrection, even when no one can explain it to anyone else's satisfaction. . . . God loves bodies. I mean that in some way that defies all understanding, God means to welcome risen bodies and not just disembodied souls to heaven's banquet table. The resurrection of the dead is the radical insistence that matter matters to God.[19]

We learn further from Barbara about the practice of getting lost, whether in the woods or in an unfamiliar city or foreign country, or the experience of being lost from one's plans in life—a marriage, one's children or career, even one's health. The experience of being uprooted, of becoming the stranger ourselves, puts us in the shoes of so many who are themselves migrants, dispossessed, newcomers, travelers, and pilgrims not necessarily by choice but because of war or poverty or the end of relationship or sickness. To be a stranger often means being alone, misunderstood or incapable of making oneself understood, being afraid and dependent. How many in the Bible went through this, from Abraham and Sarah down to the wandering Israelites, eventually Jesus in the desert. Though the GPS has become standard in our cars and even cell phones, the experience of being lost and being a stranger is there for us all.

> You can get lost on your way home. You can get lost looking for love. You can get lost between jobs. You can get lost looking for God. However it happens, take heart. Others before you have found a way in the wilderness, where there are as many angels as wild beasts, and plenty of other lost people too. All it takes is one of them to find you. All it takes is you to find them.[20]

Finding and being found—encountering others—this is yet another practice Barbara sketches, another altar in the world closely linked with that of getting lost. How easy it is to believe that searching for God, trying to live the life of holiness, is a solo act, an individual adventure. But drawing on the desert mothers and fathers, she insists that the neighbor is the face of God always before us, that we cannot live for ourselves or by ourselves. We are ever in need of the brother and the sister. Is not the greatest of the commandments to love the neighbor as we love ourselves? As with all the other practices already looked at and to come, this one requires nothing special by way of training, setting, or equipment. It is possible, without entering into long conversations, to recognize not only the "significant" others around us each day, but the innumerable less familiar ones we encounter just in our business: the checkout clerk at the market, the toll collector, the student at the back of the classroom who seldom speaks, the fellow parishioner whose name you've never remembered, the member of the "other church," or better *masjid,* synagogue, or no religious community at all.

"Hell is other people," Sartre scowled, but "when you have seen your neighbor, you have seen God," the desert fathers and mothers assure us. So much of what passes for religion seems to direct us vertically, to the kingdom of heaven somewhere else, to a God "upstairs" or "out there." Again, such a vision could not be further from the scriptures, for whom existence meant belonging to this family or tribe, this city or village, to the people of God here and everywhere. And all of the details in the Torah on treatment of the slave injured or the neighbor whose crops have been trampled by your herd or the one injured unintentionally by your ox—not to mention someone robbed or raped or assaulted or taking a life in self defense—no matter the specific circumstances, the common truth affirmed in all is that we are always obligated to the one before us, that each person and every relationship is important, in fact, sacred.

Having discovered the fire escape of a Victorian building on her college campus as a better place to pray and meditate than the chapel, Barbara wondered out loud to God one night, sitting up there, what she was supposed to do with her life. She imagined hearing God actually reply: "Do anything that pleases you . . . and belong to me."[21]

Here is yet another of the altars in life, another practice that goes with us wherever we are going—our living with purpose, with meaning. Martin Luther was but one of the many who over the years rediscovered the truth that any situation in life, any career, any work can be a vocation, a way of "preaching the gospel," as Francis of Assisi is supposed to have said, "even using words if necessary."

"No work is too small to play a part in the work of creation," Brown Taylor writes, and this tracks back on some of the earlier practices, for work connects us to both those below and those above us, to clients and vendors, those we owe and those who owe us.[22] How many of us have thought at one or another point that God had this very specific plan for us to accomplish in life, only to find that overturned, ourselves surprised or maybe disappointed, and something entirely different thrust upon us. I thought for a decade while in the Carmelites, as did Andrew Krivak in the Jesuits, that here was my vocation, as a friar and priest, serving God and his people in the order, in the church. Barbara believed this with everything in her head and heart, having done the entire academic and ecclesiastical formations, having first served in an urban and then in what seemed the dream small town parish. All of us were, to be sure, surprised at how things turned out later on.

Others we've encountered here, Sara Miles, Darcey Steinke, Lauren Winner, Diane Butler Bass, Nora Gallagher, Patricia Hampl too— all spent quite a few years searching, looking for the door that would open to . . . a life with purpose. Yet we know that only a very few of us will settle down into work that is of our own choosing and fulfilling by our definitions. Most people endure a great deal of mindless, frustrating demands and routines, as Barbara Ehrenreich's books have documented. Cleaning toilets, filling and emptying dish or clothes washing machines, taking food orders, stocking shelves, cleaning nursing facility or hospital patients—a great deal of work has little glamour or excitement. Even work that might seem to, such as writing and teaching, is for the most part perseverance, pushing on despite the boredom. Yet looking at Ghandi as well as Mother Teresa, the infinite beauty and worth of the most routine work is revealed. Glory permeates the monotony: "The glory of God is a human being fully alive." No job title or salary level or academic degrees are stipulated, no allusions about excitement or social or political importance are presumed, and moral perfection is not assumed in this most biblical reflection.

One of the richest of the practices or altars is that of keeping Sabbath, the extremely difficult art of saying "no" in our lives, even for a few hours, one day a week at minimum. After decades leading the services every Sunday morning, the first Sunday after Barbara stepped down from the Clarkesville parish was a revelation for her. (It is an experience I too have had on snowed-in Sundays and on vacation.) The thought that Sunday could not be Sunday without all morning in church—at the liturgy, coffee hour, with the singing, preaching, communion, conversation—no denying this is the pattern that many faithful follow. And it is of course what the clergy pound away at, always to those already in church, hence "preaching to the choir." Yet the original biblical sense of Sabbath was not restricted to the obligation of the Shabbat services, or even Shabbat supper. The Shabbat candles, in Brown Taylor's understanding, represent both rest and freedom. We rest, you might say fast, from what we do all the rest of the week, work yes but quite a few other things too—we can turn off Blackberries and laptops and TVs and iPods. God rested on the seventh day, and we, created in his image, bearing God in ourselves, we too are to rest from the creative work we otherwise are also called to do.

Sabbath is one day of saying no in a culture of "getting to yes," Barbara observes. In rest we stop, we are allowed to really be with the others around us, to think without background noise, to eat without hurry, to be free. The other candle is for many freedoms that keeping Sabbath reveals—our essential equality with one another, our dependence on each other and on God, the realization that we cannot save all our wealth or ideas or possessions and take them with us into the grave and life after death. In the Bible, Sabbath extends to Jubilee—to leaving fields fallow, freeing slaves, recognizing you don't really own the land your family had for generations or the house you worked so hard to purchase.

The Sabbath in the Bible is not just one more "thou shalt," in a wearying list of numerous rules to obey. Like other of the *mitzvot,* which are "good works," far more than obligations, Sabbath keeping is connected with all of the rest of a life with God and others. It is not

so much that one "keeps Sabbath" to make God happy, but rather
that the Sabbath is a gift from God to us. "The Sabbath is for us, not
us for the Sabbath." So, stopping—resting, praying, eating—strips
away so many layers of meaning and value that obscure the way
things really are.

Barbara's front porch on the first Sunday she was not a parish
pastor could have seemed like a gaping, frightful abyss, the vacuum of
not having that church altar, the reminder of her weakness and failure.
But on the contrary, it was heavenly, with a new attention to the birds
and the quiet, with spacious duration of time. How rarely we have
such feelings, even when on vacation, when we are often more sched-
uled and soon long to go home to the regular grind.

And if I can say no on one day, might it not be possible for me to
do so through the rest of the week? Could this not also be a liberating
asceticism, as Paul Evdokimov says? In our time, it is not just fasting
from food that is needed, but also fasting from our addictions—from
power, control, needing to be seen and liked, needing to achieve and
accumulate, needing to always win.

Yet as we turn from our obsession with work, Brown Taylor
points us to another practice that is a form of worship. She calls it, in
summary, "carrying water." This comes from the story she tells about
being snowed and then iced in, without power, and thus without heat
or light, and surviving through lots of trips carrying water. But the
point of her experience during the power outage was not merely a
dreamy return-to-simpler-ways-and-times. Physical work, accepted
as such in earlier times, was constantly the target for inventors. Countless labor-saving devices were created and patented and used even by
the spiritually deep and technologically savvy Shakers. A visit to their
preserved interpretive locations in Hancock, Massachusetts, Sabbath-
day Lake, Maine, or other places will attest to their numerous techno-
logical discoveries, from better brooms and looms to ingenious har-
nessing of water power and forward-looking methods for preserving
and packaging foods to herbs and salves for natural healing. They
considered work sacred and the products as well, but they valued re-
duction in both working time and physical effort. Surely many people
who pride themselves on doing their own gardening, preserving of
food, maintenance, not to mention various crafts, employ sophisti-

cated technology to enable these activities to be done efficiently and with quality. Brown Taylor emotes about getting dirty, putting one's fingers into the earth while gardening.

> The earthling's first divine job is to till the earth and keep it. . . . Keeping the earth is hard work. You get dirty doing it. You break fingernails and wear holes in the knees of your pants. You wear yourself out. You also remember where you came from, and why. You touch the stuff your bones are made of. . . . If you have nerve enough, you also foresee your own decomposition. This is not bad knowledge to have. It is the kind that puts other kinds in perspective.[23]

Even less noble activities such as the kind of housework that Merry Maids and other cleaning services do, their workers earning minimum pay, also put things in perspective, as does the feeling of making a meal from scratch and seeing others enjoy it. To any misty thoughts about ordinary housework and service work, say in the food or hospitality industries, one simply has to turn to another Barbara—Ehrenreich—who dispels any romanticism in her accounts of wait-ressing, house cleaning, stacking shelves in Walmart, and the like.[24]

Continuing in the realm of the physical, the experience of the body, Brown Taylor moves to the seemingly counterintuitive claim. She argues that intense suffering, in particular, exquisite physical pain, is also an altar, a practice that connects us with God and our neighbor. No one in their right mind looks for pain, especially the monstrous, exquisite physical pain that results from injury, disease, or torture. She again tells a gripping story of her experience with just such pain in an accident resulting in a corneal tear. Her absolute fear of needles in childhood also led, once more counterintuitively, to dental work without local anesthesia—the needle making this out of the question. No matter one's pain threshold or peculiar pain phobias, there is the experience of watching another endure it. It is another kind of suffer-ing to hear the screams and feel the grasping of one's arms and see the pain-contorted face of my wife in an attack of sciatica due to a herni-ated disc pressing on the nerve. When asked on a scale of "one to ten" where your pain is, how can a number adequately capture what you are experiencing?

Brown Taylor skillfully connects all this to the story of Job and his every painful experience—loss of his children and property, loss of his friends' and spouse's support, his own physical pain from boils and other afflictions on top of the emotional suffering. In the Book of Job, at the end, there are no real answers to the problem of suffering in general or the suffering of the innocent in particular. The ways of God are not clarified or justified for us, yet there is some closure. Job comes to realize that suffering is neither gift nor punishment, that its justification cannot be sustained. And he comes to know that, though finite and mortal, as a person he will never be separated from God. Brown Taylor goes on to note that suffering people can and do express themselves—in words, colors, rituals, and relationships, and that sometimes the greatest expression as well as response is silence.

Finally, we come to explicitly or recognizably religious practices— those of being present to God or prayer, and that of pronouncing blessings. Barbara's transparency is again here.

> I am a failure at prayer. When people ask me about my prayer life, I feel like a bulimic must feel when people ask about her favorite dish. My mind starts scrambling for ways to hide my problem. I start talking about other things I do that I hope will make me sound like a godly person. I try to say admiring things about prayer so there can be no doubt about how important I think it is. . . . I would rather show someone my checkbook stubs than talk about my prayer life. I would rather confess that I am a rotten godmother, that I struggle with my weight, that I fear I am overly fond of Bombay Sapphire gin martinis than confess that I am a prayer-weakling. To say I love God but do not pray much is like saying I love life but do not breathe much.[25]

She knows all the seven different types of prayer listed in the catechism of *The Book of Common Prayer*. She's read David Steindl-Rast on prayer and Henri Nouwen and Brother Lawrence of the Resurrection and probably a lot more spiritual writers than she lists. But there is a difference between *saying* prayers, no matter how ancient or with what attentiveness, and *living* your prayer. I think of Paul Evdokimov and Mother Maria Skobtsova, who stress that it is not a matter of reciting prayers, attending services, keeping fasts, lighting vigil lights, or doing prostrations. Rather, one is to become prayer, prayer incarnate. At the last judgment we will only be asked if we fed the hungry, clothed the naked, sheltered the homeless, visited the sick and imprisoned—in short, if we loved.

So Barbara is pointing to the act of waiting, to thanking another, to listening even to Byzantine chants in an archaic Greek she cannot understand, hearing the chanted Torah portion, looking up at the icon of Christ in the dome of a Greek Orthodox church, staring at the candles and icons on her own home altar. Her holding up the example of Mary the Mother of God's quiet, open faithfulness is another noncognitive way to indicate what prayer is about. On the mark too is her reading of the list of names of those she is praying for.

Lastly, as an ordained person, set apart and called upon to bless everything from the Eucharistic bread and cup, the child to be baptized and the couple to be wed, the believer to be buried, but as well houses, cars, and, so very Episcopalian of her, foxhunts, Barbara knows that blessings are understood as essential actions of faith. It is not so much that the priest can impart blessing herself, rather, as in all liturgical worship, the priest calls on God, in the name of the community and the individual, to be present, to give all the gifts of peace, joy, and love that are of the very nature of God. Neither praying for, anointing, nor laying hands on a person is magic. Certain words and gestures do not hold or unleash divine power nor render certain results as in the recitation of a spell by Harry Potter or his fellow students of Hogwarts.

> Pronouncing a blessing puts you as close to God as you can get. To learn to look with compassion on everything that is; to see past the terrifying demons outside to the bawling hearts within; to make the first move toward the other, however many times it takes to get close; to open your arms to what is instead of waiting until it is what it should be; to surrender the justice of your own cause for mercy; to surrender the priority of your own safety for love—this is to land at God's breast. To pronounce a blessing on something is to see it from God's perspective . . . is to participate in God's own initiative . . . to share God's own audacity.[26]

That in his dying, Barbara's father would bless his son-in-law, her husband, Ed, perhaps conveys the depth and the beauty of blessing as not just a practice but really an epiphany, a manifestation of God among us.

It is a considerable journey through the way of holiness, the search for God that Barbara Brown Taylor gives in this "geography of faith." Her effort to map out some of the ways in which God is present everywhere and by which we can be in communion with him is echoed by many of the others we've heard—Darcey Steinke and Patricia Hampl, for example, in their attention to details of years gone by. Matthew Kelty too, with his eye and ear for connections, relationships, speaks to this presence.

> People who live by the sea are not too apt to pay a great deal of attention to it, save what is practical and useful: high tide, low tide, a stormy day, a quiet one. The same is true of those who live in the mountains, in a lovely valley, or any locale a visitor would find remarkable for beauty. Such a visitor is likely to think the inhabitants live on a constant high. Not necessarily so. Sometimes yes, now and then. . . . Though we perhaps advert little specifically to it, we are as monks submitted to an onslaught of positive, spiritual influences. We are profoundly affected by them all. The modest amount of attention that monks give to choir, for example, is not the sum of what choir does to them. The repeated exposure to such power and grace, day after day, night after night, for years on end, has far more influence on the monk than he is aware of, just as his influence on others is once both hidden and enormous. . . . We are truly embraced by the merciful Christ and we live in a country of mercy. . . . Like a stranger coming among us and saying, "What a beautiful place this is," we may almost catch ourselves and respond, "Yes, come to think of it, it is."
>
> . . . Environment does not create saints, but it sure helps. Not all who emerge from lovely homes are lovely people, and there are wise souls of stature in the slums.[27]

It is something the Bible is aware of: place and God's presence in that place. The names that dot the Hebrew Bible, each of them tells a story of the presence of God and the interaction with us there:

*Beth-el* (house of God), *Massa* (test), *Meribah* (quarrel). It not just a striking discovery, though often it is just such an epiphany, and not just the culmination of the search for God, but it is a condition or element of holiness—the reality that God is everywhere, in everything. It is not unusual, as many of the writers and others encountered here have learned, to embark on a great pilgrimage, start out to make a journey of discovery, only to realize that God was always right here, right now.

# CHAPTER EIGHT

# Transformation in Faith and Work, Liturgy and Life, the Church and the World

It is the greatest mystery of life that satisfaction is felt not by those who take, and make demands, but by those who give, and make sacrifices. In them alone the energy of life does not fail, and this is precisely what is meant by creativeness. The positive mystery of life is therefore to be found in love, in sacrificial, giving, creative love. As has been said already, all creativity is love and all love is creative. If you want to receive, give; if you want to obtain satisfaction, do not seek it, never think of it, and forget the very word; if you want to acquire strength, manifest it, give it to others.[1]

## God at Work in Us as Saints

"I don't have the slightest idea what God is like, really," Rick said in his sermon. "All I know is what I see God doing, in my own life and in the lives of the people around me."[2] The Rick who said this is Rick Fabian, one of the founding pastors of St. Gregory of Nyssa Church, San Francisco. Sara Miles cites him in her memoir, *Take This Bread*. With his statement we come full circle to where we began, with the aim of experiencing saints as they really are.

All the children of God are made in God's image and likeness. If saints are made, then it is first in their creation by God. They are like God, God is in them. We can also say that women and men are made saints, in another sense, by God's gift of holiness. The washing and receiving of the Holy Spirit in baptism, the "christening," is the revealing of the Father, Son, and Spirit dwelling in a person. We are initiated into a community, communion with God and each other. Fabian reminds us that before the coming of Christ, there was indeed holiness in the relationship of God with God's people, Israel. Sanctity is not moral achievement but more like a seal, a stamp, being marked and set apart as God's own.[3]

In baptism, as Augustine says of the Eucharist, "we become what we receive." We are saints-in-the-making. This is not the same type of sainthood as those recognized by the community and identified as saints for the witness of their lives. Some we call saints were never explicitly or formally canonized. They were simply revered as such after their deaths—the apostles, the prophets of the Old Covenant, many of the church's teachers and fathers, as well as the monastics of the desert. Then there were the martyrs by suffering and death. There are missionaries, artists, scholars, pastors. And then there are innumerable holy men and women who are confessors of the gospel in all kinds of lives: spouses and parents, researchers and healers, mediators and advocates, caregivers and cooks, bakers and farmers, craftsmen and workers of every kind. The many formally recognized is but a fraction of all the saints, one of the reasons why there has been, from early on, a feast in both East and West of all saints. As Paul Evdokimov said of those of our time, their holiness is so diverse, so omnipresent, so ordinary that it might be hidden, less noticeable than the classical categories of holy witnessing of the past.[4]

*All are called to holiness.* This is fundamental. But as I also have tried show here, religion, the institutional church, and much of the accoutrements of both can be destructive of the life of God in us. We all know the truth of this in our own experience, and the testimony of the writers listened to I hope has evoked its reality more vividly. One might want to look the other way, minimize it or, worst of all, conjure up some theological explanation for it, but for me, at least, none of these approaches are helpful. We may indeed be our own worst enemies, but what passes for the life of faith often is toxic and not in obvious ways.

*God gives holiness to each of us.* Whatever the formal processes have been, are, and will be for recognition of holy women and men in the churches, there always are countless saints whose holiness will be so ordinary and everyday as to be "hidden," less than obvious, surely not extraordinary. If anything, in the things I have written I wanted to challenge the idea that holiness should be equated with "heroic virtue," if for no other reason than that we no longer even can agree on what either heroism or virtue are. What is more, as Paul Evdokimov noted, the opposite of evil is not virtue but good, Godness, incarnate in human beings—their words and actions.

In reclaiming the "Eucharistic ecclesiology" of the early years of the church, Nicholas Afanasiev demonstrated the rooting of Christian holiness and community in both baptism and the Eucharist.[5] He reminds us that all are made priests, prophets, and the royalty of the kingdom, echoing First Peter's description of the universal priesthood of baptism. Thus, all of us celebrate the Eucharist along with the leaders and servants, the bishops, presbyters, and deacons, chosen always from among the community. All are servants of God and servants of each other. All are made one in Christ through the Spirit in baptism. All of us as prophets are to speak the word of God in our lives. All of us are to be transforming the world back into what God made it to be. We are his sons and daughters, his co-workers in redemption—this is what it means to be in baptism a "king" or "queen" in the kingdom. No one has recently thought through and expressed the fresh, provocative faith of the gospel better than the Anglican New Testament scholar and former bishop of Durham, N. T. Wright.[6] So much of what we have heard here is echoed in his writing, most particularly the need to separate authentic holiness from institutional and popular versions of piety. Wright also speaks very directly to the necessity of leaving the afterlife to the afterlife, in order to properly live out the kingdom of God here and now, in everyday life.

In the Eastern Church, the unity of all ministries and vocations and their location in daily life is expressed in their being celebrated liturgically by a procession—originally around the altar—at baptisms, at weddings, and at ordinations. Even the procession of the Christian who has "fallen asleep" in the Lord—from home to the church and then to the place of burial—is more than functional. It signifies the pilgrimage of that person's life in the life of the kingdom of God. Eventually life here, in the kingdom, which N. T. Wright has identified as the core of Jesus's preaching, will lead past earthly existence.[7] God is thus always and everywhere "wonderful in his saints," at work in us and in all those around us, as Rick Fabian said.

We have seen this presence of God active in all the writers we have heard from, in their experiences of loss and recovery, of destructiveness and healing, of sadness and joy. As we draw toward a close in these reflections, it is good to recall that while a separate chapter has not been set aside for the most difficult experiences we encounter in living the holy life—all sorts of loss in life, material, in our relationships, as well as sickness, aging, and death—these common human moments of suffering have indeed been encountered all through our listening to the writers. We began with Kathleen Norris's brave and forthright account of spiritual dryness and depression, not in the abstract but in the context of her own life and more particularly of her husband's illness and dying. Who could miss the anguish in Darcey Steinke's memoir of growing up as a PK, Barbara Brown Taylor's narrative of her failed ministry, Nora Gallaher's chronicle of her brother's dying and her own spiritual turmoil, or Sara Miles's life before and after finding Christ. For all he found of camaraderie and learning, inner clarity and commitment to serving others, Andrew Krivak was also given the gift of peering into his own loneliness and need for love and companionship. And as the former Frater Simon also learned about the "sacrament of love," the vocation of marriage, children, and family bears its own ascetic demands of sacrifice, forgiveness, patience.[8]

As we will learn, Diana Butler Bass does not hide the falling apart of her marriage and the painful experiences from self-confident believers around her at Gordon-Conwell Theological School and Westmont College. Lauren Winner experienced the turning to Christ as the turning away from her by many close friends in the Orthodox community. As lyrical and exquisite as Patricia Hampl's memoir of her parents and growing up in "old St. Paul" is, there is a great deal of sadness and hurt in her story and the stories of other relatives as well. It is not the case that the search for God requires pain and loss, degradation and depression, among other afflictions. Rather, these are the elements of life, of the human condition. The scriptures are full of them, the Psalms both wail and sing about the stress and glee of existence. The path is a way of the cross, but also the leaping joy of resurrection.

The experience of transformation in the life of holiness, of the bringing together of faith and work, liturgy and life, the church and the world is abundant in what we have heard. Now let us turn to a couple more.

*Strength for the Journey: Diana Butler Bass's Pilgrimage of Faith*

Diana Butler Bass has established herself with a number of studies of American church life and spiritual practice. Having done her graduate work at Duke, earlier studying at Westmont College and Gordon-Conwell Divinity School, she has taught at several colleges and seminaries, and written a column on American religion for the *New York Times,* among other papers. She headed a three-year Lilly Endowment–funded study on congregations of intentional practice between 2002 and 2005. Her books document that study's look at ten parishes and how their renewal made them authentic communities of faith with rich liturgical prayer, strong fellowship, and a real sense of living their faith in their families, neighborhoods, and jobs.[9] Most recently she has produced a look at Christianity—from the people of God up.[10] She appears all over the media, and rightly so, as an expert on American parish and spiritual life.

There is probably no one who has done more fieldwork on parishes across America than Diana Butler Bass, none who has herself experienced more parishes that are intentional in all aspects of their existence—liturgical and spiritual, education and fellowship, outreach and involvement. It will not be surprising that across her work she has encountered many of the same experiences and practices already seen here. For I know of no researcher who is so adept as she at letting us into the lives of parish pastors and people, allowing them to reveal their successes and failures, how they differ from one denomination to another yet face common problems with the basics of the Christian tradition.

What leads me to listen to her here is her own pilgrimage. It took her more than a decade, through a number of church bodies, perspectives, and career and life choices. This she documented in *Strength for the Journey*. Her journey is an important map in the life of holiness.

> Over the last twenty years of churchgoing, I have learned a few things about faith, about hope, and, above all, about love. I still feel afraid occasionally. But I no longer feel the wrath of a vengeful and demanding God. Rather, I fear I cannot begin to comprehend the breadth of God's love. I fear I will not be able to give away enough love—to my family, friends, church, to the oppressed and disenfranchised—before my time is done. Life is too short for all its love, to really understand its transforming power. And I sometimes fear Christians will not rise to the challenges of our times, that we will fail to embody God's love in the world.[11]

Diana started out in an urban Methodist parish in Baltimore, one short on liturgical splendor but increasingly long on social justice in a tumultuous time, that of the height of the civil rights movement. Her family's relocation to Arizona would prove decisive, for after a short stint in a Methodist parish they switched to an energized evangelical congregation. And this is where Diana would be shaped for the next decade or more. She did undergraduate work at evangelical Westmont College in Santa Barbara, and while she visited All Saints' Episcopal Church there, she was solidly shaped as an evangelical. This meant becoming a proponent of doctrinal orthodoxy, critical of liberal mainstream Protestants with their social justice vision. This was in the aftermath of the civil rights and antiwar years. Yet there were glimpses of other versions of Christianity—visits to European cathedrals and a particular impression of a weekday Eucharist in Westminster Abbey.

From Westmont, Diana came east to Gordon-Conwell Theological School, an evangelical institution in Hamilton, Massachusetts. Theology there was orthodox and rooted in the Reformed tradition. Compared to the Anglican liturgy she had come to treasure, the worship was very plain, with preaching central. It is no surprise that she guided her husband to the local Episcopal parish led by Mark Dyer, a former Benedictine monk and a professor of church history at

Gordon-Conwell, and for her a doorway into a more generous un-derstanding of the tradition in theology and a rich liturgical style. This parish was for her the first of several in which she would encoun-ter the conflicts within mainstream churches, conflicts about how broad and how deep the sweep of Christian tradition can be, both in theology and liturgy as well as in ethics. The openness of the Anglican tradition led to Diana's entering the Episcopal Church and her subse-quent work as a scholar.

When Dyer left Christ Church upon his election as a bishop, Diana experienced a parade of clergy through the various parishes she attended. Her husband, coming from a conservative evangelical back-ground, found a number of issues problematic, not the least of which was women clergy. But when he and Diana moved to Durham, North Carolina, where she began doctoral work at Duke, they experienced in greater intensity how class, social, and political identity, attitudes toward even clothing and entertainment often cut through a parish. Their lack of fit with this "country club" parish sent them to a more intentional congregation, one that focused more on worship, study, education, and outreach than social status.

> As I think about it, however, one lesson stands above all others: it is hard to be a mainline churchgoer. It is not, as some critics claim, the easy road to faith. It is hard being a pilgrim soul in a church learning to be a pilgrim community. Conflict, timidity, injustice, quiescence, insti-tutional dysfunction, and fear of change have been the cup of mainline unfaithfulness. Because of our own shortcomings, we live in congrega-tions where it can be difficult to feel God's presence. I am trying—we are trying—to hear, heed, and practice faith in new ways. But it can be tough to stay with it. For me, for all of us, it has been a strenuous journey.[12]

I am following Diana's journey in detail not only for what her pil-grimage tells us about the search for God and life with him. She also was to become an insightful student of parish life in our time—a destination of mine here because one cannot be a believer, a Chris-tian, alone. The very title of this memoir of Diana's comes from a mo-ment in which she hears a communion assistant alter the formula of distribution. Instead of "The blood of Christ, the cup of salvation," he says, "Strength for the journey." Already uncomfortable in the context of the progressive parish they were visiting, this modification of the formula produces more unease for her and her husband. But in retrospect she saw it as a symbol of the kind of release she speaks of in the passage quoted above. It became the realization that questioning and struggle with the tradition are also paths of fidelity to it. She comes to see that history, culture, even class prejudices, in addition to those of sexism and racism, often masquerade as theological orthodoxy.

There are other issues that she confronts as she moves from parish to parish in her career travels that second the important truth echoed here in earlier chapters—the church is not just divine but human, material, economic, political, cultural, and social. The Spirit is present always—*ubi spiritus ibi ecclesia et omnis gratia,* "where the Spirit is, there the church is and all is grace." Yet the very human and earthly domicile and its structures can indeed be counter to the presence contained—toxic, destructive, oppressive, prejudiced. Diana began to read the scriptures differently, not for codes of conduct or precision of doctrine but for connection with Christ, for living out the gospel, for the rule of love over the law. She describes her discovery of the ordinary, everyday character of holiness, the mundane path in spiritual practice.

There were always dishes to wash. And tables to set and linens to iron. There were vestments to keep clean and orderly. Altar cloths to press. Flowers to be arranged. Bulletins to be folded. Music to be played, and hymns to be practiced. Throughout my life I had often resisted the "Martha" tasks of housework, thinking them somehow less than the "Mary" tasks of doing theology and being with Jesus. But at Holy Family [parish] I began to see the irony in the sisters' biblical story. The "better part" that Jesus urged could be discovered among the pots and pans if the tasks were done intentionally. We did the work of spiritual housekeeping purposefully—as ways to love God and one another. As we knew God to be in the Eucharist, we discovered God's presence at the sink. As writer Kathleen Norris found to be true elsewhere, and so observed in her book *The Quotidian Mysteries,* "Laundry, liturgy and 'women's work' all serve to ground us in the world, and they need not grind us down."[13]

Diana linked this discovery to a larger trend of communities intentional toward spiritual practices, exactly the activities that we learned of from Barbara Brown Taylor. Earthy, practical, material, everyday—these are the very substance of faith enacted in the scriptures, where fishermen are called to spread the good news, where the risen Christ has fish and bread grilling for the disciples out all night fishing, where the same Christ makes himself evident in conversation along the road to Emmaus and in the grace and breaking of bread at the inn (Lk 24:13–35).

Later Diana discovered through spiritual direction the legacy of saints who would feed her spiritual life, none of which she ever encountered—Francis of Assisi, Teresa of Avila, John of the Cross, Bernard of Clairvaux, Julian of Norwich, Hildegard of Bingen, and from our time, Dietrich Bonhoeffer, Henri Nouwen, Thomas Merton. The saying of Irenaeus of Lyons also became pivotal for her: "The glory of God is a person fully alive." What did it mean, what did it look like, to be "fully alive"? After so much evangelical shaping of faithful living, a more dynamic, diverse, and creative humanity was a revelation. Whereas questions had been suspect, representing signs of doubt or, worse, wrong belief or unbelief, now Diana found, in the Anglican tradition, that questions were welcome indeed.

> I was starting to understand that earthly passion was not so bad—nor was fear or doubt or suffering or sin. All the "stuff" of humanity needed to be brought into the center of God—as God had come to the center of humankind in becoming one of us in Jesus. I was beginning to live into what Christians call the doctrine of the Incarnation—the belief that an embodied God blesses our embodied lives. God and humankind partake of each other's fullness in mutual love.[14]

Listening to Anne Howard's description of black lines on the floor of Durham Cathedral, lines behind which women had to stand as to not come too close to the tomb of the great Saint Cuthbert of

Lindisfarne because their pollution and evil required distance from the holy relics, Diana saw another breakthrough in her thinking.

> "The gospel," she [Anne Howard] exclaimed, "is the good news of God's inclusive reach, a love for all humankind—men and women, straight and gay, rich and poor, all races, adults, and children. God's love destroys thick, black lines. Indeed, the gospel proclaims that there are no lines."
>
> A faith with no lines . . . was almost beyond my comprehension. Christianity was about drawing lines—doctrinal lines, behavioral lines, lines between the saved and the damned, lines between us and them.[15]

Reading a lesson from Acts 15 as part of the daily office of the *Book of Common Prayer*, Diana encountered a remarkably similar situation to the one of the lines, namely, the first council of Jerusalem's resolution of the question of whether converts must first become Jews in order to become Christians. The apostle Peter's contribution was to proclaim that God gives the Holy Spirit to those outside Israel just as to those within, making "no distinctions between them and us." Peter would then have the vision in which he is ordered to eat of the foods formerly forbidden and to enter the house of the non-Jew, the centurion.[16]

> Faith was not easy. Love was not easy. Line drawing is easy. Walking over thick, black lines is hard. Tearing down walls of exclusion is hard. Living safely inside established boundaries was easy; there is no real faith inside lines. Only on the other side of lines can there be faith, that adventurous journey of embodying God's love in the world. . . . Anne Howard was right: Christianity was not about lines. It was about the inclusive reach of God's love.[17]

Having returned to her alma mater, Westmont College, to work as a faculty member, Diana began to experience a great deal of conflict between the school's evangelical ethos and her ever-expanding theological and liturgical openness. But even as her marriage fails and she finds herself struggling with both administration and some faculty, she also finds another door opening, one of the most significant parish communities to which she will ever belong, that of the dying but then resurrected Trinity Church in Santa Barbara. This is the same home parish of Nora Gallagher and other fascinating people mentioned in her two books: activist Ann Jaqua, priests Anne Sutherland Howard and Mark Asman. She also comes to know retired bishop George Barrett, the civil rights worker and ordainer of some of the first women priests, who writes to support her progressive approach to teaching theology at Westmont. She also meets sociologist of religion Clark Roof, the author of the important study on what happened to baby boomers in their religious lives.

If Diana was in the process of opening up her theology, her faith, her spiritual life, probably no other community encouraged her to do so further than the people of Trinity. There, particularly in the person of rector Mark Asman, she also came to confront the issue of gay and lesbian people in the church, an issue that still rages in the the mainline churches and that has caused splits in the worldwide Anglican communion as well as in the Episcopal Church in America. But while it may seem like the rifts across the American religious landscape are mostly about "culture war" issues like abortion and the status of gays and lesbians in church and society, Diana Butler Bass's spiritual autobiography and her studies of congregations reveal this to be a radical oversimplification. As tempting as it might be to impose the "red state versus blue state" model on congregations, clearly the reality is far more complex. In the parishes Diana studies, Christians of differing political, social, and theological viewpoints still gather around the Eucharist and word and find unity that transcends differences. This was also true in Sara Miles's very progressive and engaged parish of St. Gregory of Nyssa in San Francisco.

The intentional movement to deepen liturgical life, spiritual living, prayer, study, fellowship, as well as outreach is what enables congregations to cohere despite their members' differences. Further, this commitment to communion in Christ, to the life of holiness and the many practices that sustain it makes parishes not only capable of diversity but also able to change, as all living organisms must. The learning experiences at Trinity Church gave Diana a great deal of "strength for the journey," and in the process she met Richard Bass, who would become her second husband.

The two relocated to Memphis for her to take a faculty position at Rhodes College. There in Memphis their first child, Emma, was born, and they encountered yet another parish with many strong features as well as troubling ones, Grace–St. Luke's. She chronicles the division between nominal members and regular ones, a difficult challenge for the clergy and members. There she once more experiences organized religion's toxic potentiality and reality.

Like many American families, the Basses move yet again, this time to northern Virginia, where they join historic Christ Church in Alexandria's old town, founded in 1773. The spare colonial sanctuary, designed by James Wren, a relative of the more famous Sir Christopher Wren, is a link to the time even before the founding of the United States. This is a church that has seen not only the Revolutionary and Civil Wars, but the civil rights movement and so much more in between.

Thinking about the birthday of the church, Pentecost, when, despite all their different languages and cultures, thousands understood Peter's preaching and received the Spirit, Diana sums up much of what she learned and wants to pass on from her own spiritual journey. Was the pilgrimage in the end just babble, like the tower of Babel—all the idiosyncracies of the many parishes to which she'd belonged? In the end would she simply cling to the open door and minds and hearts of Trinity in Santa Barbara and hold it up as the model against which to judge the inadequacies, bickering, and partisanship of the others? Not at all. She employs Pentecost as an image of the church and, in turn, of the life of holiness. Looking back on her former parishes she can see how all contributed to her journey, even if she did not grasp this at the time. While looking at them also through the lenses of several studies of American church life by the likes of Holifield and Stark and Finke, she observes a number of aspects useful to us here, considering the real shape of searching for God and living the spiritual life today.

While past eras may have been better served by communities that were comprehensive, then more devotional, and still later social, in our time the characteristic is that the parish is participatory and intentional. In a society of enormous diversity and complexity, in which we are saturated with information and yet the demands on our time are staggering, it is no longer possible to insist on timeless, changeless patterns of religious belonging and participation. Americans marry out of their church bodies of origin more than they marry within them. Studies of the baby boomers by Roof and Wuthnow suggest that while some return to membership and participation in communities of faith later on in middle age, after long years of absence, others never come back to the church.[18] As for younger generations, it is simply too early to know whether they will be as religiously active as their parents or grandparents. Panic struck when a small decrease in religious belief and activity was announced in the Faith Matters survey in 2006 and the Pew religious landscape survey of 2007.[19] A Pew Religion in Public Life survey in 2009 however questioned whether there was a surge in "nones," people reporting no religious belonging at all.

Diana Butler Bass is right, I think, in arguing that while parishes will continue to change, the turn back to the basics of prayer, liturgical worship, study, fellowship, and outreach are what seem to keep them alive, capable of the renewal, the transformation, or *metanoia*, that is at the core of the New Testament and therefore of the life of the church. "Behold, I make all things news."

> My pilgrimage, like that of the mainline, has not been a predictable, smooth path, traveling from victory to victory in Jesus' name. Rather, mainline's rough way has often been hard, following paths overgrown with brambles and thistles, up theological mountains of terrifying heights, and down to the depths of conflict and broken fellowship. Of the true pilgrim soul, John Bunyan claimed "that they have met with hardships in the way, that they do meet with troubles night and day." Fear, doubt, despair, and temptation mark the pilgrims' path. Most days, a vision of God keeps me going, usually visible to me at Sunday morning Eucharist. . . . But sometimes the fog obscures even that.[20]

*Parishes: Gathering around Tradition, Practice, and Openness*

Diana Butler Bass had a journey of many joys and frustrations, of growth in faith and real doubt. In this she was not unlike many Christians in the later part of the twentieth century. It was a personal pilgrimage of discovery and change, but also disappointment and loss.

But somewhere in the struggle of it all, she really did find in her faith the "strength for the journey"—the formula, admittedly an alternate one—that the communion assistant once used in administering the Eucharistic chalice to her. Building directly on her own experience, she planned and applied for funding for a study of congregations where vibrant Christianity—"Christianity," as she calls it, "for the rest of us"—was in evidence.

She has done perhaps the best, most discerning research in recent years on local congregations, their common life and the lives of their members. Her work shows many different Christian church traditions confronting life in America in this new century. The parish of the past has passed, though most church bodies hold onto the models of it from rural village, urban enclave, or even the post–World War II suburbs. No longer is any parish just a collection of like people, similar in ethnicity or language, in class or economic status, in social and political perspectives. True, because of the sociological specificities of "place," of location as in real estate, many congregations remain racially homogenous. But as the faces of Americans change, as for example more than two-thirds of Greek Orthodox marry outside both the Greek and Orthodox communities, we are increasingly mixed in our backgrounds. And not only these, but also our religious belongings, our cultural experiences. Mobility of every kind—geographic, economic, professional—has become standard. In my own family, members have belonged to five or six different church bodies, and there are eight different ethnic lines—this for two parents and two children.

Change, as Butler Bass's personal narrative indicates, can be terrifying, whether relocation to another part of the country, another school system, a different church body or congregation, a different college or job. Change, some of us used to think, Diana included, should never happen when it comes to the set text and pattern of the Christian liturgy or doctrine, or even the stance of a political party. Yet in just the past few decades we have seen the radicalization of political parties as well as religious communities. Some, as say the evangelicals at Gordon-Conwell, have become ever more conservative in response to the increasing liberalism in other church bodies, in for example the Democratic party, or in the youth culture that boomed

in the 1960s, one of dissent and protest, experimentation and searching. Yet for the Falwells and Dobsons of the religious right, there are
Jim Wallis, the "emerging church" movement, the probing criticism of
a Gary Wills, Jimmy Carter's progressive Baptist faith, the continuing
memory of the prophetic stances of Martin Luther King Jr., Daniel
Berrigan, Thomas Merton, and Dorothy Day.

Contrary to "red" versus "blue" political orientations, however,
the parishes Butler Bass passed through on her own journey of faith,
as well as those she studied, do not settle into one or another of these
categories. There are mixes of perspectives as well as inconsistencies
even in individuals. While one is tempted to think that Diana's journey witnesses primarily to individual transformation as the key to the
life of holiness in the twenty-first century, this is not accurate. Rather,
as I have tried to suggest from her own narrative, it was the constant
interaction with others, with both supportive and similar but also
with challenging, opposed points of view that moved her along, that
very often and painfully disturbed her stability. She was forced to re-
consider many of the defining "lines" around doctrine, liturgy, and
ethics, as well as many other issues of everyday life including politics,
outreach, the situation of gays and lesbians in church and in society
more broadly.

What she discovered in both her own journey as well as in the
parish research was that the old Mary-Martha dichotomies—between
contemplation and action, personal conversion and outreach, liturgy
and life, the church and the world—were false oppositions. The intentional communities of faith she found in her study were dynamic
because they transcended these dichotomies, because they refused to
pit prayer against caring for those in need, study against fellowship,
church services against free time for family and recreation. The old
antinomies began to appear quite differently. Whether law/gospel or
faith/reason, science/religion, sacred/profane—these and many others were redefined, as Christians, whether they knew it or not, returned to earlier forms of tradition in which community belonging
was indispensable. The life of faith could not be simply my decision
for Christ or my religious needs any more than defending the authentic, unchanging form of the liturgy, or just the attachment of family:
"Grandma was married here, my mother baptized here."

As I step back from what Diana Butler Bass offers, both in her spiritual autobiography as well as her parish studies and her most recent book, a look at Christianity and the church from the bottom up,[21] what I sense is a reintegration of believer and community, of the person with not just this parish but the sweep of lived experience of the faith we call tradition. What is most striking is that, in her account, Christianity returns to what it was in the beginning—a lived faith, the collective experience of the saints, not simply canon law, a particular ecclesiological structure, nor doctrines defined once and for all in some distant century—whether the sixteenth or the third.

Moreover, what I also take from her work is the elasticity—in the Eastern Church it would be called the "economy"—of Christian faith and life. This is a sign of life as well as hope, of a parish both living the gospel as well as seeking new ways, responding to new situations without compromising the basic content of the Christian faith. By this I also mean that since it is the place—better, the assembly—where the Spirit is, the Spirit then must always be speaking to the church. When members of this community speak, we have to think it possible that we are hearing the Spirit—asking us to stretch our old definitions, erase former lines or walls of restriction, perhaps rethink through the scriptures and sacraments what the life with Christ, the path of the kingdom of God, looks like, as Merton said, "now, here," in "this" situation. The transformation that is the essence of the "way," as Christianity was called in the New Testament, is personal. Diana's story of her pilgrimage, as well as the accounts of the others we have listened to here, affirm this. But in the life of the Spirit, nothing remains just with the individual. The community of the parish, the neighborhoods beyond it where members work and live, all of the society and world are also transformed.

*Singing for the Kingdom: Matthew Kelty*

When one lists the writers on the spiritual life in the last century, it is certain that Thomas Merton will be mentioned as one of the greatest if not the major author. Merton was so many things in addition to being a master of the spiritual life. Yet we are now going to hear from an articulate preacher, really a poet in the art of both the homily and memoir. Matthew Kelty, who died in 2011 at the age of ninety-five, had been a monk of Gethsemani Abbey for over fifty years. He was himself a novice under Merton, even though he entered as a priest and former missionary and journal editor for the Catholic community of the Society of the Divine Word. Kelty had also been head of a small experimental monastic community sponsored by Gethsemani in Oxford, North Carolina, from 1970 to 1973. He walked to Washington DC from there to protest the Vietnam War. He also returned to Papua New Guinea, where he had earlier worked as a missionary, to live a hermit life from 1973 to 1982. From there he came back to Gethsemani where he worked in the tailor shop and in administration. For quite a few years he was chaplain in the guest house.

Over the years, though he never thought of himself as an author, several volumes of his homilies, talks, and reflections have been published. The one that was published in 2008 had as a subtitle *The Last of the Homilies,* since in 2006 at the age of ninety-one, Father Matthew asked to be relieved of the task of preaching at the monastery. He still celebrated the Eucharist every morning in the cloister chapel and attended all the daily office services in the monastery church, using a motorized chair to get around. I once went up to him, said that we'd corresponded briefly—I had asked for an essay he wrote on monastic life, a really stellar account of what the life is. I also told him that I had enjoyed all his talks and homilies that had been published. "Oh yeah?" was his reply, as he zoomed off.

I turn to him for several reasons. Consider all he has been and done in his life. Beyond that, something only reading his work can bring is his combination of poetic sensitivity to beauty in everything, an almost journalistic frugality in expression, but also a generosity and sense of humor not often found in people of faith, who are often way too serious and emotional. Kelty reflects on his Irish Catholic upbringing, but he does not indulge in nostalgia, there is no wistful longing for the days gone by in preference to the present. He talks of his parents as though they were still alive, similarly his old novice master, Thomas Merton. He says being a novice under Merton was not easy, for Merton was "tough."

I frequently had occasion years ago to be in on it when Father Louis [Merton's monastic name] would meet someone or other, usually in connection with vocation work. It was interesting to note how many were frankly disappointed with the real Thomas Merton. Not all, but many. They had their own idea of what he must be like but, when confronted with his person, were at a loss to adjust to reality. He was so bland. Indeed, at his very last appearance, as it were, when he gave that last conference in Bangkok, two monks who heard him to the end were not impressed. In the blunt way of scholars, one said to the other, "Well, that wasn't much." Maybe it wasn't in terms of what the monks expected, no doubt some dazzling performance that would leave all breathless and on their feet with applause. He has not measured up to expectations. It happens all the time. To me. To you. . . . Thomas Merton was a constant annoyance to many in and out of the monastery because he catered to no one's pious delusions. Even now it is amusing to ask someone how soon they think Merton will be canonized and the 10th of December become his feast day? The very idea strikes those who knew him as ridiculous. Their faces cloud in distress at the very idea. Their notion of sanctity and Merton have nothing in common.[22]

Elsewhere he recalls that at the age of forty-five, having already been ordained and acting both as a missionary and the editor of his religious community's periodical, he was given a typing assignment by novice master Merton. He's a lousy typist, he's having a lousy day in an equally lousy period of time as a novice and refuses. Back and forth the two go until Kelty gives in, at which point Merton smiles and tells him that it was the "old man," the "Adam" in him that was talking. My sense is that even in the retelling, decades later, Kelty was still not happy with the exchange.

Yet in one of the best memoirs of Merton, in a collection of monastic reminiscences and tributes, Fr. Matthew speaks at length about Merton "the Man," the person. And once more, what he has to say about this world renowned spiritual writer who was once his boss and for years his colleague says as much about Kelty as it does about Merton. The Merton he describes is an "original," a person utterly without affect or pretense, completely at ease in his own skin, with his own thoughts and feelings, totally free in his experiences and personality. He had his weaknesses and his deficiencies to be sure, but perhaps the reason there was so wide a variety of responses to Merton in print as well as Merton in person was this authenticity.

> He was a kind of dividing spirit, a sign spoken against, a sort of question demanding an answer. Thus, he raised issues, and there was no way out but to reply one way or another. In this he was unsettling, disturbing, not comfortable to live with. Put in other words, there was a kind of truth about him that got under your skin, into your heart. He belonged to nobody, free as a bird. He could not be categorized, labeled, pigeonholed. And he had vision. Putting this together makes it clear that the fire in him burned not only himself, but burned many around him as well.[23]

Matthew Kelty is for me a great poet and preacher of the realities of everyday life, of the transformation that comes only with time, attention, effort, and, most of all, mercy. Just before Lent and Easter, when we all come back each year to the dying and rising at the root of it all, he brings it back home: "Begin in your own heart."

> As if the yearly encounter with the salvation story is not enough, we have it daily in the Eucharist. . . . Christ's Passion, Death and Resurrection are transcendent events, surpassing time, in the world until it is all over. . . . In the face of such cosmic realities, it seems rather lame to speak of noting the splinter in your brother's eye rather than being aware of your own hampered vision. Is that to be taken as an answer to the world scene? It seems so, for if the flaw in your brother is a problem with you, does that not indicate a critical view of your own flaws? You cannot treat others any way except the way you treat yourself. If you can be savage in your comments on another, no one need doubt you are just as savage in your own heart, revealed in your speech. The beam in your own eye has never been removed in mercy nor the speck you see in your brother's eye.
>
> We need to meet mercy if we are to do mercy to others. Anything less is sheer waste. The sinful heart that has accepted Christ's mercy approaches another in quite a different mode than the one foreign to it.

The healing of the world does not begin is some far-off land that we must hasten to help, but in the geography of your own heart. There the sinner is washed in mercy and becomes thereby an instrument of mercy, not merely in his prayers, but in everything he does. He is a vessel of grace. We cannot heal all the world's problems, but we begin with our own heart if our help is to amount to anything.

Our response is not limited to prayer for the afflicted. We practice justice, feed the hungry, clothe the naked, visit the sick, bury the dead. We forgive injury and do not resort to revenge, to reprisal, to contempt. In our world. Where we are.

It costs nothing and is worth more than anyone can tell. It is the way the world is healed, with Christ dying daily everywhere and we with him.

Since the healing process is so slow, as it always is, we need to look ahead to the triumph in the end when Christ, put to death by humankind how many times, rises in glorious mercy.

Amen.[24]

It was the apostle Paul who said each Christian would in baptism die in Christ and be raised with him. He also said that we would bear within ourselves the marks of the cross and of the resurrection, as he did. The search for God and the living out of holiness go wherever we are, wherever we go. It could be the trip back in time that some of our writers here made, into their childhood or students days or younger adulthood, to see where they had first encountered God, learned what the life of faith was all about, perhaps even where and how this was given up or lost. For some it was this journeying back that made it possible to recover their faith, to move on ahead. Preaching at Gethsemani Abbey on a Sunday, after a week in which a monk had been buried and a new one taken vows, Father Matthew connects both to the actions of Christ.

As in the mysteries of faith, we do not merely read about them, study them, reflect on them. We do them. The Passion, Death and the Rising of Christ are not merely recalled and celebrated. They continue through history, and we participate in that continuation. Christ lives and dies and rises among us. His life and grace permeate the whole of us. Here is art of another sort. Here is a witness of staggering beauty and significance. It is God in the human scene in a most specific way.[25]

Clearly, while preached to the Gethsemani monastic community, this was also addressed to everyone else in the monastery church, and for that matter to everyone who reads *Singing for the Kingdom*. In all his homilies, reflections, and talks I have been able to get hold of, Kelty's realism shines very brightly. No glitter, no issues, no complaining, no nonsense. Following Christ, living one's baptism, is to do the hard work of whatever vocation and place in life we find ourselves, monastic or not.

In hearing his no-nonsense but compassionate approach, we hear what we have heard in the diverse voices and tones earlier. The real place for searching for and finding God is the various ordinary tasks and relationships in which each of us find ourselves. But does that exhaust our reflection here? Might there also be things to change, to add or subtract from the mix at the level of our parish communities, the most tangible, significant "local churches" to which we belong, and in addition, at a more public level? Diana Butler Bass's research on intentional communities—*Christianity for the Rest of Us*—has some further points to make about transformation.

## *A Faith We Can Live with, and that We Can Live*

Much of Diana Butler Bass's work has been on intentional communities, that is, parishes which have been deliberate in thinking about living out the gospel together in the complex situation of America in the twenty-first century. It is important to consider at least a few of the features she identified as crucial ones for Christian communities in our time, so that the issue of transformation might be seen as not just an individual but a communal, and also a public, reality.

What she found in the study of parishes is both unsurprising as well as provocative. None of the spiritually and humanly vibrant communities employed the techniques of megachurches, such as the "niche marketing" of Willow Creek of Bloomington, Illinois, to ecclesially disaffected, religiously indifferent clients. None reduced or eliminated symbols of the faith or classical elements of Christian life. One would search in vain for Joel Osteen's and T. D. Jakes's success and personality centered approaches, or even for Rick Warren's formulaic "purpose-driven" model.

However, when it comes to the "basics" of rich liturgical worship, seriousness about prayer, study, social outreach, and a true delight in fellowship—in eating together, being together—the ten parishes she focuses on are predictable. They are also diverse not only ethnically but in terms of social and political perspectives. These are not "red" or "blue" communities. All have somehow found ways to re-root either where they have been historically located or where they have relocated. Some are urban, others in older suburban settings, still others in exurban situations. They include mainline denominations— the United Methodist Church, the Presbyterian Church in the USA, the Evangelical Lutheran Church in America, the Episcopal Church in the USA, the United Church of Christ, and so on—but no Roman or Byzantine Catholic or Eastern Orthodox parishes, and none from Pentecostal, evangelical, or independent categories, though for sure, what Butler Bass found in the mainline congregations would also be found in these others. The validation group of another forty parishes pretty much mirrors the same denominational groups and widens the regional location as well as the urban, suburban, and exurban settings. One might object that significant parts of the American church landscape are missing—this is admittedly so, though what Butler Bass and her associates found is surely not limited to the denominations or the parishes sampled.

There is one characteristic that I believe shows up in all of the parishes Diana examines: an openness to God and to the world around them, which makes change natural instead of a threat. In the larger American religious scene, such an outlook would for many be heretical. It would be taken as a sell-out to the spirit of the times, to the amoral or immoral secular society and its values. It would fly in the face of the utterly antihistorical attitude that has emerged among Eastern Orthodox, Roman Catholic, Anglican, and a variety of other Christians, namely, that the way they celebrate the liturgy, the form doctrine takes in their expression of it, the style of life they follow— that all these are the great tradition of Christianity unchanged and in need of no reform. The parishes in Butler Bass's study are nowhere nearly so self-confident or self-righteous. They neither canonize what is usually one historical version of the liturgy, one cultural expression of doctrine or life, nor do they idolize everything the culture around them serves up.

In describing the Episcopal Church of the Redeemer in Cincinnati, she follows the rector's yearly report which he chose to include as part of his sermon.

It is March 2005, and this is Bruce Freeman's first report in his new congregation. For more than twenty years, the people at Redeemer have intentionally engaged Christian practices as the heart of their communal faith. At a time when many mainline congregations still tried to do church as their grandparents had, Redeemer reconfigured itself as a pilgrimage community, a place of personal transformation based in the life of study, prayer and discerning the work of the Holy Spirit. It has not always been easy. . . . In his first months Bruce listened carefully to the language of this pilgrim community, trying to understand its distinctive practices and the way the church organizes its communal life. They have many gifts, including a special practice of the "ministry of encouragement" and unique practices of discernment. On the first day of his new ministry, Bruce was given an extraordinary gift—a member who had just passed away left Redeemer more than $12 million to be used at the congregation's discretion. In today's sermon, Bruce reflects upon Redeemer's many gifts. To Bruce, gifts should not occasion self-congratulations. Rather, gifts are an invitation to change. He talks about the call of Jesus' disciples and the relationship between abundance and risk. The New Testament reading is about the great catch of fish, whose very abundance threatens to sink the apostles' boats. "This is a metaphor for the church in general and the Church of the Redeemer in particular," Bruce says. "We have caught onto an abundance of Spirit, an abundance of gifts. But this call involves risk; it is both a challenge and an opportunity." Bruce highlights Redeemer's many successes as a parish—its faithfulness, intelligence, humor and commitment. Yet he gently reminds them that these gifts are a renewed call to "open itself and share itself with new and wider communities."[26]

I can say from many years preaching in at least four different parishes, having helped build a new church in one, expand the facilities in another, that there is no telling what a change a gift the size of $12 million would bring! But when this priest, new as pastor, calls the recipients of such gifts to recognize it as only the most recent and only a material gift, one of many they have been given, and when he tells the members they are called to new people, communities, and ways of being, no gasps or panics. They have had two decades of learning to be open, to welcome change, the new, the different. They believe in the Spirit living among them, guiding them. Nothing is completed, a finished product in their church. Rather everything is a work in progress. All of them are patient because they understand themselves to be the disciples of Christ who "is the same, yesterday, today, and forever."

Contrary to the Christians for whom this Pauline saying means that nothing can change in the church, for the people of God, the "local church" which is the parish of the Redeemer in this Ohio city, it means that they are being led now as they were two decades earlier, by the Spirit whose work is never done. For them Pentecost, in Sergius Bulgakov's phrase, is "permanent," continuing. The needs of the 1980s were not quite those of the first decade of the twenty-first century. And what their grandchildren will encounter will be something else again. And such an outlook, Diana found, was not tied to a parish so generously endowed as Redeemer. Just as the people there had prayed, studied, discussed, and experimented with their vocations to be light, salt, bread for "the life of the world," and had generously themselves given to this work before they received the legacy, so too would they proceed in the same way having received it. Other congregations not so richly endowed, St. Mark's Lutheran in suburban Yorktown, Virginia; Holy Communion Episcopal in Memphis, Tennessee; Calvin Presbyterian in Zelienople, Pennsylvania; Cornerstone Methodist in Florida; Epiphany Episcopal in DC—all were not just communities in transformation. Rather, as the old monastic adage says: *aliis contemplata tradere*—they were eager to give away, to share the spiritual gifts they had received.

As Diana shows—or rather, as the parishes showed her—the transformation experienced within flowed out to their neighborhoods in so many wonderful ways. And if we have become disheartened at American retreat from outreach and generosity, we need only confront Robert Wuthnow's recent assessment of this activity.[27] This indefatigable student of American religion finds substantial evidence to claim that Christianity has not simply migrated to South America or Africa, as some interpret from Philip Jenkins's work. Just as earlier he identified the rediscovery and reclaiming of practices of the faith, so now does he see American Christians committed to the world beyond their shores.[28] No longer is the thrust solely missionary either, but humanitarian in the name of the Lord, the works of lovingkindness in medical aid, food, shelter, disaster relief, environmental improvement.

It may seem counterintuitive that rich, classical liturgy—following the tradition in Eucharistic assembly as well as daily prayer and scripture study—is not introversion. There is a long legacy of such liturgical centers being equally intensive in their outreach. The Anglo-Catholic proponents of restoring traditional liturgy in the Church of England in the Oxford movement were among the first inner-city church activists. In our own time clerics as theological and politically opposite as Richard John Neuhaus and Bishop Paul Moore Jr. spent the early years of their priesthood in inner city ministry in Bedford-Stuyvesant and Jersey City. Maria Skobtsova and Dorothy Day both had the chapel and the Eucharist at the heart of their houses of hospitality. H. Richard Niebuhr saw the social theology of the Anglican F. D. Maurice as an example of the vision of "Christ *transforming* culture."

Tracking the search for God and the effort to live a life of holiness thus far has immersed us in the experience and accounts of a number of women and men, myself too. In all of these, especially in Diana Butler Bass's journey and travels through many intentional communities of faith, it seems as though we are now, toward the end, moving from the individual to the communal dimension of holiness. That is the case, and I will say that it is where I will be going in the next thing I write. Of course it has been the case that all the lives of our writers were not lived in a vacuum but very much in relationship to worshipping communities, to friends and pastors, for good as well as for ill. But before going a bit further in the ecclesial realm, I want to briefly sum up where we have been.

# CHAPTER NINE

# "The Church has left the building"

*Belonging to the Christian Community in the*
*Twenty-first Century*

### *Memory, Holiness, and Living on: Summing up*

In almost every writer we have listened to, no matter the difficulties faced in church, no matter the clashes between religious conservatives and more progressive believers on doctrine and life, there is the realization that faith is rooted in one's everyday life. As Peter Berger pointed out, the road of experience can be one of doubt, of questions as well as affirmation. I would say pain and disgust are also part of the experience, considering the toxic sides of religion. Yet in the end Schleiermacher, Fichte, Schelling, and Kierkegaard, our teachers in modernity, were right all along. The truth that builds us up, that feeds and nurtures us, is the faith that we have encountered, incorporated, experienced ourselves. Closer to our own time, Edward Schillebeeckx stressed the centrality of experience as the path to God and God's to us.[1] In the last volume of his trilogy he modified a classic phrase that claimed "outside the church there is no salvation." Schillebeeckx contended *extra mundum nulla salus* — "outside the world there is no salvation." In writing about the centrality of Jesus, in the original Dutch he calls it *het verhaal van een levende* — "the story of the living one." We do not just seek the historical Jesus or the Christ of the scriptures and the church: we are also looking for ourselves, for meaning in Christ, and we continue to write the gospel in our lives

To consult our experiences, both the good and the bad, as the writers we listened to have done, is not merely ransacking our pasts but constitutes a crucial way in which to view our present and future. For a long time such reflection has been recognized as useful in the spiritual life, the models stretching back to Augustine's *Confessions* and to Paul's self scrutiny in his letters. In thinking back on periods in one's own journey, as Diana Butler Bass and Andrew Krivak did, along with myself, we see and understand much better going backwards, as Kierkegaard said, than going forwards. Revisiting the faces of a Father Albert or Father Vincent brought the deeper kind of happiness that I did not grasp back in the novitiate. "You want to be HAPPY?" Father Vincent roared at my immature and naive selfishness. Little then did I know what sick children, tons of dirty laundry, bad roads, and little sleep would mean when this was the pattern always—it seemed—as parents of small kids.

Searching into the experiences of women and men seeking to live a godly life by no means should be taken as a rejection of all that is given—the revelation of God in the scriptures, the gift of God in the Eucharist and the other sacraments, the lives of saints and their writings, the feasts of the church year—and constitutes the legacy of faith, that which is "handed down," the "tradition." Every writer whose thoughts we have listened to here was nurtured by many of these gifts of the tradition. Our listening to them is an education in precisely how the tradition is received and then lived, experienced by brothers and sisters, both those passed into the kingdom and those still among us.

"Experience," as the saying goes," is the teacher of fools," but one can try to share what one has already endured. Since our parish is very close to the seminary, we usually have one or more students assigned to do a parish internship with us. Typically, they are very energetic and idealistic young men and women with small children. Sometimes both spouses are students. Seminarian couples and families are always cash and sleep deprived—there are many services at seminary, and often one spouse is working. So I hear from them, both during their internships and afterwards when they are in parishes or graduate study, almost the same recitation of unceasingly full diapers and toddler vomit and tight money. I cannot recall how or if, back in the day, Jeanne and I ever did try to integrate such wall-to-wall childrearing into our "spiritual lives." I suspect we too were naïve enough to think that cleaning up kids and a messy house was something other than "spiritual." Ah, but we learned!

And thus I now try to share with them the things I have learned as a spouse, a parent, a teacher, and a pastor—when they ask. I urge these young parents to be kind to each other, to be easy on themselves, not to worry about how the house looks, just get through it, survive! I remember that an older priest once told me that we make a big mistake in restricting ascetic practices of fasting, giving generously, prayer, and reading to the season of Lent. He believed that we should be doing these things, not in any extreme fashion, but consistently, all through the year. And he noted that if we were looking for opportunities to endure hard things, to make demands on our patience and forgiveness, our moderation and stewardship of time— well, look around, for we have just such opportunities every day of the year, at home with our families, at work, in our parish communities. We could fast, as Paul Evdokimov suggests, from mindless wasting of time, from the addiction to work, our fears about financial security—the list goes on.[2] For me, passing on what I learned, often the hard way, has been a much more effective way of talking about the search for God and the holy life than any paper or lecture I have given and with no need of cracking the covers of this or any other book.

I confess to wondering who would read yet *another* book about spirituality.[3] For most of us, the leisure to read or to ponder is more often than not a luxury about which we dream. Even vacations deliver little in the way of quiet and open time. Yet, from another angle, the specific circumstances of life—the intense demands of caring for very young children, the way our jobs tend to suck away most of our alert hours, anxieties in hard economic times about keeping a job, finding a job, one's health insurance and pension, about care for aged parents— life goes on, and the search for God and the life in and with God nevertheless continue, whether or not one reads (or writes) books about this.

The search for God may at times lead people to especially revered locations such as the Redwoods monastery or the Assisi of Francis and Clare or the shrine of the Mother of God at Lourdes in the Pyrenees, all visited by Patricia Hampl. Today's sites include monastic communities such as Thomas Merton and Matthew Kelty's Gethsemani Abbey—where one has to reserve space many months in advance. Darcey Steinke has her spiritual director Sister Leslie. Sara Miles looks to the clergy and lay leadership of her parish. We followed in detail Barbara Brown Taylor's descriptions of the path toward finding God in the many practices and places of everyday life. Nora Gallagher and Lauren Winner employed the liturgical calendar, the fasts and feasts and seasons of the year, as the grid to follow, in addition to the ordinary civil calendar with its fewer holidays and vacation weeks and its seemingly endless deadlines and schedules, the ones that seem to rule our lives, even into our restless sleeping.

With Kathleen Norris and others, we have traced the suffering and disruption that our lives bring us, without any asking or planning of our own. Sickness, aging, death—of those close to us and ourselves—these are unavoidable. The wisdom of holy people before us teaches that these are not merely problems to be solved, eliminated as our everyday experience often suggests.

Listening to these writers, I hope, puts flesh and bones on, gives voices and feelings to the search for God and the attempt to lead a holy life. There are many other writers that I could have added. I have mentioned some of their names already and will not do so again. What each one does is to bring to the search her or his own unique past and vision. Of necessity, spouses and friends, colleagues and neighbors have also been drawn in—the networks to which we all belong. While by my choice, all here are within the Christian tradition, what a diversity of expressions of the faith and its life they provide, from Trappist monasteries and Jesuit houses of formation to Episcopal parishes and Carmelite priories and Orthodox churches.

All of this plus a few other exchanges have led me to want to shift attention, here at the end, to the communal or ecclesial dimension of how communities of faith are locations for the life of holiness in the twenty-first century. I think Diana Butler Bass's work was a strong push in this direction, as are ongoing conversations I have had for some time now with former interns at our parish who are discovering pastoral work in our time and other colleagues in pastoral ministry from various churches. But before moving in this direction, I want to sum up where the effort of three different books has led me. A friend felt that all I wanted to say could be put thus:

> Despite our looking for what is like God—what is good, beautiful, and true—given our human nature and condition, we cannot help but collide with the misery we often create ourselves, but which is also there in abundance, lurking where we least expect it: within the community of faith and even among ordained and other religious professionals.[4]

Sarah Hinlicky Wilson is a most gifted writer in addition to many other things—pastor, parent, spouse, professor. Her reading of an early draft of this book was discerning and her questions exacting. Her summary could not have been more accurate. Others who read this had further queries. I do not know why so many of the writers I selected are Episcopalian, but I would say that the Anglican tradition is a rich liturgical one that also is open to many cultural, ethnic, and intellectual perspectives. I think there are clearly more women writers here and beyond in the religious/spiritual memoir genre simply because men are challenged when it come to self-scrutiny and revelation. I realize that there are many other rich and provocative memoirs of the kind featured here. Merton's, Nouwen's, and Schmemann's letters and journals come to mind, and I have used some of these. Patricia Hampl has written a great deal about the crafting of memoirs, particularly the inherent problems of remembering and expressing them with accuracy and power. I selected the writers here in an act of faith, trusting in their accounts of what happened to them both good and bad. It was necessary to follow their experiences of the search for God and the living out of holiness.

After looking at a number of remarkable persons of faith and their lives and thought, and thereafter a fascinating group of further women and men whose actions and words expressed holiness both visible and hidden, we have now heard from a diverse collection of "saints" who are articulate in telling what kind of women and men they really are. This is what we have been hearing—doubts and delight, despair and defiance.

Precisely because the gift of and call to holiness is for all, there is no need for a new or special theology of universal holiness. In the past century I can think of a number of individuals and documents that pointed out its roots in the first, ancient church of the New Testament. Surely both the constitutions on the church and the church in the world of Vatican II were milestones in the rediscovery of the church as the people of God, of the vocation of all the baptized as priests, prophets, and the royalty of the kingdom, of the need of the church to be reading the "signs of the times" and working "for the life of the world." Whatever writer or theologian one thinks of, the recovery of the vision of holiness of the early church was coming for a long time and in many different ways.[5]

I am only one of many who have raised questions about how we select saints and which of our sisters and brothers we choose. The various church communities will always differ in how they go about this, yet even more crucial—so the saints themselves would and do say—is that each of us keep confronting the daily opportunities to love God and serve God in the sister or brother before us. For myself, whether in the Carmelites or in the Lutheran or Orthodox communities, the accents and emphases are just local ones. The variety of types of liturgical music and celebration, sacred art, theological writing, and preaching testify to the unifying presence of the Spirit. Whether Coptic or Ethiopian, Malabar or Melkite, Roman or Greek Catholic, American or Greek or Russian Orthodox, or Lutheran or Anglican there is but one Lord, one faith, one baptism. As Bulgakov argued long ago in "By Jacob's Well," we are still united more than divided— in prayer, the scriptures, baptism, and the Eucharist.[6]

The reality of living out the gospel is the same. To feed the hungry, clothe the naked, shelter the homeless, visit the sick and imprisoned is to love the one Lord in the faces of many suffering children of God. Beyond this, in our own homes, schools, offices, and neighborhoods there are many to forgive, to listen to more patiently, to encourage and assist. All of us struggle to hold on to so much that is beautiful, good, and true from the past without turning it all into museum displays, texts and rites, and thinking frozen in time—what one hears and sees, say, at Sturbridge Village or Colonial Williamsburg from the actors who play at being eighteenth century in order to "interpret" the way of life preserved in those buildings and artifacts. Perhaps we would do better if we looked for the effects of the works of mercy done by the saints rather than abstractly try to establish criteria for their recognition as holy women and men. Jesus said he looked more to the results, what people did, than the rules they observed or the doctrine they recited. The teaching and order of the church have their rationale, their importance. But first comes the person, then the Sabbath. And as for holiness, it cannot be a question of those few Christians identified and then recognized as saints. We are all called to holiness: "Go and do likewise."

## The Church in Our Time: Twenty-first-century Assembling

Have we heard enough talk about renewal and reform, about "church growth," more than anyone can stomach of new and exciting strategies for "the church in our time"? Most periodicals like *Christian Century*, *Commonweal*, and *America* and numerous online sites carry articles on these topics and advertise conferences with speakers from among some of the writers we have listened to here. But have we heard enough of *aggiornamento* and of "discerning the signs of the times"? Surely since the days of Vatican II, and before that of the "back to the sources" and liturgical movements, the Oxford movement, and the "inner mission" impulse to renew the cities full of impoverished industrial workers, such slogans have been battle cries. In very different ways the "emergent church" movement in the past decade or so has been raising questions about what church is in the twenty-first century. Is it keeping the roof on this historical but now impractical building? Is it re-rooting venerable parishes in neighborhoods completely different in population and use than when they were begun? Is it facing the reality that most of our formerly "village parishes" no longer draw from the immediate environs where the church bell could be heard, where people could walk to and from the sanctuary?

To delve into the complex questions and issues that face the local church and parish of the twenty-first century is beyond the scope of this book. Yet the church at all the various levels—historical, tradition, denomination, national organization, the parish—has of course figured throughout in the accounts of the writers or pilgrims to whom we've listened. In the cases of Barbara Brown Taylor, Nora Gallagher,

Darcey Steinke, and Sara Miles, all of these played significant roles, both for good and ill—the ordained ministry, the larger institutional settings of seminary and denomination, along with the structures and dynamics of the parish. This more corporate, that is, churchly dimension of the search for God and the life of holiness will be the next focus for me. (I recognize that things that are mentioned at the end of books often become road signs pointing to where further reading and reflection and writing should go.) Yet as Diana Butler Bass's probing look at intentional parishes and their practices reveals, such communities are strong supports for persons on the journey. The attachment and importance of a parish like Trinity Episcopal in Santa Barbara is so strong in her memoir, as it also is in Nora Gallagher's two accounts.

What is telling in so many of the first-person accounts we have listened to is the damage that religion can do. Perhaps it can be put more precisely—the toxicity and destructive side of religion is to be seen in what people of faith do to themselves and others. However in the very same accounts, in some cases long after, the other side of faith also emerges. The search for God, the living out of the gospel, of holiness, is transforming—of oneself and others. St. Seraphim of Sarov's best known saying is "Save yourself and thousands around you will also be saved." (We heard Matthew Kelty say exactly this on his own.)

As Paul Evdokimov notes, this was hardly the urging of exclusion, of running from the world, rejecting the works of lovingkindness. At every stage of his life, Seraphim transcended what was customary, the accepted form, to live ever more intensely the gospel that he read and prayed every day.[7] At the end of his life, his cell was open to everyone, regardless of background. In his service of the suffering, he revealed the point of monastic and the hermit life as well as ordained ministry, namely, communion with God and loving care for the neighbor. This little monk showed very powerfully that faith is inherently social, worldly, communal. If the point of the Christian life is to live in the Holy Spirit, this existence in turn breaks down all barriers and divisions, "healing all that is afflicted," as the baptismal and ordination prayers say in the Eastern Church. As many writers on the spiritual life have emphasized, it is pointless to pit Mary against Martha, the contemplative versus the active dimensions of the one life of the gospel. Often this is exactly what adversaries drift into—Eastern

Church members condemning Western "activism," Westerners criticizing Eastern introversion and passivity. One can find even discerning figures like Alexander Schmemann descending into caricatures of the protest and activism of his time, perhaps his sense of what they were about but that only. Today, after decades of the "culture wars," what might be called the "religious wars" have emerged. Coalitions of like-minded people of faith engage in activity for or against particular issues such as congressional efforts to reform health care insurance, state legislature attempts to grant legal status to gay and lesbian marriages, as well as perennial issues such as immigration, abortion, and stem cell research, among others. In fall 2009 a group that otherwise would agree on very little signed the Manhattan Declaration, taking positions on most of these issues mentioned while deploring the secularism of America and expressing fear that their religious conscience would be challenged by liberal and antireligious legislation.

Yet as Diana Butler Bass observes in her study of parishes, more often "red" and "blue," that is, more conservative and more progressive groups, did not end up savaging each other. A community united in liturgy, prayer, hospitality, and outreach became the rare locations in which those of otherwise polarizing viewpoints could still be at peace with each other. Bass hypothesizes that their *koinonia* or "communion in the holy things" in effect made them "purple." Tradition, expressed in the scriptures and sacraments, was their living memory of Jesus and of the community gathered around him from the past. In ways that are startling, old denominational distinctions and divisions crumble in the parishes she studies. Partly this is due to the increasingly diverse backgrounds of members of any congregation in the U.S. It is also a function of the other important aspects of practices that parishes take upon themselves. Study of the scriptures and the history of the church show that there is far more that unites than divides Christians. The practical action of communal events, of reaching out to the community, enables parishioners to transcend all kinds of differences that have been and still are divisive. Stepping back from her narrative it is clear that the liturgical movement, one that has restored traditional forms, has enabled Christians of differing backgrounds to see how the Eucharist unites us with Christ and with each other. A more Eucharistic sense of church is further supported by the identity of all the baptized as disciples and apostles. Baptism reveals the priesthood of all, without negating those called and set apart by ordination. All Christians are to bear the good news of Christ and of the kingdom of heaven to the world.

Sara Miles, herself a radical social activist, found out the hard way that there were some more conservative and introverted members at her apparently progressive parish in San Francisco. Her invitation to the parish to become a place of service through a food pantry was not met universally with enthusiasm. The problems with having all the needy into their beautiful new sanctuary was a shock for Sara. But it was the unifying force of the scriptures, of baptism and the Eucharist that enabled her to come to terms with her fellow but doubting members, as well as them to come to terms with her fervor. It was also a journey of deepening for Sarah herself. In *Jesus Freak,* she gives a sustained narration of day-to-day ministry in the context of her parish. Though the strains of living the gospel are presented honestly, the common commitments to prayer and community, to the Eucharist and care for those in need seem to transcend the very human disagreements and frustrations.

Nora Gallagher likewise, in her years at Trinity parish in Santa Barbara, saw individuals courageous enough to venture out and learn the other's perspective, and irenic enough to accept differences whether on public policy or questions of sexual identity. What enabled members at Trinity to challenge each other without hatred, to accept the huge task of re-rooting their parish, literally work for its resurrection from likely death, came not from any church growth strategies, not from ideas about pastor-congregation dynamics but from the heart of church life: the scriptures, the Eucharist, prayer and study, fellowship and service to those in need. The year they had to survive in their church hall for everything, from liturgy to meetings, while the beautiful Gothic nave was made quake resistant, actually turned out to be a blessing. Likewise was the arrival of an interim priest, Mark Asman, who would eventually become their new rector.

It is not the case that the elements or "practices" Diana Butler Bass identified as both crucial and common to the different intentional communities she studied are a "formula" for success. There is nothing particularly mysterious, unusual, or trendy about them.

Rather they are essential practices of the Christian tradition from the very beginning, those mentioned in the New Testament. Only the size of the community and its location in a building are different from the domes, spires, and steeples to which we have become accustomed. They might be said to each incorporate a number of other activities directly related or connected to another practice. To liturgical worship are also connected individual prayer, as well as reading and study of the scriptures and other texts. And one surely could call the fellowship—from coffee hours to other meals and gatherings—a continuation of the liturgical gathering. Likewise, hospitality, both to visitors and to the surrounding neighborhood and community, as well as outreach at the local level and to areas of need nationally and internationally—are not these the very "liturgy after the liturgy" described in the fourth century by John Chrysostom and Basil the Great and in our own time by the likes of Mother Teresa, Dorothy Day, and Mother Maria Skobtsova?

There are all sorts of possible ways in which to celebrate the liturgy, to engage in the practices of hospitality and service, and to make prayer and study regular in one's week, one's everyday. Traveling along with Diana across the country to the ten parishes of intensive study and the forty others also investigated, quite a range of variations are seen. One parish had as it specialty outreach to Hispanic immigrants, documented or not. Cornerstone United Methodist Church in Naples, Florida, was particularly flexible and welcoming of all kinds of visitors—those who came while on vacation, one-time worshippers, as well as the visitor in and out of correctional institutions due to abuse problems. Epiphany Episcopal Church in Washington DC appeared to have a large homeless congregation at their early service, with a meal and groceries available afterwards. What a contrast to some parishes I have visited where a new face is stared at, looked up and down as if in the wrong place, yet never welcomed. How different the communal sense of responsibility to welcome the stranger from the person in one of my parishes who ran up as soon as I came to the coffee hour, grasping my hand and telling me excitedly: "See that family over there, I don't know 'em, they must be visitors, so ya better go over and talk to 'em, Father!" There are the informal "welcoming committee" too who do not wait for clergy to do the honors, but eventually bring newcomers over to meet the priests.

Some parishes establish houses of retreat where those wanting time apart can go for prayer. Others set up houses of hospitality where food is available as well as temporary lodging. A visiting nurse regularly appears to do basic health screening, and there is a social worker for consultation. Butler Bass describes how a ride down the escalator to the DC Metro became a moment of conversion for Renee Grayson, a member at Epiphany. One Ash Wednesday while heading home from work, the brief moments going down the escalator to the train platforms was for her *metanoia*—a turning upside down, inside out. She turned around and rode back up and went to services and a special evening program at the church. One thing led to another, and eventually she left her job and headed for seminary and ordination, to serve more fully in the work of not just her own parish but the larger church. I have seen nearly the same happen with people who came to visit one Sunday at my parish and then stayed to make it their church home, themselves now active members of the parish community.

Others in Butler Bass's study describe how after years of church membership, attending church-related colleges, even theological school, they finally discovered that prayer was not just something done on Sunday morning for about an hour, not just a number of paragraphs one recited together or sang with others. The experience of weekday liturgies with just a few gathered around the altar for the Eucharist; of the rite of laying on of hands and anointing for healing; of centering prayer; of *lectio divina*, the slow, thoughtful ruminating on a scripture passage, even one word; the use of the Jesus prayer and icons as focus for prayer; exposure to monastic communities; and the sanctification of time by daily prayer at set times—these are but a few rich practices of the tradition of the church, East and West, which members of the congregations encountered and from which they grew immensely in their spiritual lives.

Unlikely as it might sound, the parish that specialized in the ministry of healing was Calvin Presbyterian in Zelienople, Pennsylvania. The Reformed tradition is not known for rich liturgical celebration, rather a spare service of scripture and hymn and sermon. Yet in this parish, intercessory prayer, the laying on of hands, and anointing for healing became important components of the community's life. Likewise, Holy Communion Episcopal in Memphis was anything but a staid, upper-class congregation. It regularly invited cutting-edge, even controversial scholars as guest lecturers. It conducted an evening service in the Celtic tradition, using material from the Iona community book of hymns and prayers, with candlelight and time for silence in the service. Others in the parish, following the lead of Esther De-Waal, used the rule of St. Benedict as a framework for a balance in their lives of work, study, and prayer even though they were married, parents, professionally employed, and living in an urban setting rather than a rural monastery. While many Western churches now routinely have pauses for silence and prayer, usually after scripture readings and communion, this remains almost unknown in the Eastern Church tradition where the length of liturgies often means relentless progress through them by celebrant and choir. Yet the monastic communities of New Skete have made silence part of both the daily morning and evening services and at the liturgy, after the homily and after communion. Trinity Church in Santa Barbara was enlarged and encouraged by the quiet example and hospitality of Calvary monastery in the hills above them, a house of the Episcopal monastic order of the Holy Cross, now destroyed by fire. Kathleen Norris, whom we heard earlier on *acedia*, has for decades been an oblate, a lay associate of the Benedictine order. Her books on monastic life and prayer are among the best and for many an introduction to this ancient form of Christian life. How many have discovered the richness of silence and prayer from reading authors such as Henri Nouwen and Thomas Merton, David Steindl-Rast and John Main.

Nearby to Yale Divinity School, under Lillian Daniel's pastoral leadership, the Church of the Redeemer discovered the practice of personal testimony—once considered the province solely of Pentecostal and Evangelical churches—a wonderful form of reflection, encouragement, and insight. Either in the service or in classes, the sharing of one's "faith stories," the main path we have used here in this book, is a community building practice, one that immediately knits together people who previously had been only names and faces to each other. In the telling of their pilgrimages, Christians not only become friends but see their unity, despite so many differences, in Christ.

Although it is not the custom of all church bodies, most of the parishes explicitly opened their Eucharist to all, regardless of church background. While some would see this as brushing aside theological differences, ignoring still-real schisms or divisions among the churches, there is clearly more theological substance to the practice of Eucharistic hospitality. It is hardly just the fear of offending or hurting someone's feelings. Sara Miles describes in great detail the Eucharistic as well as baptismal theology put forward by Richard Fabian and Donald Schell, St. Gregory of Nyssa's founding pastors. While breaking from traditional practice, it must be admitted that their practice is more sensitive to the effect of schism and unbelief in our time rather than the conditions of various canons in the practice of the fourth or fifth centuries.

Yet as important as learning about the scriptures and liturgy is, the parishes Diana Butler Bass places before us have as a common characteristic a profound sensitivity to the neighborhood, their city, and the place and time in which they are trying to follow Christ. As we have seen, this does not mean, as was evident in earlier decades such as the '60s, a disregard for the past and tradition, but rather a passion for connecting all the elements of Christian worship and life with the society of our country, in our time. Granted, there is a good deal of improvisation, mixing elements of the past with the present, the classical Eucharistic liturgy with all sorts of music—jazz, African American spirituals, Gregorian and Byzantine and Russian chants, as well as new forms of sacred music from Taizé, the ecumenical monastery in France, and the Iona community. Purists might object, but then liturgical historians remind us of what is not obvious, mainly that Christian liturgy has down the ages used dozens of languages, forms of music, rhythms, and colors, and cultural borrowings. Witness the selection of the Eucharistic bread from many loaves and its preparation in the Coptic church. Consider the days, usually three to four, of celebration of the birth and revealing of Christ in the Ethiopian church. The dance of celebrants and the congregation at St. Gregory of Nyssa in San Franciso is mirrored by the same group choreography in the stone-carved churches of Ethiopia—where the Gregorians got the idea, along with the umbrellas and crosses and wide-eyed icons of the Ethiopian rite.

No matter the pastor, Diana Butler Bass finds real leadership in service to the community. Ecclesiastical pomp or power is not insisted on. The congregations do not experience the clerical divide—those ordained ruling over the rest of the flock. In my parish at an important meeting for restarting and dividing the work load, an amazing incident unfolded that is worth describing. The rector had introduced the task before all of us, but how to proceed was not at all clear. There could be his own perspectives and hopes, those of the parish council, then possibly discussion and presentation of various models of parish sharing in work. Up sprang my spouse, Jeanne, a corporate as well as churchly soul. She said we were spinning our wheels and drowning in talk. She thus proposed we get out of our chairs and try an exercise she knew from the corporate sector for identification of teams and their responsibilities.

Imagine the face of a clock. So then starting at the top, at twelve o'clock, beginning with, let's say, the liturgical life of the parish, then at one o'clock maintenance of the property inside and out, at two Christian education, at three outreach into the community and evangelism, at four internal parish groups, at five the building expansion, and so on. The understanding, she thought, was that the parish council members and clergy would spread themselves out along with others interested in serving the various points on the clock. Then each of these would be a ministry/service team. One of our seminarian interns interjected that the clergy, of course, could by grace of office not be anywhere but outside of or above the clock face. What a revelation of ecclesiology or better clerocracy.

Suffice it to say, this was not the natural inclination of the pastor and myself, the attached associate. While over time there has been change in who commits to doing what, there has also been a striking consistency in dedication to the spread of tasks necessary in the everyday life of the parish. And the communal willingness to share responsibility reflects a strong sense of community in other ways that might be expected. There is healthy attendance at both Sunday and feastday services, at coffee hours and other occasional events such as food prep or baking days, the Christmas food fair, the parish picnics in June and September, as well as parish life cycle events such as weddings, funerals, and memorial services. Normally, baptisms are at the

Sunday liturgy, and are celebrations of the entire community, not just the family of the one baptized.

No matter the congregation that Butler Bass studied, the liturgical service never separates the members from the worlds they come from and to which they return. There really is what some of the émigré theologians in Paris called the "churching of life." This was not merely the placing of more vigils lamps before more icons in a house, nor just more services held in church. Rather it is what one finds in the pages of the New Testament. There are no cathedrals or basilicas there, in fact very little activity takes place in houses of worship. Rather the kingdom of heaven comes among us, confronts in everyday life. It does so in the crumbs from the Eucharistic bread and the slosh of the wine in the chalice—reminders always that this Eucharist, the table of the Lord, is not some ethereal communion but a real meal, material, with dribbles and fragments left behind.[8] The splash of the baptismal water is no different, the smear and fragrance of the anointing oil and chrism speak no less to the senses. Likewise assembled and using all these material things with words and song are the old and the young, women and men, people of all kinds of ethnic and class backgrounds and political viewpoints. Long before any of our historical liturgies and creeds, the people of God gathered and with greater simplicity broke the bread and were united in prayer and service.

Reformation churches like the Lutheran, Presbyterian, and Episcopal have been rediscovering and reclaiming ancient Christian liturgy, icons, symbols, processions. The celebration of holy week and Easter has become one great *anamnesis,* a remembrance and real presence of the death and rising of Christ and of every Christian. This is the central image of the life of holiness and the movement of us all as we follow Christ. Those traditions not represented in Butler Bass's study, the Roman and Byzantine Catholic and Eastern Orthodox, who have held onto so much in the church's tradition—the liturgies of John Chrysostom and Basil the Great, the icons, the fasts and the feasts of the church year—these are challenged to again discover the marketplace, the city square, the slums and the suburbs and small rural villages where this wonderful tradition originally began, as Aidan Kavanagh and Robert Taft, the great liturgical scholars of our time, insist on in their writings.[9]

Whatever part of the Christian tradition one comes from or is in, the search for God and the life of holiness are not solitary endeavors. We are never alone in the journey and we always have at hand the practices, the elements of the tradition that remain living and effective. The basics of church life Diana Butler Bass examines in her study of intentional parishes—liturgy, study, fellowship, hospitality, outreach, and service—transcend denominational identities, even theological differences. They have been with us all along the path taken in this book, maybe more the backdrop, the space in which many of those to whom we have listened live and move. Perhaps they could and even should be the focus of separate examination in the future. Nevertheless, they are the real sources of Christian life, all sacramental in bringing the divine and the human, the spiritual and material together. These are the means by which transformation takes place—how liturgy finds its way into life, how each individual remains part of the church community, how the church encounters the world.

*Conclusion: "The Church has left the building"*

I cannot claim to have thought up this colorful riff on a popular phrase. I found it on the Religious News Service website. It evoked for me the fact that the New Testament understands "church" not as a building but a community. The church assembles or meets in various homes of Andronicus and Junia, Aquila and Priscilla or Lydia, or even a rented space. It assembles in the upper room, in a Jerusalem square, on the seashore where Jews came to pray, perhaps in a garden or tavern after synagogue services. Yet by the third century we find a private home retooled for church assembly, for baptism and for the Eucharist, in Dura-Europos in Syria, a town also possessing a frescoed synagogue. Only much later are Roman basilicas similarly adapted and original structures for gathering built. Whether it is the plain white clapboard New England meeting house or the squat domed cube found in Greece and later across Eastern Europe, the church was not at the start such a structure.

In the books and blogs of emergent church communities, one hears a great deal about faith and life in our time. Brian McLaren, a

pastor and theologian of some standing, has written about living tradition in our time, about a "generous" orthodoxy that welcomes, is
open rather than adversarial and confrontational.[10] Others like Doug
Pagitt of the Solomon's Porch church community in St. Paul, Minnesota, have also addressed how to be church in the twenty-first century, in a diverse, secular, religiously pluralistic, technologically savvy
society.[11]

One hears that "the church has left the building" in many ways.
People distinguish between buildings and the "body of Christ," between denominations and the *una sancta*, that is, the "one, holy catholic and apostolic church," and between this jurisdiction or church
body and the people of God. Parish members are both unable and unwilling to reduce being church to continuing to finance the roof, the
heating plant, the aging windows and walls of structures, whether
urban or rural, or for that matter to fully support a pastor and family.
While this is not the place to launch off on this related but different
issue, the stance of people and clergy in the emerging churches is more
creative, as one put it, "traditionally innovative" and proactive. In
Butler Bass's study the label "intentional" was used. In a fairly thor-
ough look at such communities both in America and the UK, Eddie
Gibbs and Ryan K. Bolger found that their informants had a lot to say
about what drew them to alternative forms of church, both to liturgy
and fellowship as well as organization.[12] While on the one hand it
would be too much to say that every congregation of this sort is
unique, it is also necessary to note the wide range of ways in which
these communities form, develop their practices and perspectives,
and, of course, change over time. Many simply disappear with members starting or joining yet other alternative communities. There are
even some denominational efforts at supporting alternative forms of
worship and fellowship, such as the "Fresh Expressions" in the
Church of England, alongside renewal movements such as "Alpha
Course."[13] There are in the greater New York City area several nontraditional parish communities. One now in existence for over twenty
years, under the leadership of Timothy Keller, is Redeemer Presbyterian, with several planted communities and a greater number of affiliated ones, belonging to the conservative Presbyterian Church in
America (not the larger Presbyterian Church [USA]). Another is

Trinity-Grace City Parish, with a network of related congregations.[14] Redeemer has a pastoral staff of ten and an elaborate organization rivaling any large mainstream denomination parish, while Trinity-Grace is far less complex in structure and not affiliated with any denomination. There are variations on these themes wherever alternative emerging or missional communities are found.

Understanding the church as part of a larger living tradition, with diverse forms of worship and assembling in the past, at present, and for the future—I would call this a response that is overwhelmingly positive. There is however the default situation, the conditions in many parishes that can no longer continue to function as they formerly did for a variety of reasons. A friend in her later sixties told me that she is now the youngest member of what was once a suburban mission parish plant, a community now mostly in their eighties, with a "good Sunday" meaning perhaps thirty at the liturgy. All across New York, Methodist and Lutheran parishes are gathered into clusters, with a pastor caring for two, three, four, or more on a rotating basis. Even in the bucolic, affluent Hudson Valley where I live many parishes are cared for by "weekend" pastors, both retired and "worker priests" with fulltime professions, who live and work elsewhere, traveling up for Sunday services, with other sacramental needs and meetings also sandwiched into the day. Many of these parishes are more than a century, in some cases two hundred years old, once the hub of hamlets in farming country, now the counties—northern Westchester, Putnam, and Dutchess, along with nearby Fairfield, Connecticut— are all the exurbs, with residents commuting into New York City and across into Connecticut and New Jersey and many locations in between. Most of these parishes have till now been kept open, somehow. But it is no longer an oddity to drive past a church that has become a restaurant or antiques dealer or even a private home.

What this says to me is that we are in the midst of profound change in the lives of local churches, that is, church communities not at regional or national but very local levels. In his study of the eucharistically centered life of the church in the first five hundred years of the common era, Nicholas Afanasiev found that the self-understanding of the assembly, of the Eucharist they celebrated together, and the various ministries exercised by members of the assembly—all of this was interactional, interdependent, and local.[15] This was before the "rule of law" and the stratification system dividing the assembly into clergy and laity hardened into a hierarchical caste-like division. Also, "local" here cannot be condemned as "congregational," a much later turn in ecclesiastical polity. Contrary to some of his critics, Afanasiev says over and over again that the local church was fully the church in itself—not merely a branch of some larger entity. However it was fully the church always in communion with all the rest of the local churches that comprised "the Church of God in Christ," the Pauline sense of ecclesiology.[16] When one considers the disappearance of "brand," that is, denominational loyalty, for all sorts of reasons, and when the investment of trust and generosity is more often with a local and visible community rather than the more distant, even abstract levels of diocese or national church, I think Afanasiev's findings have gained an unforeseen and powerful new relevance for us in the early years of the twenty-first century. In an essay published in 1937 in a collection entitled *Zhivoe predanie,* or *Living Tradition,* Afanasiev made a strong case for the living adaptation of the church to changing times.

> The Church is founded on a rock. "You are Peter and on this rock I will build my Church and the gates of hell shall not prevail against her." These words could be inscribed on the front of the principal churches of all confessions, including Rome, but of course, without the Roman Catholic interpretation. The belief that the Church of Christ is unshakeable and unconquerable comprises one of the most basic convictions of Christianity. In the age of profound world crisis and in the dusk of humanity's historical paths this unshakeable quality of the Church is a haven for the Christian soul. The face of the earth is changing. Mankind is entering unknown and unexplored paths, and we ourselves, just like our children, do not know under what new conditions we will be living. When the soil on which we are accustomed to stand falters and shifts out from under our feet, the rock of the Church will remain. "Everyone then who hears these words of mine and does them will be like a wise man who built his house upon the rock; and the rain fell, and the floods came, and the winds blew and beat upon that house, but it did not fall, because it had been founded on the rock" (Matt. 7:24–25). She

will withstand the storms of man even more: "Heaven and earth will pass away, but my words will not pass away" (Mk. 13:31). In the midst of the changing and the ever new, she alone remains changeless. In the midst of the temporal, she alone is eternal.

But how should we understand and to what should we attribute the unalterable in the Church? Is everything in the Church changeless and in what sense is the Church herself changeless? Such are the questions that, under various aspects, stir modern Christian thought. These are not only academic questions. They are questions vital to Christian life, since the solution of another question depends on them; i.e., what should and must be the attitude of the Church towards modern life and its problems. If everything in the Church is changeless and there is nothing temporal in her, then this means that modern life concerns the Church only to the degree in which the Church must keep and preserve her sanctity in the life of the world in order to bring it to the time of fulfillment. This presupposes that the Church to a certain degree is withdrawn from the world, that there is one road—from the world into the Church—but there is no road from the Church into the world. This would be correct only if the Church, together with its members, could leave the world. But she does not lead them out of the world "since then you would need to go out of the world" (1 Cor. 5:10) and, accordingly, the Church cannot leave her members in the world alone. The Church faces the world, not the desert. She abides in the world and builds in the world until "the fullness of time." In relation to the world the Church, aside from a concern for self-preservation, also has positive concerns. If this is so, then there must be in the Church not only that which is unalterable, but also that which changes—along with the eternal, that which is temporal. Where then is the eternal and temporal in the Church, where is the dividing line between them, and what are their interrelationships?[17]

Perhaps one could say that the two thousand years of Christian history have been one long attempt to sort out what is essential and unchangeable from that which is variable, adaptable, that can be diverse with there still remaining unity in the faith.[18] How many efforts have there been to describe the essentials that unify? I cited Bulgakov's still powerful essay, "By Jacob's Well." There was the *Lambeth*

*Quadrilateral* of 1884 and the *Baptism, Eucharist, and Ministry* document of Faith and Order in 1982, as well as a substantial literature of response to and reflection on these dominical sacraments and the ordained ministry as essentials of the church.[19] In over a quarter of a century the revelation of so much unity in basic faith and worship, in addition to the published papers of so many international and national official dialogues (among Roman Catholics, Orthodox, Lutherans, and others), have not opened the impasse of division, despite so many affirmations of unity on the Trinity, Christ—the principal dogmas—as well as on baptism, Eucharist, and ordained ministry. Robert Jenson has lamented the reality that when one agreement is reached automatically new disagreements surface.[20] And even more regrettably, discussion on what would appear to be the unifying elements of the church have shown deep rifts among members of the same church.[21] Among many Christians, younger ones to be sure but older as well, there is weariness with the inability of the churches to act upon that about which they have already affirmed they are in agreement. Beyond this, I have seen and heard disillusionment, not with the search for unity, but with the chief pastors of the churches, the bishops. They have shown themselves unable and unwilling to confront the search for church unity, just as they have been unable and unwilling to deal with abuse of various kinds, including financial and clerical. Possibly the "church leaving the building" also has to do with the building's superintendents.

To confront more of the fascinating, even terrifying changes of the twenty-first century, as already noted, goes far beyond our focus here. Yet with so many parishes unable to support a pastor, unable to meet their other operating expenses, the reality of this change is already with us, and the number of such congregations is growing. A quick assessment might be that there is a clergy shortage—looking at the situation with Roman Catholic parishes and some other church bodies could lead one to this conclusion. However, in most cases it is precisely the opposite, namely, a shortage of viable parishes. This is so, in some cases, because of redundant congregations—parishes that formerly were ethnic in origin but of the same church body or parishes of church bodies not previously but now in communion with each other. The presence in a small coal region town in Pennsylvania

or in a formerly urban industrial area in New Jersey of several Orthodox and even more Greek and Roman Catholic parishes would be an
example. Likewise in Brooklyn, parishes of formerly autonomous
Lutheran church bodies, now long merged into the ELCA, would
be another, as would be multiple plants of parishes of the same
denomination—Presbyterian, Episcopal, Methodist. Where I live in
the Hudson Valley, many formerly independent small towns all have
their very own set of denominational outposts—Lutheran, Methodist, Episcopalian—now within minutes' drive of each other, clearly
duplications. Yet efforts to regroup and re-root such into a regional
parish have been resisted. Catholic parishes have constructed new,
very large exurban plants, when older inner-city buildings and locations are far from members' homes. Seating hundreds of people, these
new buildings enable a single priest with many lay Eucharistic ministers to service very large congregations for the Sunday Masses. Perhaps the Catholics could qualify for clergy shortage, but they too
have many parishes that are no longer viable.

For me, it is always the case that one thing leads to another.[22]
When a friend asked if I intended to keep cranking out books on holiness in our time, my immediate reaction was to say no. There were already so many that I had probably contributed enough of my ideas
and of writers I wanted others to hear. I think that there will continue
to be contemplation of the search for God and the struggle to live in,
with, and through God. But over the past few years, conversations
with other clergy and with the seminarian interns from our parish
started to coalesce. A visit I made to a former intern at the parish he
took in the coal region of northeastern Pennsylvania, where my father's family had lived and my uncle had served over fifty years as a
priest, was an eye-opening experience. The decline of so many parishes in that area, of all denominations, connected with other accounts
I had heard from urban as well as rural locations. It was not that
people were abandoning the church, rejecting Christian faith, liturgy,
or life. Rather, there had been profound changes in the demographics.
With mines and factories gone, the second and third generations of
immigrants moved away to where jobs were, and very beautiful,
cathedral-like churches were now attended by a few dozen retirees.
The challenge of keeping buildings heated and cooled, of maintaining

the roof and other structural aspects, as well as supporting a pastor and family—this was becoming impossible. In some churches such as the Methodists, Presbyterians, Lutherans, the problems were addressed by forming multipoint parishes—combinations of formerly independent units now linked together for church school, being served by one pastor who might rotate services, or people would gather in different sanctuaries on various Sundays. A colleague who is now a diocesan administrator in the Episcopal Church described a growing number of small town and rural parishes that could not support their own pastor. While there were available clergy, in theory, there was the further difficulty of matching any of these "worker priests"—that is, clergy with fulltime occupations unable to relocate from their homes or jobs—to fill the parish spots. The use of lay pastors by some church bodies is also an interesting strategy, though not without problems.[23]

I add to all this a number of exchanges among myself and a few colleagues about how to practice parish life—worship, fellowship, study, outreach—when so much about who we are and where we live and work has changed. In short, all of this has convinced me that Diana Butler Bass's path is the one that needs more study and reflection. I mean by this the cluster of questions so threatening to church leaders and seminary faculty and, sadly, often invisible to many parish pastors and churchgoers, about the shape, the arrangements, and the activities of the life of a Christian community, a "local church" or parish in the twenty-first century. This is a complex reality, for it includes not only the central liturgical worship of the assembly, but how it organizes itself as a community, how it prays outside the services, and where it locates itself. It also involves how the community will raise funds, what it will do with its financial resources, what kind of outreach it will make to the local neighborhood and other parts of the church and the world. Also connected here would be relationships of the parish to other churches in the same area, without regard for their tradition. Obviously too, the extent to which a community continues to learn, to challenge itself and be challenged, to be able to see change as other than a threat—Butler Bass found that such were the characteristics of intentional and dynamic parishes in her research. And these parishes were neither clericalized nor laicized in their sense of community, rather seeing all members joined in the living out of the gospel.

While these and related issues are likely then to be the focus of future analysis and reflection, here at the conclusion they do leave us with an important truth. The church may be leaving this or that building, but the church as the people of God, the search for God and for the life of holiness is not leaving America in the twenty-first century by any means. From Peter Berger to Charles Taylor to José Casanova and many other students of religion in our time, the former consensus about progressive secularization has been rejected.[24] While nonbelief, even in some vigorous forms, and religious indifference are part of the landscape, the last decades with the rise of the religious left, the resurgence of fundamentalism and traditionalism, the clashes, sometimes violent, as in the killing of Dr. Tiller and shooting of Rep. Gabrielle Giffords, should put to rest the idea that religion is on the way out.

How we live the life of holiness, what we believe, the ways in which we worship, gather, study, reach out—all of these have changed and will continue to change. Here we have tried to listen to a number of writers as they recount their own experiences in the spiritual life. And we have tried to hear the accounts of these "saints as they really are," in Dorothy Day's words. Of course these writers are, like ourselves, God's "living icons," saints-in-the-making. Their lives are sometimes classical and traditionally correct, other times quite singular, deviant from the norm, messy, skeptical. However the aim has not been to discredit the search and the life, nor to discard it as worthless in our time, with so many other pressing problems and needs. Rather what I have wanted to say here—and those we listened to say it better—is that the search for God and the life of holiness goes on among us.

Introduction

1. Robert Ellsberg, ed., *Dorothy Day, Selected Writings* (Maryknoll, NY: Orbis, 1992), 215–16. Also see Jim Forest, *All Is Grace: A Biography of Dorothy Day* (Maryknoll, NY: Orbis Books, 2011), and her autobiography, *The Long Loneliness* (New York: Harper & Row, 1952), as well as Robert Ellsberg, ed., *The Duty of Delight: The Diaries of Dorothy Day* and *All the Way to Heaven: The Selected Letters of Dorothy Day* (Milwaukee: Marquette University Press, 2008 and 2010).

2. See http://www.catholicworker.org/dorothyday/canonizationtext.cfm?Number=82.

3. Michael Plekon, *Living Icons: Persons of Faith in the Eastern Church* (Notre Dame, IN: University of Notre Dame Press, 2002). In *Living Icons,* I profiled a number of persons of faith from the twentieth century, looking for the distinctive features of their spirituality and their work for others.

4. Michael Plekon, *Hidden Holiness* (Notre Dame, IN: University of Notre Dame Press, 2009).

5. Kenneth Woodward, *Making Saints* (New York: Simon & Schuster, 1990); Elizabeth Johnson, *Friends of God and Prophets* (New York: Crossroad, 1999); Robert Ellsberg, *All Saints* (New York: Crossroad, 1997); and James Martin, *My Life with the Saints* (Chicago: Loyola Press, 2005), *Becoming Who You Are* (New York: Hidden Spring, 2006), and *Between Heaven and Mirth* (New York: HarperOne, 2011).

6. Paul Elie, *The Life You Save May Be Your Own* (New York: Farrar, Straus and Giroux, 2003).

7. Another effort along these lines is Marian Ronan, *Tracing the Sign of the Cross: Sexuality, Mourning, and the Future of American Catholicism* (New York: Columbia University Press, 2009), a listening to the voices of writers James Carroll, Mary Gordon, Donna J. Haraway, and Richard Rodriguez. Also see Jana Reiss, *Flunking Sainthood: A Year of Breaking the Sabbath, Forgetting to Pray, and Still Loving My Neighbor* (Brewster, MA: Paraclete, 2011).

8. *Mother Maria Skobtsova: Essential Writings,* trans. Richard Pevear and Larissa Volokhonsky (Maryknoll, NY: Orbis, 2003), 81.

9. Kathleen Morris, *Acedia and Me: A Marriage, Monks, and a Writer's Life* (New York: Riverhead, 2008).

10. Sara Miles, *Take This Bread: A Radical Conversion* (New York: Ballantine, 2007), and *Jesus Freak: Feeding, Healing, Raising the Dead* (San Francisco: Jossey-Bass, 2010).

11. Joan Didion, *The Year of Magical Thinking* (New York: Knopf, 2006); Mary Karr, *The Liar's Club* and *Cherry* (New York: Penguin, 1995 and 2001), and *Lit* (New York: HarperCollins, 2009); Elizabeth Gilbert, *Eat, Pray, Love: One Woman's Search for Everything Across Italy, India, and Indonesia* and *Committed: A Skeptic Makes Peace Through Marriage* (New York: Viking, 2009 and 2010). Gilbert's first book, her account of a year of pilgrimage and searching, was on the *New York Times* and other bestseller lists for many weeks and was made into a movie, attesting to broad interest in one person's search for meaning and experience of the sacred.

O N E   Bringing Saints down from the Walls and Pedestals

1. Robert Ellsberg, ed., *The Duty of Delight: The Diaries of Dorothy Day* (Milwaukee: Marquette University Press, 2008).

2. Robert Ellsberg, ed., *All the Way to Heaven: The Selected Letters of Dorothy Day* (Milwaukee: Marquette University Press, 2010).

3. Among these were her common law spouse, Forster Batterham, and writers and radical political activists such as Rayna Raphaelson, Mike Gold, and Peggy Baird. See Jim Forest, *All Is Grace: A Biography of Dorothy Day* (Maryknoll, NY: Orbis Books, 2011), 12–55. Dorothy Day wrote an early autobiographical account, *From Union Square to Rome* (Silver Spring, MD: Preservation of the Faith Press, 1939) but her later effort (though still not complete) is *The Long Loneliness* (New York: Harper & Row, 1952).

4. Among these were Ammon Hennacy, Eileen Egan, Jim Forest, the Berrigan brothers, Gordon Zahn, Karl Meyer, and Thomas Merton, to mention only a few. She nurtured the gifts and aspirations of Russian émigrés Helene Iswolsky and Catherine de Hueck Doherty as they settled in America. Helene would set up an ecumenical discussion group, the Third Hour, modeled on philosopher Nicholas Berdyaev's salon in suburban Clamart, outside Paris. Catherine, like Dorothy, would establish houses of hospitality, first in Harlem in New York City and later on in Ontario.

5. This mirrors Cardinal Donald Wuerl's defense of the exclusion of her contemporary and colleague, the noted writer and Trappist monk, Thomas Merton, from the *Catholic Catechism for Adults.* Each section of this catechism was to begin with the story of a notable American Catholic. When Merton's

biography was removed, Wuerl argued that he was not well known among younger Catholics. Questions about Merton's openness to Asian traditions and his beliefs toward the end of his life were also raised. Such criticism plagued Merton during his life, along with indignation at his radical stances on civil rights, the proliferation of nuclear weapons, and his antiwar position.

6. Mark Shaw, *Beneath the Mask of Holiness* (New York: Palgrave/Macmillan, 2009). I should note that the consensus of Merton scholars is that this is not a careful, well-researched study of Merton but for all practical purposes a smear campaign posing as new investigation.

7. Alexander Schmemann, *Journal (1973–1983)*, ed. Nikita Struve, trans. Anne Davidenkoff, Anne Kichilov, and René Marichal (Paris: Éditions des Syrtes, 2009). The abridged and edited English version is *The Journals of Father Alexander Schmemann, 1973–1983*, trans. Juliana Schmemann (Crestwood, NY: St. Vladimir's Seminary Press, 2002).

8. Andrew Greeley, *Confessions of a Parish Priest: An Autobiography* (New York: Simon & Schuster, 1986), and *Furthermore! Memories of a Parish Priest* (New York: Forge, 1999); Paul Moore, *Presences: A Bishop's Life in the City* (New York: Farrar, Straus and Giroux, 1997); William Sloane Coffin Jr., *Once to Every Man: A Memoir* (New York: Athenaeum Press, 1977); Warren Goldstein, *William Sloane Coffin Jr.: A Holy Impatience* (New Haven, CT: Yale University Press, 2004).

9. Rembert G. Weakland, *A Pilgrim in a Pilgrim Church: Memoirs of a Catholic Archbishop* (Grand Rapids, MI: Eerdmans, 2009); Stanley Hauerwas, *Hannah's Child: A Theologian's Memoir* (Grand Rapids, MI: Eerdmans, 2010); Eugene H. Peterson, *The Pastor: A Memoir* (New York: HarperOne, 2011); and Anne Lamott, *Traveling Mercies: Some Thoughts on Faith* (New York: Pantheon Books, 1999), *Plan B: Further Thoughts on Faith* (New York: Riverhead Books, 2005), and *Grace (Eventually): Thoughts on Faith* (New York: Riverhead Books, 2007).

10. Mother Teresa, *Come Be My Light: The Private Writings of the "Saint of Calcutta,"* ed. Brian Kolodiejchuk (New York: Doubleday, 2007).

11. See in particular the collections of his sermons and talks: Edward Schillebeeckx, *God Is New Each Moment* (Edinburgh: T&T Clark, 1983), *God Among Us* (New York: Crossroad, 1983), and *For the Sake of the Gospel* (London: SCM Press, 1989).

12. See http://www.saintgregorys.org/worship/art for images, interviews, and an essay on the dancing saints.

13. Elizabeth Johnson, *Friends of God and Prophets* (New York: Crossroad, 199), 100–101.

14. Ibid., 102.

15. Ibid., 103.

16. See Michael Plekon, *Hidden Holiness* (Notre Dame, IN: University of Notre Dame Press), 59–69.

17. When my *Living Icons* was published in 2002, except for Seraphim of Sarov (whose canonization had been opposed and postponed for almost a century in Russia until royal pressure forced it to occur), none of the other persons of faith in the Eastern Church profiled there were officially recognized as saints. Since then, Mother Maria Skobtsova was canonized in Paris in 2005 after the bishops' synod of the Ecumenical Patriarchate in Istanbul authorized this. For decades, petitions for her canonization and her portfolio had been ignored by the Moscow Patriarchate, which to the best of my knowledge has yet to include her and her companions on their calendar. The church to which I belong, the Orthodox Church in America, has finally listed her and the others on July 20 along with a reproduction of the canonization icon but without any biographical material or liturgical texts. Mother Maria has long been the target of criticism in the Moscow Patriarchate by those who reject her form of monastic life and social activism as well as her critical writings as the result of poor theological formation and the effects of living outside Russia. Another contemporary martyr who spent his entire life in Russia, Father Alexander Men, has likewise been condemned for his ecumenical openness and for his stress on study groups and fellowship, both considered "Protestant" traits incompatible with Russian church life. Further, most of the figures in *Living Icons* have not been and most likely will never be canonized for similar reasons, especially their ecumenical spirit, theological creativity, and their criticism of ecclesial decadence. Here I would include Nicholas Afanasiev, Alexander Schmemann, and John Meyendorff, among others. It should be noted that the books of these three along with those of Alexander Men were burned by the former bishop of Ekaterinburg. More recently the publication of Schmemann's journals, full of critical and creative thinking, have been greeted with enormous enthusiasm in Russia, although they remain in print and translation here in America in a very reduced, censored version.

18. The Episcopal Church, for example, lists and commemorates Sergius of Radonezh, the great Russian monk, on September 25 and the Lutheran Maximilian Kolbe, the Polish Catholic martyr, on July 14. The monastic community of Bose celebrates the Christianizers of Rus', Olga and Vladimir, on July 11 and 15, with all of them commemorating Francis and Clare of Assisi on October 4 and August 11.

Another place in which the embrace of the ecumenical diversity of the modern era is most evident is in hymnals. No longer restricted to a single tradition, say, Lutheran hymnody, contemporary hymnals range all over the denominations. The most recent Lutheran hymnal includes, for example, hymns from the patristic period early in church history, from the Anglican, Reformed, and Catholic traditions, as well as from churches in Latin America, Africa and Asia (*Evangelical Lutheran Worship* [Minneapolis: Augsburg-Fortress, 2006]).

19. There is a history of icons or images of holy people who have not been officially recognized as saints. There were icons of Seraphim of Sarov for decades before he was canonized. As noted one can find such images in the monastery of New Skete, in St. Gregory of Nyssa church, and one of Dorothy Day has been used in the cover of this volume.

20. Consider, for example, Central American martyrs such as Archbishop Oscar Romero; Maryknoll sisters and lay workers Maura Clarke, Ita Ford, Dorothy Kazel, and Jean Donovan; the Jesuit martyrs Ignacio Ellacuría, Ignacio Martín-Baró, Juan Ramón Moreno, Amando López, Segundo Montes; and Joaquin López y López and Elba and Celina Ramos who worked for them.

21. Examples include lay theologians Elisabeth Behr-Sigel, Paul Evdokimov, and William Stringfellow, and the African American Franciscan Sister Thea Bowman, among others.

22. George P. Fedotov, *Collected Works*, vol. 1, *St. Filipp: Metropolitan of Moscow*, vol. 2, *A Treasury of Russian Spirituality*, vol. 3, *The Russian Religious Mind: Kievan Christianity: The Tenth to the Thirteenth Centuries*, vol. 4, *The Middle Ages: The Thirteenth to the Fifteenth Centuries* (Belmont, MA: Nordland, 1975).

23. Plekon, *Hidden Holiness*, 55–96.

24. Matthew Fox, *Original Blessing* (San Francisco: Tarcher/Putnam, 2000).

25. Karen Armstrong, *The Spiral Staircase: My Climb Out of Darkness* (New York: Anchor Books, 2004).

26. Roberta Bondi, *Memories of God: Theological Reflections on a Life* (Nashville: Abingdon, 1995).

27. Tony Hedra, *Father Joe: The Man Who Saved My Soul* (New York: Random House, 2004).

28. Henri Nouwen, *The Genesee Diary: Report from a Trappist Monastery* (Garden City, NY: Doubleday, 1976), *The Inner Voice of Love: A Journey Through Anguish to Freedom* (New York: Image Books, 1999), and *Sabbatical Journey: The Diary of His Final Year* (New York: Crossroad, 2000); see also Michael Ford, *Wounded Prophet: A Portrait of Henri J.M. Nouwen* (New York: Image Books, 2002), and Michael O'Laughlin, *God's Beloved: A Spiritual Biography of Henri Nouwen* (Maryknoll, NY: Orbis, 2004).

29. Thomas Merton, *Seven Storey Mountain* (New York: Harcourt, Brace, 1948). The best biography is Michael Mott, *The Seven Mountains of Thomas Merton* (Boston: Houghton Mifflin, 1984). See also Monica Furlong, *Merton: A Biography*, new ed. (Ligouri, MO: Ligouri Publications, 1995), William H. Shannon, *Thomas Merton: An Introduction* (Cincinnati: St. Anthony Messenger and Franciscan Press, 2005), and Laurence S. Cunningham, *Thomas Merton and the Monastic Vision* (Grand Rapids, MI: Eerdmans, 1999).

30. Jenkins, along with others mentioned, pointed to the explosion of Christian communities in Africa and South America. The United States, despite some recent slippage, remains a strongly religious society. There are also indications of a smaller but dynamic religiosity in unexpected European locations as well as in post-Soviet Russia and Ukraine. But of course the major object defying the secularization theory is the intensity and diffusion of Islam.

31. Provocative statements of this theological independence are Peter L. Berger, *A Rumor of Angels: Modern Society and the Rediscovery of the Supernatural* and *The Heretical Imperative: Contemporary Possibilities of Religious Affirmation* (New York: Doubleday, 1969 and 1979). The closest to a memoir Berger has produced is his latest book, *Adventures of an Accidental Sociologist* (Amherst, NY: Prometheus Books, 2011).

32. Peter L. Berger, *A Far Glory: The Quest for Faith in an Age of Credulity* (New York: Free Press, 1992).

33. Peter L. Berger et al., eds., *The Desecularization of the World* (Grand Rapids, MI: Eerdmans, 1999).

34. Peter L. Berger, ed., *Between Relativism and Fundamentalism* (Grand Rapids, MI: Eerdmans, 2011).

35. Peter L. Berger, *The Precarious Vision* and *The Noise of Solemn Assemblies* (New York: Doubleday, 1961 and 1961).

36. Peter L. Berger and Thomas Luckman, *The Social Construction of Reality* (New York: Doubleday, 1966), and Peter L. Berger, *The Sacred Canopy: Elements of a Sociological Theory of Religion* (New York: Doubleday, 1967).

37. Peter L. Berger, Brigitte Berger, and Hansfried Kellner, *The Homeless Mind: Modernization and Consciousness* (New York: Random House, 1973); Peter L. Berger and Richard J. Neuhaus, *Against the World for the World: The Hartford Appeal and the Future of American Religion* (New York: Seabury Press, 1976).

38. Berger pursued this from the beginning of his career, from *The Precarious Vision* to *A Rumor of Angels* on through *The Heretical Imperative* and *A Far Glory* and beyond, as we will see.

39. Berger, *Far Glory*, 186.

40. Ibid., 189.

41. Richard John Neuhaus, *American Babylon* (New York: Basic Books, 2009).

42. See Jon Butler, Grant Wacker, and Randall Balmer, *Religion in American Life* (New York: Oxford University Press, 2003). Also see Randall Balmer, *The Making of Evangelicalism from Revivalism to Politics and Beyond* (Waco, TX: Baylor University Press, 2010).

43. Peter L. Berger, *Questions of Faith* (Malden, MA: Blackwell, 2004).

44. Ibid., 62.

45. Ibid., 66; italics in original.

46. Ibid., 67.

47. Ibid., 176.

48. Patricia Hampl, "You're History," in *Tell Me True: Memoir, History, and Writing a Life,* co-edited with Elaine Tyler May (St. Paul: Borealis Books, 2008), 142.

49. Patricia Hampl, *I Could Tell You Stories* (New York: Norton, 1999), 29, 35–36.

50. Ibid., 36–37.

51. Patricia Hampl, *The Florist's Daughter* (New York: Houghton Mifflin Harcourt, 2007), 14–15.

## TWO Messy Lives, Imperfect People

1. Kathleen Norris, *Acedia and Me: A Marriage, Monks, and a Writer's Life* (New York: Riverhead, 2008), 14.

2. Ibid., 17–18.

3. Ibid., 284–85.

4. Ibid., 285.

5. Barbara Brown Taylor, *Leaving Church: A Memoir of Faith* (San Francisco: HarperSanFrancisco, 2007), 97–98.

6. Ibid., 98–99.

7. Ibid., 102.

8. Ibid., 113.

9. Ibid., 150, 168.

10. Ibid., 209.

11. Nora Gallagher, *Things Seen and Unseen: A Year Lived in Faith* (New York: Vintage, 1999), 11–12.

12. Ibid., 12–13.

13. Nora Gallagher, *Practicing Resurrection: A Memoir of Work, Doubt, Discernment and Moments of Grace* (New York: Vintage, 2004), 206–8.

14. Personal e-mail, June 17, 2009.

15. Gallagher, *Things Seen,* 233–34.

16. Karen Armstrong, *The Spiral Staircase* (New York: Anchor, 2005).

## THREE Dangerous Faith

1. Barbara Brown Taylor, *Leaving Church: A Memoir of Faith* (San Francisco: HarperSanFrancisco, 2007), 4–6.

2. G. Lloyd Rediger, *Clergy Killers: Guidance for Pastors and Congregations Under Attack* (Louisville: Westminster–John Knox, 1997); Kenneth C. Haugk, *Antagonists in the Church* (Minneapolis: Augsburg, 1988).

3. Sara Miles, *Take This Bread: A Radical Conversion* (New York: Ballantine, 2007), xiii–xv.

4. Ibid., 251–52.

5. Ibid., 253–54.

6. Ibid., 254.

7. Ibid., 256.

8. James Pain and Nicholas Zernov, eds., *A Bulgakov Anthology* (Philadelphia: Westminster, 1976), 15–16.

9. Ibid., 17.

10. Ibid., 20.

11. *The Journals of Father Alexander Schmemann, 1973–83,* trans. Juliana Schmemann (Crestwood, NY: St. Vladimir's Seminary Press, 2002), 284, 295, 315–17.

12. Ibid., 284.

13. William Mills, "Cracking the Clerical Caste: Towards a Conciliar Church" *Logos* 3–4 (2009): 1–17.

14. Schmemann, *Journals,* 311.

15. Ibid., 231.

16. Donald Cozzens, *The Faith That Dares to Speak* (Collegeville, MN: Liturgical Press, 2004); Geoffrey Robinson, *Confronting Power and Sex in the Catholic Church* (Collegeville, MN: Liturgical Press, 2008).

17. Matthew Kelty, *Gethsemani Homilies,* ed. William O. Paulsell (Quincy, IL: Franciscan Press, 2001), 64–65.

18. Sara Miles, *Jesus Freak: Feeding, Healing, Raising the Dead* (San Francisco: Jossey-Bass, 2010), xviii.

19. Ibid., xix–xx.

20. Ibid., 120–21.

21. *Mother Maria Skobtsova: Essential Writings,* trans. Larissa Volokhonsky and Richard Pevear (Maryknoll, NY: Orbis, 2003), 142–60.

22. Ibid., 161.

23. Miles, *Jesus Freak,* 165–66.

24. Ibid., 16.

25. Kelty, *Gethsemani Homilies,* 65.

FOUR   Holiness and the Search for Joy

1. Andrew Krivak, *A Long Retreat: In Search of a Religious Life* (New York: Farrar, Straus and Giroux, 2008).

2. Ibid., 49–50.

3. Ibid., 311.

4. Ibid., 315.

5. Lillian Daniel and Martin Copenhaver, *This Odd and Wondrous Calling: The Public and Private Lives of Two Ministers* (Grand Rapids, MI: Eerdmans, 2009).

6. Ibid., 187–88.

7. Ibid., 6–7.

8. Ibid., 170–82.

9. Ibid., 211–19.

10. Ibid., 119–27.

11. Ibid., 148–57.

12. Ibid., 234.

13. Dean R. Hoge and Jacqueline E. Wenger, *Pastors in Transition: Why Clergy Leave Local Church Ministry* (Grand Rapids, MI: Eerdmans, 2005). Also see Anthony P. Kowalsky, *Married Catholic Priests: Their History, Their Journey, Their Reflections* (New York: Crossroad, 2005); and Stephen Joseph Fichter, "When Priests Leave the Church," *America*, Oct. 5, 2009, available online at http://www.americamagazine.org/content/article.cfm?article_id=11896.


F I V E  "You want to be *happy?*" My Carmelite Years

1. The rule was originally given to the hermits — many former Crusaders and Western European pilgrims — living on Mount Carmel in imitation of the brotherhood that surrounded the great prophets Elijah and Elisha. Its author was Albert Avogadro, Latin patriarch of Jerusalem, who drafted the text between the years 1206 and 1214, with parts taken directly from the rule of St. Augustine. It was finally approved by Pope Innocent IV in 1247 and later underwent mitigations that were not in the original text.

2. The Rule of St. Albert can be found at http://carmelnet.org/chas/rule.htm.

3. See Mary Margaret Funk, *Into the Depths: A Journey of Loss and Vocation* (New York: Lantern Books, 2011).

4. My recollection was assisted greatly by other St. Albert's alumni from my class and others: John Ramsay, Creig Doyle, James Hess, and James Miller. My special thanks to Robert Linderman for filling in many gaps and for his excellent memory. The late Fr. Alfred Isacsson produced historical overviews of both the Carmelite province of St. Elias and of St. Albert's Junior Seminary. These can be accessed at http://carmelites.com/main/content/carmelites-province-st-elias-0 and http://www.carmelites.com/history/sites/default/files/stalberts1.pdf respectively.

5. A former teacher of mine produced the best history of the Carmelites: Joachim Smet, *The Carmelites: A History of the Brothers of Our Lady of Mt.*

Carmel, 4 vols. (Darien, IL: Carmelite Press, 1975). Also see John Welch, *The Carmelite Way: An Ancient Path for Today's Pilgrim* (New York: Paulist Press, 1996); Wilfrid McGreal, *At the Fountain of Elijah: The Carmelite Tradition* (Maryknoll, NY: Orbis, 1999); and Eltin Griffin, *Ascending the Mountain: The Carmelite Rule Today* (Dublin: Columba Press, 2004).

6. Alexander Elchaninov, *The Diary of a Russian Priest*, trans. Helen Iswolsky (Crestwood, NY: St. Vladimir's Seminary Press, 1982), 117.

s i x  Conversion and Community

1. Patricia Hampl, *Virgin Time: In Search of the Contemplative Life* (New York: North Point Press, 1992), 120–22.

2. Ibid., 146–47.

3. Ibid., 175.

4. Ibid., 179.

5. Ibid., 207–8.

6. Thomas Merton, *The Other Side of the Mountain, The End of the Journey, The Journals of Thomas Merton*, vol. 7, ed. Patrick Hart (San Francisco: HarperSanFrancisco, 1998), 262.

7. Lauren Winner, *Girl Meets God* (New York: Random House, 2003), 269–71. Winner has updated her spiritual journey with *Still: Notes on a Midfaith Crisis* (San Francisco: HarperOne, 2012), an account of her response to failure and sorrow in her own life.

8. Lauren Winner, *Mudhouse Sabbath* (Brewster, MA: Paraclete Press, 2003), and *Real Sex: The Naked Truth about Chastity* (Grand Rapids, MI: Brazos, 2006).

9. Veronica Chater, *Waiting for the Apocalypse: A Memoir of Faith and Family* (New York: Norton, 2009).

10. Susan Campbell, *Dating Jesus: A Story of Fundamentalism, Feminism, and the American Girl* (Boston: Beacon, 2009).

11. Jon M. Sweeney, *Born Again and Again* (Brewster, MA: Paraclete Press, 2005); Christine Rosen, *My Fundamentalist Education* (New York: Public Affairs, 2005).

12. Frank Schaeffer, *Crazy for God* (New York: Carroll & Graf, 2007). See also his *Sex, Mom, and God* (Cambridge, MA: Da Capo Press, 2011).

13. Jeff Sharlet and Peter Manseau, eds., *Believer Beware: First-Person Dispatches from the Margins of Faith* (Boston: Beacon, 2009).

14. Winner, *Girl Meets God*, 59; italics in original.

15. Jim Forest's is a recent effort: *Road to Emmaus: Pilgrimage as a Way of Life* (Maryknoll, NY: Orbis, 2007)

SEVEN  God Is Everywhere

1. Thomas Merton, *The Asian Journal of Thomas Merton*, ed. Naomi Burton, Patrick Hart, and James Laughlin (New York: New Directions, 1975), 306–7.

2. Ron Seitz, *Song for Nobody: A Memory Vision of Thomas Merton* (Liguori, MO: Triumph Books, 1993), 131.

3. Merton, *Asian Journal*, 233–35.

4. Ibid., 338.

5. Ibid., 305–17.

6. Ibid., 318–19.

7. Thomas Merton, *The Springs of Contemplation* (Notre Dame, IN: Ave Maria Press, 1992), 197.

8. Ibid., 196.

9. Ibid., 197.

10. Ibid., 201.

11. Darcey Steinke, *Easter Everywhere: A Memoir* (New York: Bloomsbury, 2007), 178.

12. Ibid., 179–80.

13. Darcey Steinke, *Milk* (New York: Bloomsbury, 2005), 70–73.

14. Barbara Brown Taylor, *An Altar in the World* (New York: HarperOne, 2009), 5–7.

15. Ibid., 15.

16. Michael Pollan, *Omnivore's Dilemma* and *In Defense of Food* (New York: Penguin, 2004 and 2008).

17. Julian of Norwich, *Showings*, ed. Edmund Colledge, O.S.A., and James Walsh, S.J. (New York: Paulist Press, 1978), 342.

18. Brown Taylor, *Altar*, 41–42.

19. Ibid., 62.

20. Ibid., 86.

21. Ibid., 110.

22. Ibid., 115.

23. Ibid., 151.

24. Barbara Ehrenreich, *Nickel and Dimed: On (Not) Getting By in America* (New York: Holt Paperbacks), 2008. Also see her *Bright-Sided: How the Relentless Promotion of Positive Thinking Has Undermined America* (New York: Metropolitan Books/Holt, 2009).

25. Brown Taylor, *Altar*, 176.

26. Ibid., 206.

27. Matthew Kelty, *Gethsemani Homilies*, ed. William O. Paulsell (Quincy, IL: Franciscan Press, 2001), 19–21.

258  ⚭  Notes to Pages 195-204

EIGHT  Transformation in Faith and Work, Liturgy and Life

1. Nicholas Berdyaev, "The Ethics of Creativity," in *Ultimate Questions,* ed. Alexander Schmemann (Crestwood, NY: St. Vladimir's Seminary Press, 1977), 262.
2. Sara Miles, *Take This Bread: A Radical Conversion* (New York: Ballantine, 2007), 257–58.
3. Michael Plekon, *Hidden Holiness* (Notre Dame, IN: University of Notre Dame Press, 2009), 162.
4. Paul Evdokimov, *In the World, of the Church: A Paul Evdokimov Reader,* trans. Michael Plekon and Alexis Vinogradov, and *Ages of the Spiritual Life* (Crestwood, NY: St. Vladimir's Seminary Press, 2001 and 1998).
5. Nicholas Afanasiev, *The Church of the Holy Spirit,* trans. Vitaly Permiakov, ed. Michael Plekon (Notre Dame, IN: University of Notre Dame Press, 2007).
6. See N. T. Wright, *Surprised by Hope: Rethinking Heaven, the Resurrection, and the Mission of the Church* and *After You Believe: Why Christian Character Matters* (New York: HarperOne, 2008 and 2010).
7. However, the obsession of so many with the afterlife, evidenced by the wild popularity of a recent book, is an aberration. See Don Piper, *Ninety Minutes in Heaven: A True Story of Death and Life* (Grand Rapids, MI: Revell, 2004).
8. The "sacrament of love" was John Chrysostom's description of marriage. See Paul Evdokimov, *The Sacrament of Love,* trans. Anthony P. Gythiel and Victoria Steadman (Crestwood, NY: St. Vladimir's Seminary Press, 1995).
9. Diana Butler Bass, *The Practicing Congregation* (Washington DC: Alban, 2004), *Christianity for the Rest of Us: How the Neighborhood Church Is Transforming the Faith* (New York: HarperOne, 2006), and *From Nomads to Pilgrims: Stories from Practicing Congregations,* with Joseph Stewart-Sicking (Washington DC: Alban, 2006).
10. Diana Butler Bass, *A People's History of Christianity* (New York: HarperOne, 2009).
11. Diana Butler Bass, *Strength for the Journey: A Pilgrimage of Faith in Community* (San Francisco: Jossey-Bass, 2002), 281.
12. Ibid., 281–82.
13. Ibid., 148.
14. Ibid., 174.
15. Ibid., 178.
16. Brian McLaren identifies a similar moment of insight into Christianity's openness to strangers in the case of the Ethiopian eunuch's welcome by the apostle Philip in Acts 8:26–40. He discusses this in *A New Kind of Christianity* (New York: HarperOne, 2010), 175–90.
17. Butler Bass, *Strength for the Journey,* 179–80.

18. Wade Clark Roof, *Spiritual Marketplace: Baby Boomers and the Re-making of American Religion* (Princeton, NJ: Princeton University Press, 2001); Robert Wuthnow, *The Restructuring of American Religion* (Princeton, NJ: Princeton University Press, 1990).

19. Robert D. Putnam and David E. Campbell, *American Grace* (New York: Simon & Schuster, 2010), 126, 136.

20. Butler Bass, *Strength for the Journey*, 282.

21. Butler Bass, *A People's History of Christianity.*

22. Matthew Kelty, *Singing for the Kingdom: The Last of the Homilies* (Kalamazoo, MI: Cistercian Publications, 2008), 32–34. This passage, about his famous novice master, is from a homily titled "Fantasy versus Reality," based on Matthew 14:22–33, where Jesus walking on the water is taken by his disciples to be a ghost.

23. *Thomas Merton/Monk, A Monastic Tribute*, ed. Patrick Hart, new enlarged ed. (Kalamazoo MI: Cistercian Publications, 1983), 34–35.

24. Kelty, *Singing*, 66–67.

25. Ibid., 11.

26. Butler Bass, *Christianity for the Rest of Us*, 239–40.

27. Robert Wuthnow, *Boundless Faith: The Global Outreach of American Churches* (Berkeley: University of California Press, 2009).

28. Robert Wuthnow, *After Heaven: Spirituality in America since the 1950s* (Berkeley: University of California Press, 1998).

NINE   "The Church has left the building"

1. See Edward Schillebeeckx, *Christ the Sacrament of the Encounter with God* (New York: Sheed & Ward, 1963), and his trilogy: *Jesus: An Experiment in Christology, Christ: The Experience of Jesus as Lord*, and *Church: The Human Story of God*, (New York: Crossroad, 1979, 1980, and 1990). Also see his *Ministry: Leadership in the Community of Jesus Christ* and *The Church with a Human Face* (New York: Crossroad, 1981 and 1985).

2. Paul Evdokimov, *Ages of the Spiritual Life*, trans. Michael Plekon and Alexis Vinogradov (Crestwood, NY: St. Vladimir's Seminary Press, 1998), 64.

3. I now see the comical in such pondering, given that it was just such a book that I previously completed and that it was the product of a thick slice of uninterrupted time that I had on a sabbatical a little more than a year ago. I also had the summer and my wife's recuperation in which to block out the rough draft of this text you are reading.

4. Personal correspondence, March 2, 2011.

5. I think of Catholic theologians Yves Congar and Karl Rahner, of Orthodox ones such as Sergius Bulgakov and Nicholas Afanasiev, of activists and writers Dorothy Day and Maria Skobtsova, among many others.

6. Sergius Bulgakov, "By Jacob's Well," in *Tradition Alive: On the Church and the Christian Life in Our Time, Readings from the Eastern Church*, ed. Michael Plekon, 55–66 (Lanham, MD: Rowman & Littlefield, 2003).

7. Paul Evdokimov, *In the World, of the Church: A Paul Evdokimov Reader*, trans. Michael Plekon and Alexis Vinogradov (Crestwood, NY: St. Vladimir's Seminary Press, 2001), 129–46.

8. Robert F. Taft, S.J., *Through Their Own Eyes: Liturgy as the Byzantines Saw It* (Berkeley: InterOrthodox Press, 2006).

9. Aidan Kavanagh, *On Liturgical Theology* (New York: Pueblo, 1984).

10. Brian McLaren, *A New Kind of Christianity* (New York: HarperOne, 2010), *Finding Our Way Again* (Nashville: Thomas Nelson, 2008), and *A Generous Orthodoxy* (Grand Rapids, MI: Zondervan, 2006).

11. Doug Pagitt, *A Christianity Worth Believing* (San Francisco: Jossey-Bass, 2009), *Church Re-Imagined* (Grand Rapids, MI: Zondervan, 2005), and *Listening to the Beliefs of Emerging Churches* (Grand Rapids, MI: Zondervan, 2007).

12. Eddie Gibbs and Ryan K. Bolger, *Emerging Churches* (Ada, MI: Baker, 2005), 41–46, 235–38. Also see http://www.solomonsporch.com.

13. See http://www.freshexpressions.org.uk/, http://www.htb.org.uk/, and http://alphausa.org/.

14. See http://www.redeemer.com and http://www.trinitygraceparkslope.com/about.

15. Nicholas Afanasiev, *The Church of the Holy Spirit*, trans. Vitaly Permiakov, ed. Michael Plekon (Notre Dame, IN: University of Notre Dame Press, 2007), 133–254. The "rule" or primacy of love is stressed by Afanasiev as what constitutes and holds the Church together (255–76).

16. Nicholas Afanasiev, "L'Église de Dieu en Christ," *La pensée orthodoxe* 13, no. 2 (1968): 1–38.

17. Nicholas Afanasiev, "The Church's Canons: Changeable or Unchangeable," in *Tradition Alive*, ed. Plekon, 31–32.

18. The enormous diversity of Christianity is emphasized in the masterful new study by Diarmaid MacCulloch, *Christianity: The First Three Thousand Years* (New York: Viking, 2009).

19. Also see *Ecumenical Perspectives on Baptism, Eucharist, and Ministry* (Geneva: World Council of Churches, 1983), *Baptism and Eucharist: Ecumenical Convergence in Celebration* (Grand Rapids, MI: Eerdmans, 1983), and the volumes of responses from churches to the document, *Baptism, Eucharist, and Ministry*.

20. Robert Jenson, *Unbaptized God* (Minneapolis: Fortress, 1992).

21. Gennadios Limouris and Nomikos Michael Vaporis, eds., *Orthodox Perspectives on Baptism, Eucharist, and Ministry* (Brookline, MA: Holy Cross Orthodox Press, 1985).

22. Writing about Kierkegaard's theological criticism of modernity led me to his criticism of the modern church and society. Later, this connecting of social and theological inquiry in turn led me to Paul Evdokimov's distinctive work bringing theology and social concern, the church, and the world together. This was almost typical of the scholars and teachers and others in the Paris School centered at St. Sergius Institute—Sergius Bulgakov, Nicholas Afanasiev, George Fedotov, Mother Maria Skobtsova. They were teachers and mentors to Alexander Schmemann, John Meyendorff, Elisabeth Behr-Sigel, Lev Gillet. And the adventuresome thinking of these twentieth-century writers led back to lesser known individuals like Gregory Krug, Joanna Reitlinger, and Paul Anderson, and forward to Dorothy Day, Thomas Merton, Alexander Men, Simone Weil, Etty Hillesum, and eventually to Sara Miles, Darcey Steinke, Rowan Williams, and at last to the other writers we have listened to here.

23. Lawrence Wood, "Called but not Ordained," and Barbara Wheeler, "The Problems with Lay Pastors," *The Christian Century* 127, no. 14 (July 13, 2010): 22–33.

24. Charles Taylor, *A Secular Age* (Cambridge, MA: Harvard University Press, 2007), and José Casanova, "Rethinking Secularization: A Global Comparative Perspective" and "After Secularization," *The Hedgehog Review* 8, nos. 1 and 2 (2006): 7–24.

# INDEX

# MICHAEL PLEKON

is a professor in the department of sociology/anthropology
and the Program in Religion and Culture at Baruch College,
City University of New York. He is also an ordained priest in the
Orthodox Church in America. He is the author or editor of a number
of books, including *Hidden Holiness* (University of Notre Dame
Press, 2009) and *Living Icons: Persons of Faith in the Eastern Church*
(University of Notre Dame Press, 2002).